APR 21

ALSO BY WILLIAM M. ARKIN

History in One Act: A Novel of 9/11

Unmanned:
Drones, Data and the Illusion of Perfect Warfare

American Coup:
How a Terrified Government Is
Destroying the Constitution

Top Secret America:
The Rise of the New American Security State
(with Dana Priest)

Divining Victory:
Airpower in the 2006
Israel-Hezbollah War

Code Names:
Deciphering U.S. Military Plans,
Programs, and Operations in the 9/11 World

Operation Iraqi Freedom:
22 Historic Days in Words and Pictures
(with Mark Kusnetz and Neal Shapiro)

The U.S. Military Online:
A Directory for Internet Access
to the Department of Defense

Nuclear Weapons Databook, Volume IV:
Soviet Nuclear Weapons
(with Thomas B. Cochran,
Robert S. Norris, and Jeffrey I. Sands)

The Untold

Story

of Our

Endless Wars

SIMON & SCHUSTER

New York   London   Toronto   Sydney   New Delhi

THE GENERALS HAVE NO CLOTHES

* *

WILLIAM M. ARKIN
with E. D. Cauchi

Simon & Schuster
1230 Avenue of the Americas
New York, NY 10020

First Simon & Schuster hardcover edition April 2021

SIMON & SCHUSTER and colophon are registered
trademarks of Simon & Schuster, Inc.

For information about special discounts for bulk purchases, please
contact Simon & Schuster Special Sales at 1-866-506-1949
or business@simonandschuster.com.

The Simon & Schuster Speakers Bureau can bring authors to
your live event. For more information or to book an event, contact
the Simon & Schuster Speakers Bureau at 1-866-248-3049
or visit our website at www.simonspeakers.com.

Interior design by Lewelin Polanco

Manufactured in the United States of America

1   3   5   7   9   10   8   6   4   2

Library of Congress Control Number: 2021931214

ISBN 978-1-9821-3099-2
ISBN 978-1-9821-3101-2 (ebook)

To Rikki and Hannah

CONTENTS

chapter one

PERPETUAL WAR

In today's perpetual news machine, the unspoken first commandment is to never stop. I've borne witness to this, working as an on-air analyst, journalist, and national security expert over two decades. I've been in the news trenches covering the 9/11 attacks, wars in the Middle East and Africa, and everything from nuclear weapons to domestic watchlists.

During the 2016 presidential campaign season, NBC News asked me to join their new investigative reporting unit. My job was to bring in the big national security stories— beyond the day-to-day.

What I proposed to report on was perpetual war, a deeply entrenched and inherently invisible system that has taken hold of our government and our society—one that not only controls how we navigate our way in the world but also influences every other priority. Wars in Afghanistan and Iraq have spread throughout the Middle East and into Africa. Somehow, no matter what happens in the countries where we are fighting, despite continual declarations of success—killing terrorist leaders, winning battles, freeing territory—the fighting never diminishes. And, to put it bluntly, despite so much activity, despite the sacrifice of so many lives, despite enormous cost, and despite countless excuses and justifications behind why we cannot stop fighting, we are neither defeating our enemies nor do we ever become more secure.

Then Donald Trump happened.

When in the first *week* of the administration a disastrous special operations raid went down in Yemen and the new national security advisor, retired general Michael Flynn, rushed to the microphone to threaten Tehran, I thought, with 9/11 fading and a seemingly more aggressive president taking over from Barack Obama, that America might finally pay attention to its many wars, that this system would finally have its reckoning. Pentagon sources told me that officers felt pressured to produce a quick win for Donald Trump and that, in rushing to do so, a Navy SEAL died unnecessarily. An operation justified to weaken Al Qaeda was dragging America into Yemen's civil war. What is more, these same sources said, the raid would never have happened had the Obama White House not approved it.

To me, that Yemen raid seemed a tangible way not just to illustrate our lack of attention but to serve as a metaphor for how the never-ending fight sustained itself. Over the months that I worked on the investigation, I uncovered the clandestine fabric of American special operations, secret agreements with the United Arab Emirates and Saudi Arabia—even a clandestine war with Iran. And yet because Donald Trump had taken over the news, all the public heard was former Obama administration officials and national security gatekeepers telling them how Donald Trump was doing everything wrong and how they had done everything right.

Over the next six months my investigation into perpetual war grew increasingly out of step with this now singular message. A long investigation scheduled to appear on *Dateline*,

NBC's marquee prime-time investigative program, got cut back and buried to air on a weekend morning. And even there, a story that I thought should span two administrations and show an autonomous system operating regardless of who was president transformed into one centered on an interview with the dead sailor's father, who was denouncing Donald Trump.

Then North Korea rocketed into the news. As the Navy built up an armada, and as the Air Force brought in bombers, news coverage skewed. It was as if Donald Trump were at the helm of every aircraft carrier and the pilot of every airplane. And even worse, in the frenzy to convey how dangerous Donald Trump was, as if he were responsible for Pyongyang's pursuit of a nuclear weapon, the news media filled with scaremongering and superficial accounts: that North Korea could not only now attack Hawaii and the West Coast but that it could also destroy a powerless South Korea and defeat any American counterattack. News stories lazily reported that Kim Jung-un possessed "the fourth largest army in the world," the exact formulation used decades earlier to justify war with Iraq. It was a misleading picture of military might. The message conveyed was that America had no real options other than a perpetual standoff. No one seemed interested in the fact that over the last twenty years the U.S. military had transformed its war-fighting capacity, accruing advantages that not only explained the North's fears but also paved the way for new solutions.

Then interest in North Korea waned as the next story took over. By the end of Donald Trump's first year, reporting anything that did not feed the breathless machinery of presidential missteps and wrongdoings floundered. And not only that, but NBC and the rest of television was saturated with former national security bigwigs and retired generals telling America how things should be done. I tried to point out that these paid commentators, Obama and Bush administration officials alike, were the very makers of our global mess. On their watch, everything—*everything*—had gotten worse. They had presided over quagmires in Afghanistan and Iraq. They had overseen North Korea going nuclear. Under their tenure they had watched as the Islamic State rampaged, lodged the United States in Yemen, and moved perpetual war into Africa. They had even presided over the creation of a new cold war with Russia and China, backing a new generation of nuclear weapons.

Stranger still, then, was a subtle narrative building (not just at NBC) that somehow these makers of perpetual war and the secret agencies of government that they represented—the so-called deep state—were going to save America from the new president's recklessness—or, even worse, his supposed treason. Forgotten in the deification of these supposed saviors were their legacies, their histories of misdeeds, their violations of civil liberties, and, more recently, their forays into torture and secret prisons and warrantless surveillance. Former officials now spouted purported wisdom about the world and the threats, those giving them airtime ignoring how they and their very agencies had proven wrong so many times in the past, misinterpreting everything from the fall of the Soviet Union to Iraqi weapons of mass destruction to the very emergence of ISIS.

When I say Donald Trump happened, what I mean is that he is such a gigantic presence that he shifted our definition of national security. As the new president proposed a Muslim travel ban and pushed a border wall, as he attacked friends and allies, as he insulted his own intelligence community while complimenting Vladimir Putin, *he* came to embody instability. Amidst mounting allegations of wrongdoing and even lawbreaking, and with a backdrop of Russian interference in America's domestic affairs, many people came to believe that President Trump was the greatest threat to America. And not only that, but that the new president was going to blow up the world.

But to give him some credit, Donald Trump, in his own impetuous way, was also questioning what he called America's endless wars. He was right to do so, just as many in the national security establishment were right to worry about how he would go about withdrawing. And yet the debate became the national security status quo versus Donald Trump. And whether they intended to do so or not, the news media and the national security experts ended up arguing that nothing should or could change. With Syria and Afghanistan, when Trump said he wanted to withdraw, they supported continued fighting. On North Korea, when Trump said he wanted to denuclearize, they argued that it wasn't possible, and even that it wasn't worth trying. On Russia, they questioned why the president wasn't being *more* offensive. On Iran, they practically pushed for Trump to expand America's battlefield.

When I suggested to editors and bosses that Donald Trump might be right in some of his scatterbrained intuitions, I remember being met with astonishment. I argued that we'd long ago stopped asking what it was we were really fighting for, how much we were accomplishing, or what was the desired ending. After nearly two years of arguing, and as the scope of news coverage shrunk to this one man, I left in frustration, writing an open letter to my colleagues in which I bemoaned the "Trump circus" and the news media's transformation into one of perpetual war's many enablers.

"I find it shocking that we essentially condone continued American bumbling in the Middle East and now Africa through our ho-hum reporting," I wrote. "I find it disheartening that we do not report the failures of the generals and national security leaders."

That letter went viral in January 2019. I was flooded with invitations to speak out. Those requests instantly affirmed my unease. For all across the news media, as I tried to make the case that we had done a disservice in not reporting more aggressively on perpetual war, I found myself being asked about Donald Trump. And the news media.

"The national security community itself has gotten stronger and has gained strength under Donald Trump," I said on CNN, "and part of our responsibility as journalists is to cover the government, not just the president." To demonstrate our lack of engagement with and knowledge of America's wars, I asked the host Brian Stelter if he could name the ten countries around the world that the United States was currently bombing.

"I can't," he responded.

And here's the tragic punch line: I'm not sure that I got that number right. It's probably more countries than ten. Officially, I knew then that on any given day the United States was killing terrorists and bombing in *at least* ten different countries. But there were others, more obscure—Burkina Faso, Nigeria, Cameroon, Chad, Uganda—where I also knew that American forces were secretly operating. In fact, the so-called global war on terror engaged the U.S. military in fifty-five different countries. And there were more places where our "allies"—a total of eighty nations and counting—were killing on our behalf. Indeed, American special operations forces were routinely present in more than ninety countries, sometimes with partners and sometimes unilaterally. And only a quarter of those countries were officially acknowledged.

I've been a student of this world for more than forty-five years, since I joined the Army in 1974. Trained as an intelligence analyst and assigned to West Berlin, I was focused on the physical manifestation of the Cold War—Soviet weapons, bases, military units—a *where* and a *what* that cut to the core of what really goes on: "capabilities and not intentions" we used to say, beyond the words of politicians and the news media coverage. When I got out of the military and started writing about the American military, I approached the United States in the same way, endeavoring to methodically piece together a big picture—a true picture—from the smallest details. My belief then, as it is now, is that these tiny pieces accumulate into a physical machine, and a larger truth, more powerful than whoever is president. What is more, this machine in its many parts emits its own energies—like a black hole—with hidden and unintended consequences, provoking the other side, creating crisis, constraining change.

Given that we are talking about national security, another feature of this machine is that so much of what it does is intentionally kept secret. That secrecy, I've also come to learn, is not just directed at America's adversaries. It also serves to defend the machine, to keep it out of view of the public and the news media, from congressional overseers, and even from insiders with alternate views. During the Cold War, and today during perpetual war, one of the greatest consequences of secrecy is that very few people—even government officials—have a complete grasp of the total physical system. And not only that, but the stimuli emitted by the machine, demanding day-to-day decisions and constant effort to forestall crisis if a wrong move is made, keeps insiders focused on the immediate rather than the big picture.

During the Cold War, a misstep in the nuclear machine might have led to nuclear war, and this created a world of cautious deliberation and a general resistance to change. Perpetual war follows a similar pattern, the fear being that letting up anywhere might result in another terrorist attack as catastrophic as 9/11. Where the two eras further intersect is in the presence of a disruptive leader. We forget that Ronald Reagan—with all of his Star Wars craziness and neutron bomb enthusiasm—was outrageous and considered ignorant and dangerous. And yet his disruptions challenged the entire fabric of deterrence, and his musing about disarmament led to the single greatest shift in ending the Cold War. So too did Donald Trump's disregard for the conventions of perpetual war open the way to diminish its influence and find an end. Even before coronavirus I thought that would be his legacy.

Although Donald Trump continues to dominate the news, as I write this, coronavirus promises to reorder national security priorities, even to close the chapter on 9/11. As changes are contemplated, it is essential to keep the focus on the big picture of war making's physicality. Today, a gigantic physical superstructure sustains endless warfare. Given the participation of half the countries on earth, it is extraordinarily complex. It is made up of bases and outposts, air and sea operations only tentatively connected to the ground, and it includes robust clandestine forces. And, befitting this modern era, much of this perpetual war infrastructure is a globe-straddling network of communications and sensing, largely invisible even as it "wires" together the planet into a single system. Like the nuclear system that preceded it, few have a grasp of the entirety. People who work within the war infrastructure, both the decision makers and the participants, are largely oblivious to the totality.

The perpetual-war machine also reverberates and transforms the world by militarizing foreign policy and nation-state relations in areas that have little or nothing to do with terrorism. The list of additional activities—countering the proliferation of weapons of mass destruction, dealing with long-range missiles and drones now owned by all, fighting cyber threats, defeating piracy, policing the drug trade and stemming transnational organized crime, stopping illegal migration and human trafficking—creates more infrastructure and is more stimuli and more to orchestrate. Though justified as necessary to deal with the roots of terrorism, these activities have expanded military missions and diffused the main effort.

And finally, perpetual war transforms the world by promoting greater domestic militarization and challenging the liberal multilateral order. Authoritarianism flourishes around the globe. The age of cooperative globalization that many hoped would replace the five decades of the Cold War and lead to an era of peacekeeping has slowly disintegrated. Nationalism gains strength throughout Europe and spreads onto other continents. NATO—the Western heart of internationalism—sleepwalks toward global domination. The United Nations unites no one and has become a powerless bystander. Even the reliable global peacemakers of the past like Sweden are bolstering their militaries and taking sides.

* *

What started as the "global war on terror" after 9/11, what was rechristened "countering violent extremism" by President Obama, what Donald Trump calls "endless war," what the news media refers to as "forever war," and what weary generals describe as "fifth-generation warfare," "hybrid war," war in "the gray zone," and "the long war," is what I call "perpetual war."

The costs have been astronomical. Since 9/11, nearly 11,000 Americans have died fighting. More than 53,000 have been physically broken, while countless more have been inflicted with psychological injuries. Because of secrecy, that number of deaths is thousands more than most people think. That's because the widely accepted number of American deaths—that over 7,000 *soldiers* have been killed—excludes the number of private contractors who have also died. These are civilians, some highly skilled technicians, but some just security guards, who have become an increasingly large proportion of the machine, sometimes added when host countries don't want to see people in uniform, sometimes added because the military itself wants to obscure how many people are engaged in the fight. By 2018 the number of contractors killed began to exceed the number of soldiers. Not only does this say something profound about how out of view perpetual war has become; it also shows how distanced we have become from the physical realities on the ground. For a country that so reveres its fallen warriors, so many unnoticed and unrecognized American deaths are a double standard, both for the government and the public.

Beyond America, how many have died is a gigantic missing piece. After almost twenty years of fighting, the estimates of the civilian toll range from a few hundred thousand to as many as two million killed, most as a result of the chaos that has come to dominate where we fight. Millions more have been driven from their homes, causing a refugee crisis that the United Nations calls the worst since World War II. Lurking somewhere behind all of this is an even greater mystery regarding how many terrorists have been killed. No one, not even within U.S. intelligence, has a precise number. The intelligence agencies don't even know how many terrorists there actually are in the world. The consensus is that there are probably a couple of hundred thousand, although how many there are seems increasingly lost in definitions of who is a terrorist and, distressingly, how many new ones are created every day.

Fighting against these terrorists are the nearly 8.5 million military personnel of the United States, NATO, and their coalition partners in Afghanistan, Iraq, and elsewhere. Of course 8.5 million troops aren't *fighting* a couple of hundred thousand lightly armed insurgents. It's an account of the resources available. But the number should illustrate how the war on terrorism is a very different kind of war where conventional forces and arithmetic don't apply. And as will be seen, it should give some idea of how huge the superstructure is that sustains the few thousand who actually do fight.

Illustrative of how huge the larger perpetual war machine is, not just in forward deployed troops but in the physical base, communications, and intelligence network that sustains them, is an accounting of how much money we spend. Since 2001, warring in foreign lands has cost the American taxpayer more than $6.5 trillion, a sum more than twice what the government officially reports. That's more than the defense budget of all the other nations combined, *over six years of spending*. It's twice the cost of annual health care for all Americans. It's ten times the annual budget of the entire American public school system.

And what is the result? After two decades of fighting, not one country in the Middle East—not one country in the *world*—can argue that it is safer today than it was before 9/11. Every country that is now a part of the expanding battlefield of perpetual war—from Pakistan to Lebanon in the Middle East, from Somalia across Africa to Mali, in South and Southeast Asia, and even in Central and South America—is an even greater disaster zone than it was two decades ago.

Whether one is a hawk or a dove, Democrat or Republican, on the left or the right, it's hard not to concede that the world is an ever more dangerous place. Top national security officials agree. "We face the most diverse and complex set of threats we have ever seen," Dan Coats, Trump's first director of national intelligence, told Congress in 2018. James Clapper, who preceded Coats in the same position in the Obama administration, warned two years earlier with almost identical words, saying additionally that "unpredictable instability" had become "the new normal." Marine Corps general Joseph Dunford, the chairman of the Joint Chiefs of Staff under both

Obama and Trump, said that he thought the planet was in its most uncertain time since the Second World War. And Dunford's predecessor, General Martin Dempsey, wrote that "today's global security environment is the most unpredictable I have seen in 40 years of service."

In other words, things have gotten worse as we have waged war. So how did we end up here? Partly the answer is that while those engaged in national security go about doing their jobs, we haven't done ours. We can argue about why, but we, the citizenry, have taken our eyes off the ball, going about our lives unaffected by war. Much of the reason is that this is just the time we live in, that fewer and fewer people's lives are touched by war because fewer and fewer *soldiers* are needed to sustain the modern machine. The perpetual war system has advanced—and it *has* advanced, in the air, in unmanned systems, in the cyber sphere, in space, and most importantly in a network that ties together all of these parts—to where it no longer is represented by armies and navies that once demanded public participation and sacrifice. And attention.

But the machine has also changed internally, able to persist in fighting without absorbing much harm to itself. We aren't yet at the point where everyone is sitting at a keyboard, but the preponderance of people who work in national security are supporting a very small number who are actually on the ground and in the fight. It is a ratio of *hundreds of thousands* to one. The physical reality of actual combat—the sounds and smells of war—has grown distant to nearly everyone in the national security community. It's a pinnacle of achievement to maximize one's advantages and not put one's own people at risk. And yet, if that's the state of things for those *at* war, imagine how and why the public can so easily live as if there were no war at all.

It's a macabre bargain we live with. After 9/11, it seemed

that the United States would pursue terrorists with every means possible and that the war would be ferocious, bloody, and quick. But the American military has its own culture. It fights with the promise that it will not only stop terrorism but also contain the effects of fighting. The American way of war, born of the last three decades in this era of precision, is one of smart weapons and remote instruments and even the newer cyber and electronic acrobatics of hacking into enemy networks and systems. Minimizing soldier deaths and injuries and *even* civilian harm facilitates frictionless continuation. I'm not arguing that there isn't great danger and sacrifice for those few on the ground who actually do fight. But the American way has also become to make war invisible, not just because counter-terrorism demands secrecy, but also because the military assumes that the America public doesn't want to know because it isn't prepared to sacrifice. And for that reason the American way of war preserves the enterprise, minimizing outside interference.

Technologically driven and stretched out over many years, one of the unintended consequences of this style of fighting is that time has also allowed more and more terrorists to be manufactured. Despite so much focused effort, despite killing Osama bin Laden and other terrorist leaders, not a single organization has been eliminated. Indeed, new ones constantly emerge, while existing ones disperse and spread to new parts of the world. Unlike any previous conflicts, the dead and the dispossessed are not just victims. In perpetual war, many of them and their relatives become soldiers for future battles. We are now at a point where young men (and women) born after 9/11 are old enough to take up arms against us. And they do.

Still, we should not let images of American weakness prevail. In comparison to others, to our adversaries who don't have a global network and who haven't gained twenty years of experience fighting with modern instruments, the truth is that no one compares to the United States in military capacity. I reject that Russia or China are surpassing us or even catching up. They may have lots of things and even bigger weapons, and they may even have developed brute force cyber armies that seem menacing and superior. But where real military capability materializes—in integration, in choreography, in initiative, and in decentralization, and on any global scale—there is no comparison. But while the United States is the most powerful nation militarily, we also have failed in our war against terrorism. Not only is it one of life's central maxims that one can win every battle and still lose a war, but there's a more difficult truth that challenges the American self-image. We haven't won every battle. Our way of war and our style of warfare has never been well suited for this counter-terrorism fight. When we turn the fight over to secret armies, spending so much energy trying to kill terrorist leaders is the wrong approach. And killing terrorists in battle merely condemns us to our own endless assembly line of doing that forever.

* *

In the chapters that follow, I develop a more comprehensive picture of perpetual war and how it thrives, grounding it in examples of actual practices and events. I precisely identify the practitioners who support and protect it, who built this system and operate it within their own set of rules. I show also how counter-terrorism extended the fight not just geographically overseas but also far beyond military missions. The impact has been that perpetual war, particularly at home, is no longer a military affair—that it now incorporates law enforcement and the vague armies of Homeland Security, and even civilian agencies charged with protection of critical infrastructure. Warfare has never been purely a military problem, but the wages of perpetual war have infected the whole of our society while also pushing that very society to have less and less input.

I conclude with three primary proposals. First, that civil society, which has become ever more detached from all things military, develop greater literacy about matters of national security. I argue that the public reengage and make its voice heard. Second, I argue for greater civilian control. I call for a new cadre of civilian experts similar to those who existed during the Cold War: the arms controllers and nuclear experts who became knowledgeable enough to challenge the generals and the status quo. And finally, I propose a "global security index," a Dow Jones–like tracking tool that would quantitatively measure our state of security—that is, keep an eye on progress or the lack thereof in our constant warring. It is so easy for everyone—national security experts, the news media, politicians—to just focus on the day-to-day, constantly manufacturing ever more threats, never quite getting to the question of whether the continuation of fighting is actually achieving its objectives. A GSX could remedy that, arming the public with a bottom-line assessment driven by big data and not by fear or habit.

Ending perpetual war isn't a formula, and, as we shall see, its supporters are so broad and ubiquitous that any single set of policy proposals—to stop fighting in this or that country or to eliminate this or that program or organization—runs into arguments and constituencies that are powerful and overwhelming. In the final analysis, ending perpetual war really means a psychological shift, one that derives from understanding the physicality of what's going on and one that demands an unsentimental look of what we're actually accomplishing. In Syria or Afghanistan or in the rest of the Middle East, with North Korea and Iran, or even against Russia and China, I make suggestions that I believe will ultimately lead to better outcomes than the tracks we are on. In my proposals, I stack the physical reality of what we are actually doing against the enduring goal: to protect the American people and to make a safer world for our children. In that regard, perpetual war has been a failure and ending it—really ending it—is essential.

chapter two

THE NATIONAL SECURITY ESTABLISHMENT

Perpetual war has grown and flourished over four administrations: Clinton's, Bush's, Obama's, and now Trump's.

George W. Bush came into office ready to carry out "ABC": Anything But Clinton. In other words, he wanted to abandon the peacekeeping and remote war making of the 1990s, to stop "swatting at flies" in the Middle East. Then 9/11 happened, and he responded exactly as the previous president would have. Of course, he did it with anger and cowboy bravado, but still, the retaliation in Afghanistan was dominated by shooting missiles and using "safe" airpower and hidden special operators, thereby minimizing the military's footprint on the ground.

Rapid defeat of the Taliban emboldened the American military, and Afghanistan was followed by the disastrous Bush administration decision to invade Iraq. Saddam Hussein and his supposed weapons of mass destruction had nothing to do with 9/11, but the system was now primed to fight again. Almost the entire shooting air forces had been moved to the Persian Gulf region, with seemingly nothing left to do in Afghanistan. Why send them home? One Pentagon general told me this at the time. After all, there was now a leftover Clinton task to fulfill in Iraq. "We're going to kill two stones with one bird," he said.

Then what did the Bush team do? They embraced Clinton's model of nation building and humanitarian alliances, even as they completely misread both of the countries they were now fighting in. Yes, counterterrorism was the official raison d'être, but as they became more chastened while becoming more and more bogged down in Iraq, they looked to the local governments for help. So the Bush administration declared that the U.S. armed forces were now fighting for liberty and democracy, and that Afghanistan and Iraq would transform. George W. Bush's final *National Defense Strategy* stated that the United States was to be "a beacon of light for those in dark places," a phrase that could have been written by either Clinton or Bush's successor, the young senator from Illinois.

Barack Obama entered the Oval Office in 2009 intent on ending Bush's wars. But neither Obama nor his people saw the bigger picture: how the military had developed over eight years of nonstop warfare, not just learning the ways of new capabilities and weaponry but also how to reformulate their mission to correspond with prolonged fighting. Obama may have wanted to end Bush's wars, but a host of military adaptations were reaching maturity right when he took office, and those adaptations suggested that the United States could continue with a smaller ground force and a lesser negative effect, especially in that fewer and fewer Americans were at risk. The two most important of these adaptations were armed drones—which were just coming into their own—and what many would call the "cyber revolution" in intelligence. Obama did not accelerate drone killing, as many have asserted. Drone strikes just got better as the operators perfected their craft. And so targeted killing demanded more of the president's time and his signature—a deep dive into the weeds that obscured the bigger picture.

The cyber revolution similarly aggrandized more and more attention. The hunt for information had almost completely shifted from targeting foreign governments and national armies to selecting and monitoring individual terrorists. This is when we first heard about terrorist leaders as high-value targets. Constant surveillance and digital innovation opened up vast and abundant new sources of information. Obama's process and law-oriented wishes were fed by this meticulous effort. And so Obama allowed remote-controlled killing machines and the expanding system of targeting to move into Pakistan, Yemen, and other countries, the theory being that pinpoint decisions set the United States on a track to be less warlike, more thoughtful, and above all more contained. The migration necessitated a shift away from conventional forces to clandestine operators—the direct assassins on the ground and the spotters for drones to do the same work. And thus what was going on became more invisible.

In 2017, Donald Trump came into office with an isolationist streak that diverged from mainstream America, or at least from the Washington majority. He wanted out of Bush's and Obama's wars altogether. Or so he said. But the new commander in chief of "alternative facts" neither was competent enough to carry out his policies nor had the support needed to reverse the course of the previous administrations. But perpetual war by that time was also making its own rules. America was no longer waging "war" in any conventional sense, and that meant that withdrawing forces on the ground not only wasn't going to stop combat but wasn't the most important move to make.

Trump pronounced and blustered, but no matter what he said or did, the war-making structure hummed along. Airpower and special operations continued to assume a larger and larger share of fighting, while covert operatives and private contractors conveniently went about expanding in new African battlefields. Trump did attempt to disrupt things. When he watched on television that ISIS was being defeated in Syria, he called for the withdrawal of American forces. He was rebuffed by his own secretary of defense. The Pentagon said that any withdrawal, even of just a couple of thousand troops, would take months. Soon the president lost interest and the system prevailed.

The United States was still fighting in Afghanistan and Iraq, but to accommodate Obama and mask the enduring presence, the language of perpetual war changed. Washington now spoke of "ceilings" that put a cap on how many soldiers could be on the ground in any country. Where combat was supposedly over in places like Afghanistan and Iraq, the Pentagon insisted that men and women on the ground were only engaged in "train-and-assist" missions. The United States was working *by, with, and through* allied nations in these and in other countries, "building partner capacity," as the Pentagon put it. Meanwhile, the U.S. military continued maintaining a foothold everywhere, relying more and more on a network of bases far from battlefield countries and used to project air and even cyber power into new places.

During this post–Cold War era of intervention and perpetual war, each of these four presidents have had varying worldviews and declared intentions. And yet, what manifested in the physical outcome of each administration was interchangeable. The reason is that a powerful national security establishment had formed in decades of constant fighting. Today this establishment is the grand conductor of perpetual war, running on its own self-constructed and fortified track, guaranteeing steady motion. We live with the contradictions that the establishment creates: we're at war and we're not, we're in Afghanistan and we're not, we're building nations and we're not. We've withdrawn from Iraq, except we haven't. We are fighting terrorism in dozens of countries. But even there we've abandoned the goal of eradicating terrorism. And now comes even the newer brands. We're focused on Europe, and yet we are also "pivoting" on and "rebalancing" to Asia. And tomorrow, who knows? Cyber war? A new "U.S. Space Force"? Each new mission brings new demands for ever greater resources, never finishing anything that is already ongoing.

I liken the totality of these establishment practitioners and their perpetual war system to something akin to Wall Street. It is a synecdoche of clandestine power, not limited to a single institution or location. No one person oversees it, and no one person is really in charge. But each independent participant contributes to the greater enterprise. Individually, any one piece might seem like an aberration when compared to what presidents have declared or the public understands, but together they culminate in an untouchable force that operates as one. In that, the national security establishment is the very definition of "establishment": a dominant group or elite that holds power and exercises control over our society.

And, as befitting an establishment, this elite has also become so powerful that it is impervious to outside influence.

Conservative and liberal, Republican and Democrat, right and left, this establishment has no particular ideology. They have mastered all of the ways of bureaucracy: leaking, concealing, and overwhelming decision makers with technicalities, slow-rolling outcomes, and perfecting passive-aggressive responses to direction. When the establishment wants to counter the White House, it simply avoids offering options. When the

White House wants something, the establishment ponders and delays. Each part of this establishment has its own method of rejecting a presidential decision. In the national security establishment's head, every president is flawed. Those executive leaders who make snap decisions are charged with being "impetuous," and those who waver, or appear irresolute, are accused of "dithering." The bureaucracy chokes them with process and deliberation, and then pushes them to action at hair-raising speeds.

More than half a century ago, at the end of World War II and at the dawn of the Cold War, President Dwight D. Eisenhower warned Americans about the rise of a "military-industrial complex," and today it remains a powerful image. But the term gives too much power to the production of capital goods and a conventional military, and the description no longer represents the current national security establishment. Our world today is one of information, space and cyber. The armed forces are sustained more by data than by metal. One of the consequences is that the national security establishment is far more than just the generals and admirals, and even their defense industry partners. The national security establishment seamlessly combines the military, the intelligence community, the new institutions of homeland security, even the law enforcement agencies—federal, state, and local; the executive and legislative branches; uniformed and civilian authorities; the governmental and the private. sector. Membership ranges from civilian government officials, to men and women in uniform, to profit-seeking consultants, to supposed nonprofit and independent nongovernmental organizations and academics. And this establishment also includes the news media. Mainstream news outlets embrace national security, feeding off the handouts of government and building relationships with conflict-laden and biased insiders, compromising independence and objectivity.

There may be civilians galore populating congressional staff offices and agencies, and there may be a dozen civil departments seemingly doing civil things. But even there, almost all of them are dragooned into the care and promotion of perpetual war, particularly as it has reached the shores of America.

Every day, this national security establishment issues a global prognosis: telling us how bad the threat is from Russia, China, North Korea, and Iran; how bad things are with terrorism and violent extremism; how bad things are with nuclear proliferation and instability. Then the establishment warns us how much worse things *will be* if we don't continue the fight—and if they don't get what they need. The foes are as interchangeable as the subjects. Soon it becomes difficult to tell which enemy we are fighting and why. This is how war never ends. It is kept alive by a million little line items and indistinguishable "counter" missions to new and constantly changing "threats." For the national security establishment, pursuit of national security solutions—"competitive advantage," as the military puts it—is the end in itself, as important as actually bringing any conflict to a decisive close.

* *

If the superstructure of the national security system determines policies and actions, then the most influential element is the military. It is America's largest employer, its largest socialist institution, and the single largest public corporation in the world. At the top are the brass: the generals and admirals—men and women who have risen to their rank because they are more than just battlefield leaders. They are institutional and political operators. Moving up requires understanding the ways of Washington and the bargaining processes of perpetual war. Being a Washington professional unfortunately also means being a bureaucratic knife fighter and an insubordinate leaker.

The Pentagon brass creates their own independent relationships with congressional overlords and other influencers. And out in the world? These days the generals are also proconsuls and viceroys, governing and negotiating the course of American foreign policy, more powerful than any ambassador or diplomat, controlling the destiny of their perpetual theaters of war.

Backing up the generals and the uniformed commanders are hundreds of thousands of civilians who work for the military, government employees and private contractors alike. They include permanent civil servants, government technicians, and consultants. These civilians exert outsize influence over previous eras—at least in Washington—because military officers come and go while the technologies of warfare become ever more and more complex. Even military units—down to the smallest company and platoon level—can't go to war without civilian technicians and contractors. Civilians operate complex equipment and conduct over-the-shoulder coaching of the people in uniform. And in this modern era of global networking, tens of thousands more are needed to curate and move information. The support infrastructure is massive and constantly evolving.

An essential part of the technological change experienced over decades of constant warfare is the enormous growth of the intelligence community. Intelligence has become the next most important actor in the national security establishment. Although the so-called intelligence community is still one-tenth as large as the military, it has itself tripled in size since 9/11. And yet, while "human" operations—the work of agents and clandestine paramilitaries—have grown, technological collection outstrips the human-focused activities by thousands to one.

The bulk of intelligence work directly supports the counter-terrorism mission, everything from the data needed to sustain drones and special operations to the people who make the maps. When Leon Panetta became CIA director in 2009, he said he was "staggered" to learn how many people were working on locating senior members of Al Qaeda. One senior Obama official later observed that so much was focused on the war on terrorism that the Agency short-changed its analysis of the "large global trends that were just as much influencing our future—climate, governance, food, health . . . ," subjects that virtually disappeared from the President's Daily Brief.

American intelligence has failed repeatedly when it comes to analysis, but the *doing* of perpetual war and the processing of information has siphoned off resources from seeing a bigger picture. It is a fact of history that neither the CIA nor anyone else in the intelligence community produced any specific warning about the 9/11 plot before it happened. But after that, the intelligence analysts misread Saddam Hussein's weapons of mass destruction. Even after being on the ground for years, analysts never came to understand the complexities of Iraqi society. The Agency and the rest of the intelligence community didn't think that Al Qaeda in Iraq was much of a threat then, nor did they anticipate the emergence of ISIS. One former official has said that "ISIS's march across northern Iraq took Washington almost completely by surprise." When the Islamic State rolled into Mosul in 2014, President Obama confronted his aides, angry he couldn't get any good information about either the advance or America's Iraqi allies on the ground. "We didn't get a warning that the Iraqis were going to melt away?" he is said to have asked, referring to how America's military partners stripped off their uniforms and deserted.

The intelligence community also didn't anticipate the Arab Spring, nor did it predict the speed with which events would unfold after protests began in 2010, toppling dictators, triggering civil wars, and spreading across the Middle East and

Africa. The Agency also completely missed that North Korea's supreme leader, Kim Jong-il, would empower his son to be his successor. And the CIA and the other intelligence agencies failed to detect or understand the enormity of Russia's operations during the 2016 presidential election. "When it comes to predicting the nature and location of our next military engagement since Vietnam, our record has been perfect," former defense secretary Robert Gates even joked in 2011. "We have never once gotten it right."

Still, the data keeps piling up. Everyone in the intelligence community admits that they don't have the bandwidth or brainpower to analyze what they're already bringing in. Because the national security establishment spends so much time and energy trying to triage the information it collects, it also spends billions on processing software and more pleasing visual displays of information, trying to make its cadre of Generation X and Y users more capable. Again this *doing*—just struggling to keep up—is one of the hallmarks of perpetual war. Just keeping up with intelligence gathering, just caring for and feeding the soldiers, just operating the equipment—just pulling together the resources needed to keep the global machine running—leaves little room for anything else.

Given all of the *doing*, and the shift from metal to data, the prosecutors of perpetual war also naturally operate as a network. Because of this, they tend toward decentralized decision making, which naturally empowers the outposts and gives them outsized influence. On the various edges of this network, where so many actions happen constantly and simultaneously, the proverbial butterfly effect occurs. Seemingly minor activities trigger cascading and largely unforeseen consequences. And since so much happens in the shadows, many of these disparate and decentralized events often operate at cross-purposes to each other. The depth of this compartmentalization became clear in October 2017 when four Army Special Forces soldiers were killed in the West African nation of Niger. Afterward, Congress—even members of the House and Senate committees on armed services—admitted they didn't even know that the United States had people in that country. But another anecdote shows an even more pernicious effect: Defense Secretary Gates and Secretary of State Hillary Clinton both complained internally that the CIA was handsomely paying off Afghan officials at the same time that their two departments were pursuing anticorruption campaigns. Gates later remarked that they sometimes found themselves trying to convince the very people who were on the American payroll to halt corruption. Overt and covert occupied the same battle space, not coordinated as one might imagine but getting in each other's way. Nothing changed then. And so nothing changes today. No one wins.

* *

No element of the national security establishment better exemplifies the scourge of *doing* over thinking—and the allure of maintaining a wartime status quo—than the $50 billion-a-year Department of Homeland Security. At the end of 2019 it had 240,000 employees, making it the federal government's third largest agency after the military and veterans affairs. Since its founding in 2003, this perpetual war adjunct has forged a mission statement that is almost unlimited in scope: "to help create a safe, secure, resilient place, where the American way of life can thrive."

Today, Homeland Security does everything from monitoring the safety of America's infrastructure, from the phone system to roads and bridges, to preparing for hurricanes. To protect the "critical infrastructure," Homeland Security has forced every state in the Union to create its own counterpart apparatus and its own mini-intelligence establishment in the form of so-called fusion centers. In the name of thwarting cyber threats, Homeland Security pressures private corporations to march in unison under government security and performance standards.

Not surprisingly then, Homeland Security has also grown to become the largest federal law enforcement entity in the country. Today the department has almost 60,000 domestic people with badges—Immigration and Customs Enforcement (ICE), U.S. Customs and Border Protection—plus another 45,000 uniformed Transportation Security Administration officers who, although they aren't police, sure act like it. At the end of 2019, the number of Homeland Security law enforcement officers was more than four times the size of the entire FBI, and it is growing.

Underneath all this, in the shadows, is there a deep state? If by "deep state" one means a secret society that transcends partisan political boundaries and makes self-interested decisions above and beyond the law of the land, the answer is: sort of.

First, what the deep state is not. Its members are not the experts who make missiles or submarines or aircraft, nor are they the engineers or technicians who build and run the machine. The deep state does not include the soldiers or the entire mass of fighters—military, civilian, and under contract—who are out doing the *doing*.

What the deep state can be said to be are the few thousand insiders who make decisions in the name of securing public safety. Behind the scenes, they largely operate little more than their keyboards and their phone systems, issuing directives that have enormous consequences. This elite of the elite approves who lives and who dies in drone attacks or other covert operations; they decide on programs like torture and warrantless surveillance; and they set in motion covert, clandestine, secret, and now even *virtual* operations around the globe. They are the ultimate armchair generals cut off from any real world of blood and sweat. They are completely divorced from the consequences for the nation and our society of their very decisions, and are able to operate because they form a compartmented system affirmed by Congress and veiled by secrecy.

Like all bureaucracies, the deep state and the rest of the national security establishment have developed ways to slow, modify, dumb down, obscure, and even kill anything—any initiative, any program, any law—that they decide doesn't enhance their work. When the White House debates what to do about country X, the system limits the options, either directly or by leaking to the news media, publicly divulging proposals and options to influence the outcome. Presidents often find themselves fenced in, either agreeing with what the bureaucracy wants or being dismissed for rejecting professional military advice or not giving the troops what they need.

Giving the troops what they need is both an American creed and a straitjacket that undermines our system of government. After being commander in chief for almost three years, Secretary of Defense Gates still decried that Barack Obama lacked the necessary familiarity with "American military culture" to make the right decisions. When Obama was facing reelection in 2012, one well-known retired Army officer remarked that "for the first time in modern American history, neither major candidate for the presidency has any military experience," as if four years at war weren't enough and as if his claim of military inexperience—that someone had not worn the uniform—was a national crisis in itself.

Congress is supposed to oversee the national security establishment, but even the legislature has become an auxiliary member of the national security establishment. Its enlistment started long ago, after the Watergate scandals, when members began to demand, and then were routinely granted, high-level security clearances to gain access to executive branch secrets. Those "reforms" evolved into mandatory reporting requirements about covert action and other top secret programs. There is no evidence that giving Congress access to state secrets ever stopped or prevented a major disaster, certainly not 9/11 or anything that happened afterward. Congress became more a secret keeper than an oversight institution, with certain members co-opted with select official access to information while leaving the rest of the legislative body in the dark.

Not surprisingly and despite the co-option of some legislators, the national security establishment considers Congress to be an unreasonable obstacle in their way, obstreperous and selfish, incapable of following the "decorum" that is supposed to produce a bipartisan consensus on national security. The establishment accuses Congress of "complicating" its decision making and, of course, of using defense spending as a "huge cash cow" to benefit their districts and states. Even the rare times when Congress exercises its oversight, the national security establishment has nothing but contempt for it. Robert Gates as secretary of defense under Bush and Obama decried that his yearly congressional instructions on the defense budgets contained a thousand pages of "nearly paralyzing direction, micromanagement, restrictions, and demands for reports"— surely a reasonable complaint, but also exactly the balance of power our system of government intended.

And so the military, the national security establishment, and the bureaucracy fight—each other as much as our now countless accumulated enemies. That Washington infighting replaces any true debate about progress or indeed about the performance of each element of this now entrenched group. The national security establishment has obviously benefited from the money that the trauma of 9/11 made available. New organizations came into being. New weapons and capabilities emerged. The prime directive after 9/11 was greater integration of the whole, to leave no seams between disparate parts where terrorists could sneak in. To integrate, a vast network came into being. That network demands the existence of each part in order to operate, fortifying the superstructure. What we have built speaks its own language and is increasingly cut off from society as it operates within its own subculture. This creates perhaps the greatest impediment toward change: that the national security establishment became ever more obscure, so many of its parts even unknown to—and out of the control of—its participants.

Whatever you think of them, whoever you think they are, there is one critical takeaway about this establishment. What they are doing isn't working. True, a single terrorist attack of 9/11 magnitude on American soil has been forestalled but, overall, so many have died and terrorism has so dispersed, grown, and changed that we have no idea whether this success is real or will hold. The establishment issues press releases that speak of making advances, of doing better, of even saving money, but any actual benefits only accrue to itself. And now, through two Republican and two Democrat administrations, the wars we are fighting don't just continue; they expand. To understand how this establishment has become the architect, practitioner, and now keeper of perpetual war, it makes sense to go back to 9/11.

chapter three

CLOSING
THE CHAPTER
ON 9/11

In the rush to war after 9/11, it is not surprising that the national security establishment avoided taking responsibility for what happened. I'm talking about accountability by not only the officials of the new Bush administration but the bureaucracy itself. From the lowliest airline screener to the top Al Qaeda analyst, no one lost their jobs. No one had to face the consequences of failure to fulfill their basic duties. When the public demanded some kind of accountability, they were ignored or the national security establishment told them that their desire for explanation was motivated by a desire to find scapegoats. The lack of accountability produced what has become one of the hallmarks of perpetual war: that whatever the effort is on the part of the establishment, there is never an expectation that greater security will be the outcome. So the public gets neither accountability nor security. And it is subtly told that it is unreasonable to demand either.

To explain the ways of bureaucracy, and the national security establishment's reaction to 9/11, we have to start well before the events.

As the sun set on December 14, 1999, just shy of six o'clock in the evening, a passenger ferry chugged out of Victoria, British Columbia, and began its twenty-three-mile journey across the Salish Sea to the United States. Aboard the MV *Coho* was thirty-two-year-old Quebecois Benni Antoine Noris, who sat impatiently inside his Chrysler 300M rental car. It had taken him months of planning and a few close calls, but he was finally on his way.

It was a typical Tuesday for U.S. Customs Service agent Diana Dean, who waited to greet the ferry. Dean worked the port of entry lane at the Washington State border in Port Angeles, and her job was to inspect cargo and people. By the time cars began unloading from the *Coho*, it was at the end of her shift.

As Noris' sedan pulled up to Dean's checkpoint, she asked him the basic customs questions. But Noris hesitated. "There was just something—something that wasn't quite right," Dean later explained. She asked Noris to step out of the car.

Dean and two other customs agents congregated to question the man. When they opened the trunk, they found what they first thought was drugs but upon closer inspection turned out to be the makings of a homemade bomb: a set of olive jars packed with an explosive combination of nitroglycerine, urea, and sulfate, two Casio watch timers, a circuit board, and 9-volt batteries.

Noris was arrested and later identified as an Algerian named Ahmed Ressam. At an Al Qaeda camp in Afghanistan, he and two other men had been assigned to detonate car bombs at Los Angeles International Airport on New Year's Eve. The goal was to kill hundreds of travelers, cause havoc, and disrupt the millennium celebrations. As investigators untangled the plot, they learned that massive intelligence failures—by Canadian,

French, and American officers—had occurred at previous checkpoints. They had detained and even questioned Ressam on numerous occasions, then let him go, letting him move closer to carrying out his plot.

Twenty-one months later, on a sunny Tuesday morning, there was no Diana Dean. Nineteen men boarded flights in Boston; Washington, D.C.; Portland, Maine; and Newark, New Jersey. On the morning that they checked in, eight of the nineteen hijackers were flagged by the Computer Assisted Passenger Prescreening System, an automated government database intended to subject potential security risks to additional screening. Only one of those eight had his luggage inspected. And then his suitcase was wiped for explosives but never opened. Four passengers—two flying out of Boston and two at Washington Dulles—were flagged for irregularities in their documents. They were allowed to board anyhow, and although their checked luggage was held back until it had been confirmed that they boarded, their bags also remained unopened and unscreened. Another hijacker who couldn't show proper identification was allowed to pass through security and board his flight. And still another couldn't speak a word of English and couldn't answer any security questions. He was allowed to board as well. Two of the Washington travelers carrying small knives set off metal detectors while going through security. After being wanded, they too were sent on their way.

Within four hours, these nineteen men hijacked and piloted four commercial airliners, flying the planes into the World Trade Center buildings and the Pentagon. A fourth plane intended for the Capitol dome or the White House crashed into a field in Pennsylvania. Three thousand people died, making it the deadliest terrorist attack on American soil. It wasn't a nation attacking another nation or a military attacking another military. Warfare had changed and so too would the response.

Federal authorities had little information to explain the hijackings or the events. Six of the nineteen hijackers had lived in the United States for more than a year, and three had taken multiple trips in and out of the country. And yet no one in the intelligence community had any specific tip-offs. On the day itself, dozens of officials responsible for security at four different airports went through the motions of doing their jobs but did little more. *Have you packed your bags yourself? Has anyone given you anything? Have your bags been under your control at all times?* These security questions proved to be the most perfunctory of bureaucratic utterances.

In the wake of the attacks, the Bush administration maintained that *they* were not asleep at the wheel, eventually developing a multipronged argument that they were not only working hard on terrorism but had done as much as their predecessors. "We were in office 233 days," National Security Advisor Condoleezza Rice later told the 9/11 Commission, pleading that the "kinds of structural changes" that were needed to create effective security couldn't have gotten made in the preceding eight months even if they had tried. Administration officials argued that the plot carried out was so diabolical in its simplicity and so lucky in its execution that even under the best of circumstances the government could not have stopped it. In other words, no one was really to blame.

Clinton veterans meanwhile pointed to the millennium bombing plot to criticize their successors, trumpeting their success in 1999: the very apprehension of Ahmed Ressam. And yet the truth of that story is that although the Clinton White House deliberated terrorism and issued directive after directive, nothing they did had anything to do with the Algerian's eventual capture. "I don't recall anybody saying watch for terrorists," Diana Dean would later tell NBC News. She couldn't remember any alert or guidance coming from Washington. Diana

Dean *was*, in fact, simply doing her job, she said. And in this case, doing her job meant following a human, straightforward, and nonexpert standard: she either detected threats she was charged with apprehending or she didn't. It is a standard that somehow got lost after 9/11 as an avalanche of explanations and recriminations papered over what had happened and why.

Amidst all of the finger pointing, a subtle theme emerged that 9/11 was somehow the public's fault. The American people had become too soft. They insisted on due process and evidence, emboldening the criminal plotters. They had grown to love liberty too much, placing too many constraints on police power and government spying. They had become too naïve about their own safety, imagining that security was cheap and easy. If the intelligence community had failed to penetrate Al Qaeda or provide specific warning, the reason was that public insisted on oversight and legality. An immature public had too high of a regard for the constraints on the executive branch that came after Watergate, manacles that neutered law enforcers, tied the hands of the covert operators, and gutted the secret agencies. If the FBI had failed, it was because of the "wall" imposed by an overly legalistic society and by civil libertarians who valued rights over security. Those same naïve critics stood in the way of effective domestic policing, tending to their privacy and selfish liberties when no one who is innocent needs to worry about government spying. If the military had been used ineffectively before 9/11, it was also the American people's fault. They made the armed forces fight according to some version of the Marquess of Queensberry Rules. And they lacked the will and the appetite for casualties, even necessary ones. And this public in particular failed to make the sacrifices of their ancestors.

The attack on the public, perhaps veiled and not articulated as such, was particularly vicious, because for one shining moment after 9/11, despite the war drumbeat and silent coup by the national security establishment, the American people actually fought back. They did so in the form of the 9/11 "families": Americans from all walks of life, from all political persuasions, demanding accountability from the government.

Thrust into the limelight, the 9/11 families were confronted with incredible examples of government incompetence, breakdown, and sloth. They schooled themselves about government confusion and miscommunication and the lack of preparedness. They clamored for solutions, particularly for a new Homeland Security apparatus that would make the bloated and fragmented bureaucracies function and work together. Then they demanded that a reluctant government establish an independent 9/11 Commission to collect the facts and explain who was responsible and why.

Then something incredible happened. They won their demands, even managing to force Washington to appoint an outsider, New York City police commissioner Bernard Kerik, to run the new Department of Homeland Security—that is, until he had to withdraw his name due to personal scandals. Thus began the families' bitter course in civics. Special interests were already hard at work to benefit from 9/11. Money was already flowing to the very architects of failure. No one wanted to be held accountable in the way that the public might expect: by someone resigning in shame, or being fired, or even being demoted. When new departments and agencies were established, the same old people moved in. And the 9/11 families were scolded, told not to play "the blame game," not to disturb the work of those who were now toiling ever so hard to protect them, and certainly not to upset the soldiers or *their families*, because now there was a war on and everyone needed to march together.

Again, it was subtle, but the message that the establishment sent to the 9/11 families was that they needed to forgive. Not a Christian forgiveness for the attackers, but a forgiveness for those entrusted with the sacred duty to protect them. They needed to forget the miscues. They needed to let go of any anger. It was okay to ask questions, they were told, but they needed also to step aside to let the establishment do the tough work ahead. And so, while they listened to outpourings from officials and whistle-blowers and investigators about all the missed opportunities, the botched visas, the lost memos, the ignored intercepts, the hoarded intelligence, the confused names, the countless red alerts and close calls—as they learned of even more plots in the works and, of course, that it could have been even worse—any real accountability for what happened on 9/11 faded. The path to marginalization for the 9/11 families became the path for the public at large and the opening for perpetual war.

Although many tomes and countless op-eds have been written over the years decrying the failure to hold anyone in U.S. government accountable for 9/11, the public at large was effectively cowed into demanding neither better outcomes nor more security. In the months following the attacks, naturally public support for military conflict reached all-time highs. And when the Gallup organization polled Americans as the tenth anniversary of 9/11 approached, two-thirds of the public still accepted the permanent state of war, saying that they thought that the United States would still be actively and regularly fighting battles around the world twenty years into the future (in the year 2030).

Accompanying 9/11, there was a precipitous loss of confidence in whether U.S. military action abroad was making the country any safer, and it is a decline that has persisted to this day. Public trust in government has also dropped to near-historic lows, so much so that one-quarter to one-half of all Americans even believe that the U.S. government *perpetrated* the events of 9/11. When, as presidential candidate, Donald Trump floated 9/11 conspiracy theories, he was consistently applauded.

With the exception of brief outrage after intelligence contractor Edward Snowden revealed the NSA warrantless surveillance program, Americans have generally been willing to make sacrifices of their own liberties if they could be assured that those sacrifices would make them safer. Even after the Snowden revelations, the vast majority of Americans—eight out of ten—said that they approved of government surveillance so long as it targeted terrorists and not them.

By the time Barack Obama was up for reelection in 2012, only about one-fifth of Americans supported active military engagement abroad. And by the 2016 election, over half of those polled said that they would "most likely" vote for a candidate who supported withdrawal from foreign conflicts. Most Americans said that they wanted the United States to be involved around the world. But the difference between 9/11 and today is that American preference for "soft power"—for internationalism over unilateral action—has significantly grown. Today the public puts more value on diplomacy and global trade than war (85 percent), and they say they prefer to work within the framework of international bodies like the United Nations (64 percent) and NATO (75 percent).

Whatever we can surmise about "public opinion," polling indicates highly fickle attitudes about war. Americans' confidence in the government's ability to protect them goes up and down, especially when terrorist attacks occur. Immediately after the San Bernardino mass shooting in December 2015, trust in the government's counter-terror efforts dropped to 55 percent—the lowest it has been since before 9/11. And yet, after the Boston Marathon bombing that killed three people and injured more than two hundred others, public opinion didn't move.

Since at least the late 1980s the military has consistently maintained a higher approval rating than any other American institution. Some call it the "rally-round-the-flag" effect. When perpetual war got its official start date in 2001, most of the public overwhelmingly supported mounting a retaliation against Al Qaeda. Most in the public supported using military force against the government of Iraq as well. As perpetual war raged though, public worry about the possibility of terrorist attacks remained as great in 2018 as it was in 2001.

So we continue to take off our shoes and belts for the umpteenth time, are surrounded by powerful uniformed federal officers everywhere we go, and "pay the price" for our security with our pocketbooks and imposed fealty to the perpetual war enterprise. If people don't feel safer, it is because, in so many important ways, we aren't. But one thing is also crystal clear in the story of 9/11: the public has lost in every way, having been bullied into silence or intimidated into thinking that they did not know enough to engage in the complex and tangled national security debate. The establishment ultimately decides what to do and controls how it will be held accountable. And nowhere is that clearer than with a president who came to office intending to close this very chapter of American history.

chapter four

WHAT HAPPENED
TO OBAMA

If public opinion regarding perpetual war seems contradictory and even confused, one thing is clear. In 2007 the public voted not for the war veteran and hero but for the candidate who promised peace, the man who would end the war in Iraq and rededicate resources in order to finish things in Afghanistan. A constitutional scholar and an achingly mainstream liberal, Barack Obama was about as far from George W. Bush as anyone could imagine. And yet, no matter how deft the new president was, no matter how judicious he was in finding consensus, he was never quite able to implement either his promises or his desires.

Some point to Barack Obama's lack of military experience, his lack of familiarity with foreign affairs, even his outsider status in Washington. Others say he was so distracted by the economic crisis he inherited that he didn't have the political capital to challenge the national security status quo. But in the end Barack Obama was defeated by the logic of perpetual war, his very country-by-country approach turned on its head not so much in withdrawals he couldn't quite achieve but in additions that never stopped and then were never quite seen as part of a whole. Barack Obama was also defeated by secrecy, particularly by the tendency to rely more on clandestine forces as a substitution for public boots on ground. And, finally, Obama was undermined by drones, this new weapon of war that was indeed a relief to ground forces while also sucking the White House and the Obama presidency into a system of automated processes without consequential results.

Barack Obama's own bitter civics lesson began with his "withdrawal" from Iraq. One week before Christmas 2011, in an open field in the south of the country, five hundred American soldiers were loading into mine-resistant armored vehicles, eager to make it back stateside in time for the holidays—their bellies full with hot dogs and ribs from the barbecue they'd hosted to celebrate themselves. At Contingency Operating Base Adder, the sandy air was filled by the humming sounds of 125 trucks' idling engines. The mood was hopeful but tense. This was the *last* American convoy in Iraq and they were about to head home, ending nearly nine years of war. It wasn't the frenetic retreat from Saigon thirty-five years earlier, but it was done in the stealth of night, and even local Iraqi partners were kept in the dark. The final mission of these American troops was clear: Don't tip off any insurgents or terrorists. Don't open up soldiers to any "friendly" attacks by Iraqis. Avoid roadside bombs.

"You're reposturing while people are still trying to cause you harm," Army general Lloyd Austin told an NPR reporter. "It is the most difficult undertaking in our lifetime, in our military career." And so, without saying goodbye, the troops began their quiet exit. Soldiers drove cautiously across the desert in single file under the cover of darkness. U.S. drones kept a watchful eye from the skies overhead. About an hour past dawn, the last vehicle in the American convoy crossed over the border into Kuwait. While a group of guards pulled the barbed-wire barriers closed behind them, relief finally set in. The American troops cheered as if their team had just won the Super Bowl. They honked their horns, pumped their fists in the air, gave each other chest bumps, and embraced in enthusiastic bear hugs. "It's all smooth sailing from here," an Army sergeant told the Associated Press. He was going home.

The departure officially put an end to a war that had taken nearly 4,500 American military lives and cost $1 trillion. President Obama welcomed returning troops at Fort Bragg in North Carolina, telling them that the United States left behind "a sovereign, stable and self-reliant" country. In an interview with ABC News, he told Barbara Walters that the U.S. military "succeeded in the mission of giving to the Iraqis their country in a way that gives them a chance for a successful future."

Almost nothing that the president said was true. And he knew it. First, although it appeared that he was fulfilling a campaign promise to end the war, the withdrawal was hardly on Obama's timetable. President Bush had, in fact, concluded the agreement with Baghdad to cease combat in 2010. And the previous administration had also agreed that American combat forces would leave the country by the end of 2011. And it wasn't even really President Obama making the decisions. As a candidate, he promised that troops would be gone by mid-2008. Obama insisted on a "responsible drawdown of troops," ostensibly leading to a year-and-a-half delay.

But even that wasn't true. Iraq was neither stable nor self-reliant. The intelligence community was reporting that the country was deeply divided and ruled by a weak central government. As America celebrated Christmas, three prominent Iraqis penned an op-ed in the *New York Times* that opened by declaring "Iraq today stands on the brink of disaster." Prime Minister Nuri Kamal al-Maliki, a Shi'a Muslim, started targeting Sunni and Kurdish politicians and leaders, rounding them up to be arrested as soon as U.S. forces were gone. Sectarian violence and then terrorism escalated; so too did the Iraqi government's executions and use of torture.

Military advisors and American diplomats on the ground had argued in favor of a residual force—some wanted as many as 55,000 American troops—to hold the country together. But the president rejected any continued American commitment. Secretary of Defense Leon Panetta would later write that the White House was "so eager to rid itself of Iraq," they simply lost interest in any proposals contrary to complete withdrawal. As the domestic situation worsened, Republican candidates preparing for the 2012 elections were happy to suggest that the growing Iraq mess was Obama's fault for leaving too soon. "Abandoning Iraq," said former first brother Jeb Bush. "It was a case of blind haste to get out."

They weren't completely wrong. Candidate Obama had said he would make "the fight against al Qaeda and the Taliban the top priority that it should be," committing himself to Afghanistan over Iraq. Part of the reason was due to the fact that Obama's administration believed that Iraq—no matter what the security situation—was "Bush's war." As a presidential candidate, Obama labeled the Iraq war "the greatest strategic blunder in recent foreign policy."

With the Iraq withdrawal plans underway, President Obama announced in December 2009 that a "surge" in Afghanistan would enable American forces to win the fight there. Trading one country for another, Obama agreed to two packages of an additional 30,000 troops, the promise being that he would be able to start bringing home troops in 2011 as well. His commanders on the ground undertook new counterinsurgency and counter-terrorism strategies, and the Afghan army and Afghan officials were lavished with money. Obama pressured a reluctant NATO to provide their own military commitments to stabilize Afghanistan, and the administration oversaw an increase in nonmilitary aid by more than $1 billion. By the time of the 2011 Iraq withdrawal, the United States had lost 2,200 soldiers in this first fight and it had spent close to $700 million. Of course, things didn't go as planned, and in the middle of 2011, Obama promised that "the Afghan people will be responsible for their own security" by 2014.

Then came a third war. Arab Spring protestors challenged the rule of Muammar el-Qaddafi, and the Obama administration watched as Libyan military forces and security services brutally put down the civilian revolt. Military action was "the last thing that President Obama wanted to do," Leon Panetta said, referring to Libya. And yet, driven by human rights concerns and a desire to protect civilians, the president decided to throw American support behind the assault. Opening a new front in Libya was described as an example of the right way to use force, not only in an alliance with European "partners," but under Arab League and United Nations cover. Fighting was limited to airpower alone, avoiding entanglements on the ground. With this plan, the Obama administration later claimed a dictator was toppled, thousands of lives were saved, and the Libyan people were given a new chance—all without a single American casualty. "Everything went right," Obama said.

While the Libyan government disintegrated, a similar Arab Spring uprising started in Syria. Partly precipitated by the spillover from declining security in neighboring Iraq, civil war erupted. There was the usual fretting in the Obama camp that civilians were in harm's way, but it wasn't until early 2012 that the president staked another claim, saying that "it's not a question . . . if [Syrian leader Bashar al-] Assad leaves—it's a question of when." Initially the White House demurred on

CIA proposals to provide aid to the Syrian opposition. But when intelligence came in that Damascus might use chemical weapons, even possibly transfer them to Hizballah in Lebanon, opinions changed. Obama announced his now infamous "red line" that he wouldn't stand by if the Syrian leader used chemical weapons against civilians. The Pentagon, which had previously been cautious about taking on another country, now backed military action, weapons of mass destruction being the deciding factor. "Something needed to be done even if we didn't know what would happen after we took action," said General Martin Dempsey, chairman of the Joint Chiefs.

Meanwhile, Iraq rapidly disintegrated. The group that the government called ISIL (for the Islamic State of Iraq and the Levant) and the rest of the world called ISIS (for the Islamic State of Iraq and Syria) made a surprisingly rapid advance from Syria into northern Iraq, taking control of numerous cities, including Mosul (the country's third largest), and creating a self-declared caliphate the size of Great Britain. The United States had by then spent $35 billion "training and assisting" the Iraqi armed forces, only to watch them rapidly and dramatically deteriorate. When the government in Baghdad requested help from America, "a reluctant President Obama" obliged and again sent forces back. "Our objective is clear," he said on September 10, 2014, announcing the return. "We will degrade, and ultimately destroy, ISIL through a comprehensive and sustained counterterrorism strategy." In a broad campaign in both Syria and Iraq, America started dropping bombs twelve days later.

Obama took pains to declare that the new Iraq fight would "not involve American *combat* troops fighting on foreign soil (emphasis added)." Officially the United States would deploy some 5,000 "trainers." Of course, that number did not include clandestine fighters who were working in Syria and Iraq to go after the highest-value targets, nor did it count private contractors who were embedded in Iraqi military units and bases and were increasingly operating much of the forward intelligence collection devices. Although Obama stressed training and placed ceilings on the number of conventional ground troops, uncounted were the forces bombing ISIS targets from the Kurdish controlled area of northern Iraq and from Turkish, Jordanian, and Kuwait bases (and from bases even farther afield).

The president who entered office promising to end America's wars was now presiding over three different conflicts in four countries. Meanwhile, although all of the attention focused on ground forces, which were carefully counted and the subject of ceaseless attention, counter-terrorism special forces—most of them clandestine—were expanding off-the-books. Although Osama bin Laden was dead, Al Qaeda endured in Pakistan and Afghanistan and was gathering strength in Yemen and other countries. ISIS developed a second foothold in Afghanistan and then spread into North Africa and even into Asia. Al-Shabaab in Somalia and Boko Haram in West Africa expanded and got more active. Into these nations flew the drones, unmanned and armed hunter-killer Predators and Reapers backed up by spotters on the ground.

The first regular drone strikes against "high-value" terrorists occurred in November 2002, and in the five subsequent years of the Bush administration drone operators mastered their craft and grew an enormous intelligence capability, operating even from the United States. The use of drones epitomized remote warfare. Drones expanded America's military reach into restricted places like Pakistan and allowed operations into the heart of Africa, minimizing the need for men and women on the ground while facilitating counter-terrorism.

So many of the techniques of finding targets became secret

that by 2014 a president who came into office promising to be more transparent now had to tell Congress that "specific information" regarding operations and specific countries where the United States was operating could only be reported to the legislative branch in classified documents. "It is not possible to know at this time the precise scope or the duration of the deployments of U.S. Armed Forces necessary to counter this terrorist threat to the United States," Obama wrote to Congress. "The United States has deployed U.S. combat-equipped forces to enhance counterterrorism capabilities and support the counterterrorism operations of our partners and allies" in ten countries, Obama wrote to Congress in his last month in office.

The president admitted that he wasn't publicly divulging the whole picture. He only described the situation in "select countries," he said, and he was only accounting for "force management levels"—that is, official military ceilings—in reporting the number of fighters who were deployed. Despite the fact that, by Obama's last year in office, there was abundant reporting of killings throughout Africa, the White House continued to publicly withhold the names of countries where conflicts were occurring. Ever parsing words, the administration maintained that what the United States was secretly doing didn't rise to the legal definition of "war." And so the presence of American forces and contractors in places like Pakistan and Nigeria and, more centrally, Saudi Arabia was kept secret to prevent public scrutiny. By the time Obama left office, according to a classified military briefing, U.S. special operations forces were fighting on the ground at ninety-seven locations in at least twenty-seven countries worldwide.

The drone campaign was thoroughly vetted and exhaustingly discussed at the White House, particularly as the Obama administration decided to kill American citizen Anwar al-Awlaki without his constitutional right to trial. Strikes into

Pakistan were personally approved by Obama, as were other strikes involving the highest-level targets or cases where civilian deaths might occur. At the end of 2015 the administration provided the only official accounting of the result of its drone campaign. The CIA divulged that it had undertaken a total of 473 "high value target" strikes since 9/11, killing between 2,300 and 2,600 "combatants."

All of that activity to undertake fewer than 500 strikes, to kill no more than 2,600 terrorist leaders over a period of seven years. Was it worth it—the resources applied and the cost to the United States in reputation and respect for the law? Did it create greater security when balanced against the many drawbacks, not the least of which is the long-term manufacture of more terrorists? This is perhaps the most puzzling hallmark of perpetual war. "Success" in military activity—say, for instance, the killing of 2,600 terrorists by drones—is disconnected from any real assessment of greater outcome—that is, from any tangible advance in security. Even in the case of the supposed perfect war in Libya, one can't really argue that stability has been achieved or that the United States has gained greater support and respect in that part of the world. When Barack Obama announced his global coalition against ISIS in 2014, he actually inadvertently acknowledged this dichotomy: "This strategy of taking out terrorists who threaten us," he said, ". . . is one that we have successfully pursued in Yemen and Somalia for years." "Successfully pursued," he said. Based on what? That the strikes hit their targets? And yet, both countries are and continue to be basket cases. One could make the argument that the situation would be even worse had the United States not undertaken its headhunting campaign, but closer to the truth is that this is just a machine, scoring itself and operating autonomously.

The hopeful Obama of 2007 promised five goals "essential

to making America safer." These included "ending the war in Iraq responsibly; finishing the fight against al Qaeda [sic] and the Taliban; securing all nuclear weapons and materials from terrorists and rogue states; achieving true energy security; and rebuilding our alliances to meet the challenges of the 21st century." As president, he said he would "refurbish America's image abroad, especially in the Muslim world," improve the relationship with Russia as a step towards nuclear disarmament, talk to North Korea and Iran without preconditions, achieve Middle East peace between Israel and its neighbors, and expand diplomacy and foreign assistance—all while confronting terrorism without torture or the prison at Guantánamo Bay. And he would address global challenges from poverty to climate change.

Whatever Obama wished to focus on—reconciliation with the Muslim world, a new era of peace, lessening the nuclear threat and curbing proliferation, promoting democracy and human rights, facilitating global economic growth and cooperation—he and his administration were continuously defeated by the demands of perpetual war. There were high points: Osama bin Laden and Muammar el-Qaddafi were killed. The wholesale American bloodbath in both Afghanistan and Iraq were halted. As Obama was leaving office, Mosul was being recaptured from ISIS. With the use of remote airpower—and through special operations and private contractors who weren't counted as troops—the percentage of terrorists and foreign fighters killed versus soldiers engaged on the ground also increased. Certainly, as the intensity of American combat dropped, fewer foreign civilians were killed—at least, directly by America. And when Obama left office, there were indeed fewer soldiers in number engaged in ground combat than when he started, and the hemorrhaging of money from the U.S. Treasury was contained.

These achievements were more than overshadowed by the bad news. Nothing in Afghanistan, Iraq, or Syria ever got resolved, the hopes of the Arab Spring were washed away in the rain, millions of refugees flooded Europe, Guantánamo Bay didn't close, secrecy flourished and domestic spying persisted, and the war on terror expanded to Yemen and then into the heart of Africa. "We cannot use force everywhere," Obama said in 2013, speaking at the National War College. ". . .And in the absence of a strategy that reduces the wellspring of extremism, a perpetual war—through drones or Special Forces or troop deployments—will prove self-defeating and alter our country in troubling ways." It was a rather distant observation made by a commander in chief responsible for that very absent strategy. Ignoring the reality of what would become of his many wars, Obama persisted in arguing that strength was more than "bellicose words and shows of military force" and that cooperation and diplomacy "work." But what he meant by "work" remains tragically unclear, especially when as president Obama left so much unresolved.

To be fair to the president, the national security establishment is the world's most powerful opponent. Even experienced hands like Robert Gates, who served as Obama's first secretary of defense, found it almost impossible to move on anything that the perpetual war makers didn't want. Gates repeatedly complained that he was frustrated that Washington bureaucrats often acted as if they didn't care that the United States was "at war"—that is, that they carried out business as usual. Similarly, Obama's first national security advisor, retired Marine Corps general James L. Jones, later observed that too much of the outlines of perpetual war seemed to just move forward on autopilot.

"We, the people," the great orator said in his second inaugural address in 2012, "still believe that enduring security and lasting peace do not require perpetual war." And yet, that is exactly what they got. Barack Obama ended up spending every day of the rest of his presidency at war. And, tragically, wordplay and concealment helped to make perpetual war invisible and mundane, providing it the fuel to persist.

chapter five

SIPPING TEA AND SWAPPING T-SHIRTS

Six military services. Eight branches. Eleven active and reserve components. Thirteen geographic and mission focused "combatant commands." More than seventy sub-components for air, land, sea, special operations, cyber, and space. Hundreds of subordinate and independent task forces and agencies. The machine of perpetual war is a sprawling enterprise, a world-straddling organization that has been tasked with responsibility for every country and for every possible contingency. Leading it all are some 880 generals and admirals. One hundred very much juggle the *doing*, the immediate and relentless demands of perpetual war. But the rest fight Washington battles with the bureaucracy, the White House, and the Congress. And they prepare the military for every what-if, saddled as much with Chad as with China, readying everything from nuclear weapons to defense against a pandemic.

Nothing quite captures this massive organization, for the military not only fights the nation's many wars but each of these organizational entities also fights each other—for resources, for attention, and for their way of doing things. Everyone's priority is, or is supposed to be, to support men and women on the front lines of perpetual war. But the majority are in a parallel system that pursues another agenda, divorced from the increasingly segregated outlines of perpetual war. They aren't idle. This parallel world operates the nuclear deterrent, cares for the security situation in Europe and Asia, and supports a world-wide foreign policy. Keeping the weapons, the supplies, the information, and even the bodies flowing to meet the immediate needs of perpetual war may be a priority, but in actuality it is only one of many priorities. No wonder, then, sometimes even secretaries of defense can't control this seemingly mundane alternate machine, for while their missions might not be relevant today, every entity pursues its sacred duty as if indeed it needed to swing into action tomorrow.

It is a colossal jigsaw puzzle, with each mission, each piece, demanding resources and even attention. Faced with wide-ranging, overlapping, and, yes, even limited means, leaders have to constantly make compromises to accommodate real war and bureaucratic war. The enterprise engages in a constant bargaining process, one that not only struggles to fight and support perpetual war in three dozen countries on five different continents but also ponders all other possible contingencies on a far larger battlefield. The fight is fierce, and not only because perpetual war is so demanding. It is also because the United States as world military leader has taken on an almost infinite mission.

Nowhere can this bargaining process be better seen than in the story of one unit—the Army's 155th Armored Brigade Combat Team, "Dixie Thunder"—which deployed its 4,000-plus soldiers to the Middle East for nine months starting in June 2018. Assigned to the Mississippi National Guard, the 155th is entirely made up of citizen soldiers, weekend warriors whose day-to-day "service" is, in theory, to come to the rescue when there is a civil strife or coronavirus. And like other reserve components, in times of war the 155th is slated to be federalized and incorporated into the overall Army, mustered and prepared to defend the nation.

When people sign up to be part of the National Guard these days, they have to prepare for three separate missions: their domestic duties, their wartime responsibilities, and support for perpetual war. For reservists, perpetual war isn't inconsequential, for they make up just over 50 percent of all Army forces in the Middle East, being the logisticians and behind-the-scenes supporters who run the physical machine. But perpetual war is not *wartime*, for the latter connotes warfare against other nation-states; indeed, it means World War III. And although the resources devoted to wartime have ebbed since the end of the Cold War, a land battle in Europe still dominates and stands above all other conventional military missions. To ensure that reservists are ready for this distant fight, the Army has maintained what it calls a "total force" policy since at least the Vietnam War, manning and training reserve units to be nearly equivalent in readiness to their active duty counterparts.

When the soldiers of the 155th Brigade were called to active duty, taken from their day jobs, separated from their families, and sent to the Middle East in 2018, they didn't go to aid in the fight in Afghanistan or Iraq, nor was the brigade mobilized to play any part in the fight against ISIS. The 155th wasn't even sent to a country where the United States was fighting terrorism. Instead they were sent to Kuwait—in the middle of the fray, to be sure, but a relatively peaceful sanctuary where the United States has the freedom and the safety to play out every contingency, the Middle East address obscuring that even here preparation for war with Russia and China is still a demand. Nothing about the brigade's deployment had anything to do with who was president or the state of perpetual war. Nor was the mobilization of these reservists the result of any order issued by the Defense Department leadership or connected to anything in the news. The deployment instead was part of the giant choreography created to satisfy multiple commands and multiple missions, a window into how the military works but also into how autonomous and invisible its workings have become.

"The 155th stands ready to deploy for any mission within Mississippi or abroad," Colonel Doug Ferguson, the brigade's commander, told local reporters as his unit got ready to leave America. "The men and women of this brigade train year-round in preparation to defend this great Nation. We've proudly represented Mississippi in past deployments and will continue to do so now," he said. Defend this great nation. What's behind the colonel's hyperbole first and foremost is the can-do mindset of the military itself. Every commander wants to do their part, striving to be the best in a vast lineup of many parts. And every commander, at every echelon, has to believe in the mission, not only for themselves, but also for their men and women. In today's military, the commander's duty also includes convincing the families of his men and women that there is a good reason for tearing their reservists away.

When the local reporters covered the departure of the 155th—the local reporters were the only ones who did cover it—they quoted Colonel Ferguson saying that the brigade would be practicing "wartime missions with wartime equipment." Operation Spartan Shield, what the 155th was assigned to, was described by the reporters as a "combined forces contingency operation designed to deter and react to possible threats within the Middle East region."

If you've never heard of this operation, you aren't alone. Telephone calls to Pentagon and Army press relations officers in Washington sent them scrambling to explain a mission that none of them had ever heard of, either. And if the above words—"wartime missions," "past deployments," "contingency operation," "deter"—seem vague, the military isn't interested in elaborating; in fact, it's careful to keep things jargon laden and all-encompassing because both what it's really doing *and* military habit promote a culture of keeping one's head down and following orders.

The secret mission—the *wartime* focus—was to prepare the unit to fight Russia. Kuwait indeed is one of only three places in the world where there is sufficient land and environment for tanks and armored vehicles to fully maneuver, even to fire their guns, in formations and with the intensity that mirrors real combat. It is a microcosm of the entire machine—war in the Middle East, "big" war, and military-to-military relations—all subsumed in one deployment.

And then there's Iran . . .

Back to Spartan Shield: the local Kuwait-based command, one step down from the U.S. Central Command responsible for the region and an Army *component* responsible for training and equipping units for combat, describes the mission as "a U.S. military posture in Southwest Asia sufficient to strengthen our defense relationships and build partner capacity." Even in the fine print of the defense budget prepared for Congress, Spartan Shield is described in the same dense language. The operation, the budget says, "allows U.S. Army Central [the Kuwait-based command] . . . to contribute to the U.S. Central Command mission imperatives of Counter, Protect, Defend and Prepare . . ." By doing so, the budget says, Spartan Shield demonstrates that the United States "is committed to ensuring it has the capability to win decisively in conflicts in the Middle East."

"Counter." "Protect." "Defend." "Prepare." "Build partner capacity." "Defense relationships." "Win decisively." "U.S.

military posture." Each of these words and phrases has specific meaning in this colossal system, each connoting both purpose and priority in the day-to-day bargaining process. "Counter," "protect," and "defend" indicate the stages of every war plan and connote skills that every unit must attain: common fighting potential that has to be uniform across every brigade combat team. "Building partner capacity," like "total force," has been around for a long time; the mission has become increasingly important as combat troops have been "withdrawn" from Afghanistan and Iraq.

"Win decisively" is another important buzzword. Although perpetual war forms the global wallpaper, after the Russian annexation of Crimea in 2014, the American military started shifting its active attention to big war, "win decisively" being the Army's new label to describe conventional warfare with heavy forces in operations to defeat the armies of other countries. The Army doesn't have to nor does it want to say Russia, even if it is the intended enemy. That is because the contingencies also include China and possibly North Korea and even Iran, and it is the Army's responsibility, as the so-called force provider, to ready itself for every potential. Although it might seem otherwise, since 9/11, there's only been one phase, in the battle against Saddam Hussein's army in 2003, where tanks were actually called upon to fight. And so, after two decades of focus mostly on counterinsurgency and counter-terrorism fighting, all heavy units like the 155th were reoriented to reacquire and practice *wartime* skills. The 155th was the first tank-heavy brigade to deploy to the Middle East since the 2003 Second Gulf War.

The 155th Brigade flew its soldiers to Kuwait and, once on the ground, the brigade went to climate-controlled warehouses where their *wartime* stocks—everything from tanks to computer equipment—were being kept. Going back to the first Gulf War in 1991, the Army has kept tanks and ammunition in Kuwait, the stockpile originally placed there as an insurance policy should Saddam Hussein again attack his neighbors. Units deploying for war in 2003 drew from these stocks, and indeed Spartan Shield began in 2011, a quiet backup to the withdrawal from Iraq and a commitment to Kuwait that the United States would always defend the country. In exchange, Kuwait makes its land available for training and its bases available for perpetual war support. In fact, Kuwait is the busiest and most secure American foothold in the entire Middle East.

Once it readied its equipment, the 155th Brigade—armored and mechanized heavy units—moved out into the open desert of northwestern Kuwait to practice the demands of fighting a conventional war. Every squad, every platoon, every company, and every battalion practiced individual, small-scale, and then large-scale synchronized ground combat; moving, replenishing; and refueling; even communicating as if they were at war. That training meant intentionally cutting the brigade off from plug-in power, communications, the commercial Internet, and even any kind of FedEx-like peacetime logistics. The brigade had to learn to carry and move everything, from the fuel and water that sustains machines and soldiers to every folding chair and piece of paper that they might need in a real war. In the Kuwait desert, they maneuvered into place, set up their positions, and then tore them down daily, moving tens or even hundreds of miles in their training, and then doing it all over again, simulating fights. When they were done, the brigade was certified to do its part to win decisively in the future, whenever and wherever it was called. Like every other heavy combat unit in the Army, in three years' time the 155th Brigade would have to do it all over again.

But remember build partner capacity? While the bulk of the brigade trained, individual soldiers and small detachments from the 155th fanned out to work with friendly militaries, conducting individual training and participating in local exercises. In fact, the Army later said, on some days during their time in Kuwait, the 155th Brigade had soldiers spread out in twenty-two different nations, from Tajikistan in Central Asia, to Egypt in North Africa, to Oman on the Indian Ocean periphery. In most of these cases their mission was *defense relationships*, the focus of training not being *building partner capacity* for counter-terrorism but the *wartime* tasks of Middle East militaries, which in many cases means fighting Iran and, in the case of Egypt, even weirdly means potentially fighting Israel.

But of course in the parlance of the American military, "wartime" really only means the big four of Russia, China, North Korea, and Iran, and there, although no part of the 155th Brigade's written mission in Kuwait and Middle East involved Iran, the local Army commander took it upon himself to label Spartan Shield "a strategic deterrence initiative" in an interview with *Army Times*. Lieutenant General Michael Garrett didn't explicitly name Iran, but he also didn't need to. Iran is the only country in the Middle East that the Pentagon defines as having to be "deterred." Given that there was a new administration in office, General Garrett reached into the geopolitical playbook and told *Army Times*, thereby telling his own soldiers and even conveying it to Tehran, that his command "oversees possibly the most strategically important region in the world today," responsible, he said, for major shipping choke points—the Strait of Hormuz, the Bab el-Mandeb Strait, and the Suez Canal—through which flows "the resources that support the global economy."

If "most strategically important" sounds like more hyperbolic overstatement, it is. The term "strategic" as used by the Pentagon—indeed, as used even by the news media—is so elastic as to be meaningless. Was General Garrett saying that the Middle East was more strategic than Russia and Europe? Or more important than China? Or North Korea? It's a tricky word, "strategic." In 2018 alone, the *New York Times* used it to describe twenty-seven countries and regions in relation to U.S. national security. During that same time period, the *Washington Post* used it to describe twenty-two countries and regions. Of course, included in their descriptions were Russia and China (and Taiwan), Iran and North Korea. But there were also India and Pakistan, Israel and Saudi Arabia, Germany and Japan. War zones in Afghanistan, Iraq, Syria, Yemen, Somalia, and even Niger were also described as "strategic," as were rivals Eritrea and Ethiopia in Africa, Montenegro in the Balkans, Nicaragua, Rwanda, Uzbekistan, the Solomon Islands and Vanuatu in the South Pacific, and even Sweden. "Strategic locations," "strategic interests," "strategic partners," "strategic competitors," "strategic resources," "strategic infrastructure," "strategically sensitive." To paraphrase Supreme Court justice William O. Douglas, who said in the *Pentagon Papers* case that if *everything* is secret, then *nothing* is secret, "strategic" has become meaningless verbiage.

And if "strategic" is a lifeless word that appears everywhere and can connote anything, so too is the term "deterrence." It certainly involves nuclear weapons. But the word should not be confused with "stopping," as if somehow perpetual war has deterred terrorists from attacking the United States—that is, that terrorists don't do so because they fear the consequences. Nor has deterrence stopped Iran from spreading its sphere of influence into Iraq, Syria, and Lebanon. In fact, while military leaders were throwing around the word "deterrence," Iran expanded its own set of client states and proxies in a crescent all the way from Tehran to the Mediterranean Sea. Deterrence didn't dissuade Iran from establishing a second line of influence in Yemen, nor did deterrence stop Iran from attacking Western tankers, from shooting down an American drone, or from attacking U.S. forces in Iraq. But they are big words, "strategic" and "deterrence"—and, like "wartime," they serve as markers that establish priority in the internal bargaining process, a verbal one-upmanship for prominence and resources.

Here, then, we arrive at the truth of the Spartan Shield mission. It is first payment to Kuwait, a quid pro quo that ensures defense of the country in exchange for a friendly and complacent host. But it is also a bureaucratic cover for many missions and needs, where terms like "defense relations" and "building partner capacity" can be borrowed to deter Iran even as they are used to rally the troops, to make them feel important. Although Spartan Shield was used in 2018 to prepare a heavy unit for possible war in Europe or Asia, why waste the geographic messaging? It wasn't as if war was imminent. And it wasn't because of some crisis of readiness. It was merely a slot filled in a global schedule, a piece in the colossal puzzle that the military made the most of. For all the arcane terminology and all the grand articulations, in the physical and real world, Spartan Shield was little more than opportunity, nothing to do with perpetual war or even the locale, but also at the same time everything that represents the workings and requirements of the American military machine.

To begin to understand this machine, it dawns on me that it isn't just the terminology that is dense and obscure; it's also the fundamentals. Understanding why the 155th Brigade was in Kuwait demands a familiarity with a complex organizational scheme and the constantly changing military landscape. It requires understanding what the role of the Army is, what the combatant commanders do, what a subcommander like General Garrett does, what the National Guard is, what the reserves are, how contingency plans work, and how difficult it is just to prepare a military to be at its fighting standards. To tackle ending perpetual war, the public doesn't need fluency in these matters, but it does need basic literacy—enough to understand the military the way people understand how a school works, how mundane it is.

In many ways, Spartan Shield *is* mundane, and the 155th is insignificant. In the Army of 2019, for example, there are sixteen heavy tank brigades like the 155th, the so-called armored brigade combat teams. That's just sixteen heavy brigades to cover the entire world. If it doesn't sound like a lot, it isn't. Then think of the unit itself. A heavy brigade like the 155th has 102 tanks—the 70-ton behemoths that are indeed the kings of the battlefield. One hundred and two tanks, plus eighteen long-range artillery guns. That's the combat power of the heaviest standard ground combat formation of the U.S. military. It is the most potent force in the world for its size, tank on tank, and each brigade today is equivalent to multiple Army *divisions* of World War II in terms of lethality. These units have the ability *on an open battlefield* to cover geographic expanses far exceeding those of multiple divisions of old—that is, larger formations made up of three to five brigades.

But here's some modern-day arithmetic that helps to explain both how this system works and how resource constrained it perceives itself to be. In this very brigade, the 155th, less than 15 percent of the soldiers assigned are actual tankers and gunners. The rest of the people are there to guide, maintain, fuel, and repair. It is a stark calculation, how much "support" is needed to sustain combat. That arithmetic holds all the way to the top of the Army. Of nearly 1 million people in this branch of the armed services, only about a third of the people are even assigned to combat units—that is, the fighting brigades. Only about 15 percent, then, of these 350,000 people, active and reserve, are shooters.

This same type of math repeats across the other military

services, the so-called tooth-to-tail ratio being incredibly low, the reality being that no unit really fights alone. It's almost impossible to calculate what the precise ratio is. What the military calls "combat"—counting everyone in a brigade like the 155th as fighters—is far from counting the actual shooters. And that ratio only gets bigger the higher one goes up in the chain of command. Even in the case of the most elite—the special operations forces—the ratio of supporters to fighters is still greater than twelve to one; that is, for every shooter in the field, there are twelve others who are either in support positions or out of the fight.

And so, for every bomb dropped by an F-16 fighter jet or a B-1 bomber—or for every Hellfire missile fired by a drone, or for every ship that sails—there are literally thousands and then tens of thousands of people behind them in the supporting cast. The intelligence community alone is over 300,000 strong. Some are forward deployed in combat, but more than 95 percent are a supporting cast that collects and analyzes all the information that comes in, processes it and builds the databases, writes the reports, and makes the maps. Hundreds of thousands of IT workers wire the planet together and keep the networks running. And then there are the hundreds of thousands more who push paper and run the infrastructure, who fiddle at the laboratories, who stand on production lines, and who test and sustain every piece of military equipment that eventually finds itself on the battlefield.

When Barack Obama and his White House team discussed force needs in Iraq or surges in Afghanistan, they found themselves constantly flummoxed by this arithmetic. For every additional "combat" troop that the president approved, he learned that there also needed to be a supporting cast called "enablers" who were never presented in his accountings. I've heard numerous participants in the decision-making process tell stories of the president asking why these additional support elements—some as intrinsic as the medical evacuation units needed to accompany combat units—were never disclosed when he was presented with force packages. But in the ways of the military, the word "troops" had a specific meaning. The way the system worked, once Obama made his decision regarding troops, he found himself with no choice but to stand behind the American soldier and give them the enablers and supporters that they also demanded. The military thereby eked out every last drop of capability. But the euphemism was also useful to the Obama administration, for it could take credit for withdrawals, knowing that "troops" was a deceptive term, accepting that there were more forces on the ground that weren't being counted or acknowledged. Think again how we pretend that there are only a couple of thousand Americans engaged in Syria, or about 10,000 in Afghanistan, ignoring the supporting cast and the physical infrastructure and additionally not factoring in the effect that they have in the region.

As the 155th Brigade was getting ready to deploy in 2018, the secretary of the Army questioned why it and other units allocated to the Middle East were even continuing to be sent forward, wondering aloud whether they couldn't be freed up— "put in the queue" as he called it—to fulfill more important missions, which at that point were being articulated as "great power competition" and preparing for war with Russia and China. "It can't just be that we are sending soldiers out to train and they are exchanging t-shirts and sipping tea" with an endless list of "partners," then–Army Secretary Mark Esper told *Defense News*.

Like a little boy pointing out that the emperor had no clothes, Secretary Esper's suggestion that Spartan Shield should end was impudent. But his comment also revealed that even someone at his level didn't see the big picture of the physical machine—that even he didn't know the truth and didn't understand the totality of his own service. And this is the man who would become Donald Trump's secretary of defense. What he didn't understand is that Spartan Shield was merely a placeholder and not a mission. No one envisioned Iraq or Iran attacking Kuwait. But no one wanted to stop the operation, either. They didn't want to insult the Kuwaitis or signal to others that America was leaving. They certainly didn't want to expose more American soldiers to the fight, pointing out that, despite its Middle East address, it wasn't going to fight anyone.

Although Spartan Shield might have seemed like it was little more than a mission of soldiers fanning out throughout the region to interact with their counterparts, sipping tea and being personal diplomats, in the bigger scheme—in the colossal puzzle—it was just one of many tea parties that are hosted globally. I could name other operations around the world, other claimants on resources, just like Spartan Shield—Joint Task Force-Bravo in Central America, Operations Juniper Micron and New Normal in Africa—where what is done is inscrutable and impenetrable but where change would produce a cascading effect; where one commander or one region would have to be explicitly chosen over another; where someone would win and someone would lose. And this isn't just with regard to the Army. Aircraft deployments, naval patrols and port calls—even special operations missions—all contain multiple purposes, internal and external, that have become the backdrop for America's infinite national security.

And as for the military's shift to Russia and big war, the one announced with great fanfare in January 2018 as "new," that Mississippi brigade had begun the process of preparing itself to train for a high-end European battlefield two years before Donald Trump was even president. To the men and women of the 155th Brigade, national policy was a distant trumpet. Their job was just to be ready, to be a heavy armored brigade, to fulfill whatever mission they were given, and, most important, to excel at the most complex tasks, and that meant operating on the high-end battlefield. The truth is that the commanders and planners within the 155th Brigade and the Mississippi National Guard were told in 2015 that their brigade was scheduled to go to Kuwait in three years' time under president whoever.

This is how in perpetual war, official numbers and actual numbers come to differ, how geography doesn't necessarily connect to place, and where exceptions almost always exceed what is supposed to be the norm. The 155th is just an example, but it is a case study that helps to explain how the United States can throw so many resources into the war on terrorism and yet still barely tread water, fighting and even winning battles over and over again but never quite defeating an inferior force. And, finally, the hydra-headed mission of the 155th Brigade, like the missions of so many other brigades, exists because of the now-ingrained weakness of perpetual war: an actual outcome of greater security is disconnected from the activity of the machine. An immense system grinds on, none of it fully within the grasp of any one person. Consequently no one quite ever says no.

chapter six

BEYOND THE
WAR MACHINE

On September 12, 2019, for the first time, the military began accepting recruits who weren't even alive when the Twin Towers went down eighteen years earlier. For these young people born into the era of perpetual war, there was no "Everything has changed." They had lived their whole lives while America was at a state of war. And yet, that war had become largely invisible to them and their lives.

In many ways the military had done it to itself. It had evolved into such a highly specialized instrument, it no longer needed hayseed recruits or the cannon fodder infantry of yesteryear. Even with the shift to focusing on big war with Russia and China, the military wasn't anticipating getting bigger, just better. And even within the typical Army combat brigades like the 155th from Mississippi—a reserve unit—the Army needs technically competent and highly motivated learners who can operate complex equipment. But attracting them, even at vastly fewer numbers than ever before, has become a major challenge.

Contrary to Hollywood depictions of long recruiting lines and shaved heads, the armed forces need only a tiny number of young people every year to sustain itself. Together the two ground services—the Army and the Marine Corps—only have to find about 100,000 new enlistees out of a pool of more than *25 million* eighteen- to twenty-four-year-olds. But for three years in a row the Army has failed to reach its recruiting goals. It could lower its standards, but study after study has shown that lower standards have cost more due to less capability and greater attrition. So instead the Army doles out over $500 million every year in enlistment bonuses and spends $1.6 billion on advertising and marketing to attract the right recruits. And the recruiting crisis is only getting worse. The military's own polling shows that only 12.5 percent of young Americans consider the military as a possible job choice or career.

This is a confounding reality, given that the military consistently polls as the country's most respected institution. But while America loves its soldiers, it also seems uninterested in participating in the responsibilities of national defense. The result is that a third of the Army's entire budget is devoted to paying and caring for people. Overall, in the Defense Department, 20 percent of the total of $750 billion goes for personnel. Military family support, including universal health care, housing, youth programs, and even child day care, costs about $8 billion annually.

Because personnel expenses are so great, and because a smaller military has become more isolated from society at large, many people have suggested reinstituting compulsory military service, the notion being that a draft would both enhance national security while even solving many of the nation's nonmilitary problems.

Liberals see a draft as an effective way to encourage greater public participation with issues of war and peace. Their theory is that when people's sons and daughters are on the line, the slumbering populace will be motivated to be more politically engaged. A professional and all-volunteer military force, they argue, is the root cause of militarism and the perpetuity of war, since too few citizens have a direct stake in what is happening on the battlefield.

Conservatives, on the other hand, argue that drafting eighteen-year-olds into military service would instill a greater sense of patriotism and sacrifice. They point to the 16 million Americans who served in World War II—the so-called Greatest Generation—and yearn for a revival. They argue that a military made up of draftees from all walks of life would rebalance civil-military relations—not so much to instill restraint in war making, as liberals argue, but to correct the drift of a nation so distant from military service that it lacks the will and even the ability to protect itself.

Although they might not completely agree, both sides accept the proposition that the military is or should be an engine of societal change. A military draft then morphs into compulsory national service programs to oblige societal slackers to do *something*: if not become soldiers, then at least become teachers or nurses or laborers. Embedded in each of these arguments is a deep sense of anxiety about the aimlessness of America's youth, including their poor physical fitness. If there were a war today, the argument goes, seven out of ten young people, obese and unfit as they are, wouldn't even be able to meet the requirements of being a soldier.

It is largely a theatrical debate, because to be a soldier today looks very different from what it did in the past, and even different from what it did at the time of 9/11. Truthfully, a draft wouldn't be necessary even if a war broke out because our compact, efficient, and networked force is no longer defined by boots on the ground. It is no longer tied to territorial control, and no longer constrained by distance.

The military, or at least the Army—the largest and most

powerful institution within the Defense Department—doesn't understand this, for it still organizes itself to mobilize and expand à la World War II. In fact, the assumption that a future big war would look something like the past is so powerful that it largely determines how the entire military organizes itself, how it buys things, and how it plans for the future. In short, this misconception is the reason why the Army is so huge and expensive. This faulty notion also explains the existence of the many competing military commands in Europe, Asia, and even at home. But more than that, it explains the true dynamic at play in how the national security establishment stays in control. There is no longer any *war machine* that is protecting us—at least, not a machine in an industrial sense. And so, neither is there some military-industrial complex that holds the country hostage, profiting in its own interest because we have no choice but to perpetually prepare for war. If we understood this, we would stop imagining nefarious actors and evil conspiracies behind perpetual war and place ourselves in a position of greater control. The good news is that those who understand the ephemeral qualities of the modern military— particularly air, cyber, and space forces and the power of the network—see a future disconnected from the ground. Looking more closely at a draft then opens a window into understanding this bifurcation in our military, between ground and air, between the past and the future.

When thinking about mobilizing the entirety of American society for war, we have to imagine the most plausible scenario. What would happen if the United States needed to prepare the entire nation for World War III? Let's play out the idea that China builds up its military over many years, encroaching into neighboring countries, seeking more room and resources to sustain its giant population. Next, let's imagine that Beijing sweeps into the South China Sea or that it invades neighboring

Mongolia and Nepal or even takes a piece of the Russian Far East, too powerful to be either resisted or deterred. Imagine the convulsions that might follow. It's like the board game Risk.

The United States and the rest of the international community would undoubtedly protest and embark on a démarche. They would impose sanctions and indeed they would move to action, probably even "building up" their own military forces. Ships would sail and the fleet would shift into the Pacific Ocean. Bombers and fighters would move into place to get closer to the action. Spy flights and other collection assets would take up positions, exercising unprecedented intelligence surveillance. Nuclear forces might even be put on alert. I imagine that many countries would clamor to build their military forces, call up the reserves, or even eye selective service and start a draft.

In such a scenario, existing military contingency plans for World War III would look a lot like World War II, with Army and Marine Corps ground combat units rushed to friendly Kazakhstan; divisions sent to the Aleutian Islands in Alaska and to Japan and South Korea; a presence maintained in the Philippines and across Southeast Asia; and advisors sent to India and Bangladesh. Likewise, in this World War III scenario, the United States and its allies would throw up defenses along with border barriers and create a modern version of trench lines. In this—as in all the "great power" confrontation scenarios—ground forces would be central.

There's just one problem: whatever would be done, it would be constrained by time. Even as China mobilized, even as it crossed other countries' borders, it is unlikely that the American military would grow in size. And once China started moving, obtaining more soldiers wouldn't be a desirable action, not only because things move so quickly today, but also because the American military would come to see that building up World War II–like combat power isn't desirable, that fighting some throwback war on the Asian landmass would be a disaster. It would be clear because although ground units would move and do their thing, the air and naval forces, together with cyber and space forces, would dominate any real reaction.

If we wanted to repeat World War II—a linear battlefield with combat occurring along well-defined front lines—the military indeed would "need" lots more of everything: more tanks, more infantry, more bodies. In the forty-one months between the attack on Pearl Harbor in December 1941 and victory in Europe, the United States mobilized 16 million men and women, 11.2 million of them serving in the Army (and what was then called the Army Air Forces), with 660,000 more serving in the Marine Corps. During this time period (the war on terror has now been running five and a half times as long), the United States created ninety-one Army and six Marine Corps divisions. All of these units were mustered from nothing, trained, and shipped overseas as fast as the United States could create them, with an entire nation throwing support for the war effort, with policies like civilian rationing.

The calculation of how many forces were needed then was based upon the amount of territory ground units could hold. It's estimated that in World War II a ground force of 100,000 strong (six to ten divisions of 10,000 to 15,000 men each) occupied about 1,062 square miles. That's nearly the size of the state of Rhode Island. At its tip (not counting the rear area), that World War II force generally controlled a front of about 30 miles, with a depth of another 35 miles. Advances in military technology had made the reach of a division's battle space ten times the area covered by its World War I counterparts. And that's just for defense.

How many soldiers are needed for offense is a different calculation. A 3-to-1 ratio of offense to defense is often bandied about as necessary to achieve a breakthrough against an entrenched defender. Such ratios also relate to projections of how many soldiers would be killed and injured, which would then determine attrition factors, which would then determine replenishment needs, the flow of soldiers to the battlefield, how many needed to be trained, and ultimately the number needed in conscription. This "battlefield geometry" was once studied closely to determine how many units and soldiers were needed for any given scenario, and although the Army generally doesn't use scientific planning factors anymore because the modern battlefield has so changed, most contingency planning is still dominated by this type of two-dimensional ground scenario.

And yet modern war—even unconventional war—is most often described today as an enterprise dominated by speed and maneuver, one of "swirling tactics" where there is no set geographic front. Bombers, fighter aircraft, attack helicopters, air- and ground-launched missiles, and even drones roam hundreds of miles. In any future war, I can't imagine any ground unit fighting independently of these distant agnostic capabilities or against an unmolested defensive force. Airpower would constantly batter enemy ground forces and their supply lines, thus weakening even the most concerted defenses. But it's more than that. Without dropping bombs, cyber weapons would attack everywhere from military formations to the national level, negating capabilities and stymieing traditional movements. We began to see all of this gel together even as early as the 1991 Gulf War, which saw a force of almost 400,000 Iraqi soldiers hammered by airpower for thirty-nine days. When the large American (and British) armor force then attacked against this already defeated foe, they were "pushing on an open door." The same thing unfolded in 2003, except by then air and ground power operated in unison, in the same time and space. Yes, a disaster followed once the Iraqi army was defeated, but "Shock and Awe" was successful in isolating the Iraqi leadership from the armed forces, which were then dispatched in twenty-one days.

Although the unexpectedly easy victory in Desert Storm is now a distant memory, the tragedy that unfolded in Iraq after the 2003 defeat of Saddam Hussein's military colored our view as to whether the new style of warfare was successful. Physically, the record speaks for itself. In half the time of Desert Storm, American military forces in 2003 made it twice as far—all the way to Baghdad—dislodging a government that had held on to power for twenty-five years. Yes, there was a gigantic intelligence failure, both about weapons of mass destruction and the nature of Iraqi society, and taking on Iraq militarily was a monumental mistake in countless ways, but physical warfare had transformed. And although geopolitical amateurs promoted war in Iraq by claiming that military action would be a "cakewalk" followed by garlands for the liberators, the war was over so quickly that it took almost a decade for political realities to catch up.

Because of the disastrous aftermath, most in the Army, and most in Washington, reached the wrong conclusion. To them Shock and Awe failed, the implosion of Iraq afterward attributed to there being not enough troops, not enough people to occupy and pacify the country. That all might be true, but it didn't mean that modern military power had failed. Yet the conventional wisdom became that the United States relied too much on technology, that our ability to avoid setting off an uprising or coup was undermined by some nefarious desire to move too quickly, and that long, drawn-out, old-fashioned war was not only immutable but preferable to decapitation—that is, to modern warfare.

This disconnection between a World War II view and the modern reality stays alive mostly in the minds of politicians and old-style military leaders, particularly ground officers.

But every young brigade commander today who has experience fighting in the past decade knows that they not only possess unprecedented killing power, much of it facilitated by the same attributes that create air and cyber forces, but also that their "organic" capabilities are significantly enhanced by greater integration into a force-enhancing network, one made up of precision long-range weapons, unmanned systems, intelligence, and air, cyber, and space power. Ground units today don't fight apart from or without airpower and they don't expect to be bogged down in some static defense, even against China. Things just move too fast.

No sector of the military has progressed more in terms of efficiency, lethality, and precision than the air forces. Souped up with modern software and avionics and backed by a global network sensing the enemy, today a single bomber of the B-1, B-2, or B-52 variety can fly out and destroy more targets than hundreds of bombers and fighters of yesteryear—reliably. From firebombing cities in World War II to trial runs with early smart weapons during the Vietnam War, when pilots had a hard time hitting bridges and other small-size targets, today's air force can hit anything anywhere in the world almost within hours, even from a standing start. But think beyond the inventory: the United States has the intelligence and the targeting apparatus to uniquely make use of thousands of smart weapons.

Small-scale, air-delivered precision bombs and missiles make it possible to destroy even more targets with fewer airplanes. During the first Gulf War less than three decades ago, the standard laser-guided bomb had 2,000 pounds of explosives. The newest bombs weigh only 50 pounds. Just think about how much lighter that is. In World War II the United States flew almost 35,000 bombers. Few reached their target; most missed when they did. Today the Air Force has "just" 157 long-range B-52, B-1, and B-2 bombers, each able to deliver hundreds of independently aimed precision bombs—almost with a guaranteed hit. The goal is not even to physically destroy things. The targets are transportation and communication choke points and brains where the "effects" are magnified to take away the combat power of the ground force. The Big Army doesn't like to admit that it has been supplanted, nor that it would not be the dominant armed service in any actual fight against China. But that is the hard truth.

There's lots of hyperbole about whether airpower really is all that good. Skeptics abound, many of them stuck in the pre-precision era, citing firebombed cities that killed an enormous number of civilians. But nearly thirty years of fighting from the 1991 Gulf War to the present has changed things. Range constraints have been more or less eliminated. Target "acquisition" on any sort of conventional battlefield has been perfected. Stealth designs protect and augment attacks. The United States is beyond the third generation of smart weapons with accuracies reaching nearly zero feet. The main research and development effort today goes into making explosives smaller and even more lethal. When bombs and missiles weigh less, aircraft and drones can carry more of them at a time, striking with more per aircraft per sortie. If that weren't enough, a new kind of weapon entered the inventory in the mid-2000s, one that can literally "loiter" over the battlefield, waiting to receive in-flight (that is, network) commands to re-aim or autonomously find and attack a target.

Because of advances in airpower, U.S. ground soldiers fight without having to worry about being attacked from above. The United States particularly specializes at destroying air defenses and airfields, and it can reliably attack transportation means (such as bridges) and communications and fuel sources, making it more difficult for enemy forces to move and sustain themselves.

I suspect in my China scenario that the two countries

might hesitate to attack each other's territory. That might be too provocative and escalatory. But do we really think that China would invade its neighbors, trigger a looming world war, and at the same time imagine that they would do nothing as American forces mobilized in response? Wouldn't they intercept troop and supply ships in the oceans or attack Asian ports and airfields to stop local deployments? Wouldn't they attack transport aircraft bringing soldiers into the theater? Wouldn't they destroy pre-positioned equipment on the ground in the theater? Wouldn't they shoot at the brains of the operation—at the network—rather than individual soldiers? I think the answer to all of those questions is yes: they would attack as much of the enabling infrastructure as they could. Therefore we shouldn't imagine some ground war occurring independently, or some retro land war. Given enemy precision and long-range weapons, the very idea that America could mobilize and move overseas without being destroyed is absurd.

Today's military is in fact smaller by design. And this wholly modern and professional military institution has little need for endless infantry or to fill its ranks with unskilled amateurs. And this intensifies every day, given the far more influential new combat arms: airpower, cyber, space, and, most centrally, the information that fuels all of it. Whether or not some China invasion scenario happens, World War II–style conventional war isn't in the future, nor would World War II be the way the United States would want to fight. Stuffing more ground forces onto any potential high-intensity battlefield not only wouldn't yield any great combat advantages but it would increase vulnerabilities.

Don't get me wrong: there are still plenty of ugly and deadly conflicts out there, and many if not most of them are also being waged against those who are technologically disadvantaged. Whether it's ISIS in Syria and Iraq, Al Shabaab in Somalia, or the Houthis in Yemen, anywhere modern militaries are fighting these forces, the enemy knows quite well how lethal the West is. That's why they know better than to congregate in the open and why they intentionally hide behind civilians, using innocents as shields. In post 9/11 battles, air forces have ironically had to hold back because they are almost too lethal for the task at hand. Some might ascribe this soft touch in warfare to constraints from politicians afraid of civilian casualties or even the result of risk-averse military leaders. But in fact this is just a new geometry, one that we are just learning to apply. It is why since 9/11 the military has spent so much energy and human capital in building better and better special operations forces—that is, forces that can wage war while also being highly dispersed. But even here we aren't talking about eighteen-year-old draftees. It takes years and lots of experience to build this special force. Think the *Terminator* movies for future warfare, with each soldier in possession of all-seeing and all-knowing computers plugged into the network. With the cloud and with soldier-level computing devices, it's not so far away.

The Army has already been cut to its lowest manning level in decades because the efficiency of killing has already had a profound impact. The post–World War II force design demands more support organizations and civilian technicians (and private contractors). In fact, the vast majority of today's force is focused on supporting fewer and fewer exposed "shooters." Think of it in pure numbers. From 9/11 through September 2015, some 2.77 million service members served overseas. It sounds like a lot—almost 200,000 annually. But more than 75 percent of them never stepped foot in Afghanistan or Iraq. Instead, they served in Turkey, Kuwait, Saudi Arabia, the Gulf States, and many other countries, even outside the Middle East, as well as on ships and submarines, supporting and enabling the ground force. At no time were there more than 165,000 troops inside Iraq. At no time were there more than 102,000 soldiers in Afghanistan. And even there, considering that the ratio of supporters to shooters is somewhere near 10 to 1, this means that at no time during the past two decades did the United States make use of more than 20,000 shooters in Iraq or 10,000 in Afghanistan at any one time. Well, that's only if you imagine that forces on the ground are the only forces that exist.

There are two other hidden realities of today's networked and integrated force in which fewer and fewer soldiers are engaged in direct combat. First, a professional and highly technical military is also increasingly separated from society at large. Being more self-contained, it can also sustain itself with less and less interference from the public. That's why no one is marching on the streets and no one is contemplating moving to Canada to avoid military service in the era of perpetual war. Second, as the number of soldiers in the fight has declined, military leaders have shifted practices to reduce the risk to those who are exposed, thus making the entire enterprise more opaque to the public.

The U.S. military has built a very powerful network, with operations and intelligence fully integrated, and military and civilian technical skills working side by side. It is an unprecedented force in accuracy and lethality—so much so that one might think that perpetual war has been a good thing by eliminating the need for involuntary military servitude and making everything so much more efficient. But that greater lethality and precision also has a backdoor effect on civil society, which is both more dependent on centralized systems and more vulnerable to becoming a target on some future global battlefield where the nodes of centralized networks—even in the United States—would be lucrative targets. The elimination of some safe rear area—not just in the sense that the military says that America is no longer a sanctuary from terrorists, but also in the sense that the civil infrastructure is increasingly part of war-fighting—magnifies civilian vulnerabilities. Thus the disintegration of working civil infrastructure in places where the U.S. and its allies have operated in the Middle East is directly responsible for the unprecedented refugee flows that have been created.

The encroachment of the military—of perpetual war—into civil society is not the only conundrum. Networked warfare and a military more dependent on information than boots on the ground has moved greater and greater portions of military power off the battlefield—both to adjacent countries from which military power is projected onto the battlefield as well as at "home" in the United States, where the bulk of intelligence and targeting work is done. Today most drones are literally flown and directed from the United States proper. Middle East warfare employs intelligence, cyber, and space warriors—all directly contributing to the effort—from places in Maryland, Virginia, Georgia, and Colorado.

As we ponder the future of warfare in this networked and cyber age, these domestic American locations have probably risen to the level of lawful targets joining other America-based national security objects—command centers, Internet hubs, submarine cable termini, terrestrial-to-space links—to the status of being equally essential. Where the battlefield actually is then, and who is a legitimate target—uniformed military, government employee, private contractor, civilian technician—has also become less and less clear. There is no more *over there* anymore. Thus, the networked military may be increasingly modest in its need for soldiers, but the modern networked military—this generation beyond the brute force machine—has very much integrated all of civilian society. In that way it has brought war home, increasing the vulnerability of a populace that on the surface is no longer needed.

chapter seven

WAR PLAYS
OUT IN KOREA

On February 12, 2017, less than a month after Donald Trump was inaugurated, North Korea fired a road-mobile ballistic missile 300 miles into the Sea of Japan. The show of force happened at the very moment Japanese prime minister Shinzo Abe was meeting with the new president in Florida. The two leaders were embarrassed and surprised. A North Korean capability to hit the United States, Trump said in a statement, "can absolutely not be tolerated."

During the previous year in the Obama administration, North Korea conducted two underground nuclear tests and fired two dozen missiles of various types, bringing Japan and Guam within reach of potential attack. Supreme Leader Kim Jong-un promised even more, telling his people in a 2017 New Year's address that North Korea was in the "final stage" of readying an intercontinental missile.

"It won't happen!" President-elect Trump shot back in a tweet. North Korea, already the last of the world's communist hard-liners, already under UN sanctions for its various treaty violations, would soon have an intercontinental missile capable of delivering nuclear weapons? The national security establishment was alarmed, as much by nervousness that Donald Trump was at the helm during such a crisis as it was about North Korea's progress toward a workable nuclear arsenal.

The longstanding position of the national security establishment had been avoiding war with North Korea under any circumstance. "There is a reason no U.S. president in recent history has pulled the trigger on North Korea," warned former CIA director and defense secretary Leon Panetta after the February 2017 test. "We have the potential for a nuclear war that would take millions of lives," he said, evoking the darkest possible picture. A military option with North Korea would be horrific on a scale not seen since World War II, said then chairman of the Joint Chiefs of Staff General Joseph Dunford. "It would be a loss of life unlike any we have experienced in our lifetimes."

Panetta and Dunford were responsibly warning of the worst-case scenario, lest someone new in the White House got the idea that a preemptive military option would be easy or make any sense. But none of what they said corresponded to the reality of modern warfare. There wasn't going to be a nuclear war *or* another World War II. And even if North Korea provoked an all-out conflict, it wasn't necessarily going to be on the catastrophic scale that anyone suggested. And yet, the news media and the national security commentators endlessly trumpeted the warnings.

North Korea has never been a military threat in the way most define it. Its large ground force is filled with underfed and undertrained military conscripts. Pyongyang is also unable to actually carry out offensive operations—that is, other than shooting missiles and firing artillery across the border. While that capacity is significant, the United States and its ally South Korea together have developed robust counters, ones that are mostly ignored or misunderstood, even by American leaders, when the subject of North Korea is discussed. Nowhere is the power of the modern warfare network and the integration of military capabilities into new domains more consequential than on the Korean Peninsula. As a result, the military situation has shifted to clear American advantage, partly explaining why North Korea feels it necessary to develop nuclear weapons. Although I would never argue for war, or that a war in the densely populated Korean Peninsula would be anything but disastrous, I wonder how our flawed understanding of the military standoff ultimately keeps us from resolving the conflict to the advantage not just of the Korean people but also to our own security.

"The largest artillery force in the world"—that's how two U.S. Army officers recently described North Korea, pointing out that the country possessed not just long-range missiles and nuclear weapons but a seemingly omnipotent 21,000 howitzers and artillery guns, thousands of them positioned along the demilitarized zone separating North Korea and South. Those guns would cause "devastating damage" if used, wrote *Forbes* magazine in 2017. The North was "capable of raining up to 300,000 rounds on the South in the first hour" of a war, the *New York Times* reported at the same time. Another news report suggested that North Korea could fire 500,000 rounds per hour, "quickly reducing Seoul to a heap of rubble." Even the nonpartisan and scrupulously judicious Congressional Research Service gave credence to "estimates rang[ing] from between 30,000 and 300,000 dead in the first days of fighting." The U.S. military commander for the Pacific, Admiral Harry B. Harris Jr., called North Korea "the fourth largest conventional military in the world," evidently forgetting that that's exactly what the United States labeled Saddam's Iraq in 1990. At that time Iraq was also credited with having thousands of deadly artillery guns, many of them supposedly outranging those of the United States and its allies. Saddam was said to have "battle hardened" troops after ten years of war with Iran, experts opined. And they possessed—and had used—chemical weapons.

Then in 1991 came the actual war with Iraq called Desert Storm. After six months of digging into the southern desert, waiting for American ground forces to claw their way into Iraqi territory and fight a World War II battle, American airpower leapfrogged over Saddam's army, attacking the country's heart; disrupting and even cutting off communications, electrical power, and transportation routes; and devastating Iraq's air force and air defenses, making the country even more vulnerable. The world was barely on the cusp of the computer era, and only a small portion of American aircraft were then even capable of delivering "smart weapons." But a combination of long-range airpower, stealth, precision, and "special" cyber and secret operations were able to completely nullify any numerical advantages that Saddam Hussein might have had.

As the United States and its allies positioned their forces over six months to prepare for an air and ground war, Iraq didn't attack. Had Saddam chosen to move on Saudi Arabia during this long mobilization, the outcome might have been different. We now know that Iraq didn't move because it *couldn't* move. Iraqi forces didn't know how to advance. Its army didn't have the logistics structure to supply mobile forces. And Iraqi soldiers were neither trained nor trusted by their own government to be that kind of a potent force. North Korea is no different. North Korean forces are not supplied or trained to invade. The military doesn't even have the fuel to move. What is more, Pyongyang's conscript army of half-starved infantrymen exists as much to control and indoctrinate young men to fear the state as it is any kind of trained fighting force.

Once American bombing began, Iraq was immobilized. Airpower combined the old and the new. B-52 bombers unloaded hundreds of thousands of bombs on Iraqi soldier formations in the desert just for "effect" while new stealth fighters used laser-guided bombs to carefully hit targets in Baghdad. Although Saddam would have been happy to sacrifice hundreds of thousands of his soldiers' lives to war, almost everyone was surprised by what happened next. After thirty-nine days of bombing and a four-day mop up by the U.S. Army and Marines, it was over. Thousands of Iraqi tanks and guns were no match for the U.S. military. When Iraq tried to shoot its guns or Scud missiles, the shooters were rapidly silenced. Quite a few missiles were launched and the psychological effect in Saudi Arabia, the Gulf states, and even Israel was significant. Even though the United States wasn't able to find the specific mobile missile launchers, over the five-week period missile attacks diminished. By then the U.S. had won. The Iraqi conscript army turned out to be frightened young men trapped in their trenches and holes, eager to surrender.

Operation Desert Storm, like any military operation, wasn't perfect. But what began with gross mischaracterizations of Iraqi capabilities and even included images of thousands of American body bags and the possibility that the United States would have to employ nuclear weapons to win ended up ushering in a new era of warfare. Twenty-five years later these same imaginings of World War II–style warfare that governed the U.S. invasion of Iraq in 2003 dominate our picture of the Korean Peninsula. If one listens to American military and political leaders, if one watches television or reads the newspapers, one might think Kim Jong-un commands an omnipotent military force—even without nuclear weapons and missiles. This narrative imagines two armies clashing face-to-face with citywide devastation as a result of old-style industrial-era pounding.

Ignored in this picture is not only the true reason for why the United States defeated Saddam's army in 1991 but how much has changed since. By the end of the 1990s the American military had almost completely converted to precision-guided weapons and, in an airpower-only operation in 1999, the United States and NATO drove Serbian president Slobodan Milosevic to capitulate his stranglehold over Kosovo. Then came 9/11, and war in Afghanistan began combining airpower with special operations in a new kind of fighting. Then came armed drones and the era of persistent surveillance. And then came the network that tied all of the forces together. But it isn't just hardware. The American military has honed its skills to take advantage of each latest generation of technology, improving through operations and trial and error until it had become the most experienced and potent military force in the world.

It is true that North Korea possesses all the numbers. But, like Iraq, it has an overabundance of industrial-age ground equipment and a conscript army coming from an autocratic and impoverished society. Yes, North Korea could make a mess if it mounted a surprise attack on the South. But the characterization of North Korea as the fourth largest army in the world with 21,000 guns? It is misleading and irrelevant. So too are the dire projections of what the country *could* do with its military, shooting hundreds of thousands of projectiles and missiles, killing hundreds of thousands of people.

Scratch the surface of this canned scenario and it is clear that the United States—and South Korea, which has its own powerful military—have every reason to be confident that a war would unfold very differently from what either typical news media reports or conventional wisdom suggests.

First, North Korea's seemingly overwhelming artillery is far less capable than Pentagon propaganda would have us believe, inherently weak but also far outmatched as it is by the combined airpower and counter artillery capabilities of the United States and South Korea. North Korea's missile force, though upgraded significantly in recent years, is also rudimentary and aged, and would be subjected to a blistering multidimensional attack that would severely limit its effectiveness. And as for North Korean nuclear attack? The country is watched like a hawk, with all of the newest intelligence and cyber technologies and techniques brought to bear to detect and even preempt preparations to launch a nuke.

James Mattis, the retired Marine Corps general whose career followed the advancement of our modern military from Desert Storm through the present, is the rare truth teller on the subject of North Korea, militarily knowledgeable but also willing to take on the national security establishment. As secretary of defense, he repeatedly provided assurances that the North didn't stand a chance. His was a military formulation that took into consideration a holistic portrayal of capabilities rather than a static numerical assessment. "It must be noted," Mattis stated most succinctly, "that the combined allied militaries now possess the most precise, rehearsed and robust defensive and offensive capabilities on Earth." North Korea, he said, "will continue to be grossly overmatched by ours and would lose any . . . conflict it initiates."

North Korean leadership is well aware that its military—heavy equipment dependent, overly manpower intensive and painfully slow—has fallen behind. Even if claims about the capabilities of American technology (such as missile defenses) are overstated or wrong, what we have is a panther versus an elephant. The North Korean elephant is dangerous, to be sure, if it goes on the rampage. But the panther is crafty and agile and lethal to the extreme.

"The fourth largest army in the world" sounds scary. But

North Korea's arsenal of more than 21,000-plus artillery guns and short-range missile launchers are mostly illustrative of phony numbers and sloppy analysis. A significant portion of North Korea's artillery inventory is obsolete or unavailable to the combat forces. Many of the guns are in disrepair, out of commission, or allocated to training and ceremonial units. And even if we counted the 17,000 or so artillery guns (or "tubes") and short-range missile launchers that are actually assigned to the combat forces, roughly 45 percent of these have a maximum range of less than five miles. With that kind of weapon, you'd have to be firing from Times Square to hit the World Trade Center. Those guns might be important in a drawn-out war, but they are largely irrelevant in any surprise attack on the South.

U.S. intelligence assessments conclude that of North Korea's 17,000 guns and launchers, fewer than 10,000—6,500 tubes and 2,400 rocket and missile launchers—are both operational and can shoot far enough to reach over the border from their peacetime locations. Of these 10,000, more than half can't reach the capital city. That already brings us down to about a quarter of the original 21,000 number. But there's more: of the 5,000 or so guns and launchers opposite Seoul, only a small fraction—approximately 600—are long-range enough to hit the metropolitan area. Just 600 out of 21,000 are actually in place and capable of undertaking a bolt-out-of-the-blue attack.

It is still a large force. But consider that even those 600 guns and launchers have severe limitations. Most are 170mm self-propelled "super" guns manufactured forty years ago. Those guns have an impressive 60-kilometer (37-mile) range, able to hit the northern outskirts of the capital city. But the guns are also unreliable, clunky, and slow. Even under the best of circumstances, they can only shoot one to two rounds every five minutes because the barrels are such poor quality. The guns also have to be manually loaded, making the crews highly vulnerable to attack. When North Korea assembled about 400 of these guns in early spring 2017 to conduct a mass firing in celebration of the eighty-fifth anniversary of the Korean People's Army, 20 percent of the guns failed to work at all, and numerous other gun tubes were damaged when they did fire. When a second round of shells was loaded and then fired in another mass display, an even greater number of guns failed. And these were weapons (and crews) handpicked for the showcase demonstration.

North Korean rocket launchers are similarly constrained. The majority are twenty-five-year-old 240mm types mounted on large trucks, some with either twelve or twenty-two re-loadable tubes. About two hundred of the launchers are estimated to be within range of the capital. These rockets can be fired in large-volume volleys, but operational experience and practice exercises show that North Korean soldiers struggle to control their aim. In November 2010, North Korea conducted a surprise attack with these 240mm rocket launchers on the South Korean island of Yeonpyeong, killing two South Korean marines and two civilians. U.S. and South Korean intelligence concluded that only half of the rockets fired managed to leave their launchers, gain altitude, and fuse properly to explode. Of the 170 rockets that successfully took off, half also missed their targets, landing in surrounding waters, wildly off the mark. A quarter of the ones that actually hit the island were duds and failed to explode.

Overall, the "largest artillery force in the world" declines from 21,000 guns and launchers to about 600 that both function and can reach Seoul in a surprise attack. The U.S. and South Korean militaries have war-gamed these battle scenarios over and over. They figure that even if every one of those guns and launchers worked reliably, North Korea couldn't fire more than 10,000 projectiles in the first hour of a standing start attack. Once we factor in the documented problems with reliability and performance, that number drops 25 percent, for a *maximum* of 7,500 artillery rounds and rockets that might be able to fire in the first *hour*. Admittedly, accuracy is not as important in a terror strike against civilians, but even 7,500 is an impossibly perfect scenario for the North. It assumes that the United States or South Korea don't do anything, even though the North would have to amass and prepare guns and launchers first, providing ample warning to preempt. This is a far cry from the 500,000 rounds suggested in most casual and exaggerated renderings, even if one assumes no U.S. and South Korea action to preempt or respond.

What about North Korea's short-range ballistic missiles that are capable of reaching South Korea? U.S. intelligence estimates that North Korea possesses about 600 combat missiles. Most of these are based on decades-old Soviet Scud missile designs, demanding setup and liquid fuel mixing in order to prepare for attack. If North Korea started to congregate a force of these missiles for a mass launch, it would be quite observable. And, like artillery and rocket launchers, that force suffers from the same issues of aging and reliability. In fact, when the Defense Intelligence Agency gamed out a potential missile attack on South Korea, they concluded that in an all-out effort the North would likely be able to fire about one missile every two hours per launcher at most. The launchers are also highly vulnerable to counterattack once they've taken their shot or are on the move. Finding and attacking ground mobile missiles was one of the main deficiencies in the 1991 Gulf War, and the U.S. and South Korea militaries have been working on perfecting their counter-missile techniques for almost three decades.

North Korea has been upgrading both its artillery and missile forces in recent years, and U.S. intelligence says that the North recently conducted more realistic training. But, constrained by sanctions, North Korea finds itself dependent on a limited and vulnerable industrial base, admittedly a priority for the regime but not one with any kind of backup or resilience.

Meanwhile, we are spying on their every move. New satellites, reconnaissance aircraft, and high-flying drones are assigned to watch for signs of mobilization 24/7. They feed information nonstop back to command centers where officials stand ready to respond immediately to an attack, even without political approval. It's a level of synchronization and preparedness unmatched anywhere else in the world.

And then there's missile defenses. In 2017, Admiral Harris said that, even given the size of North Korea's force, he was "confident" in the United States' and South Korea's ability "to destroy any missiles that come into our defended area." Whether missile defense can actually work is hotly debated. What the United States and South Korea have built is a multi-layered ballistic missile defense system. Missile defenses aboard U.S., South Korean, and Japanese surface ships can also intercept North Korea missiles during the boost, or ascent, phase. Terminal High Altitude Area Defense (or THAAD) missiles deployed on land in March 2017 can intercept North Korean missiles inside or just outside the atmosphere during the terminal, or final, phase of flight. A third and final layer is the Patriot missile, which can also intercept ballistic missiles in their terminal phase as close as 25 miles from their intended targets. South Korea also has two other indigenously made surface-to-air missiles that can bring down North Korean missiles at this range.

According to the Missile Defense Agency, these three layers of missile defense "offer several ways to destroy incoming missiles and warheads before they reach their targets." The latest Navy Aegis anti-missile missile was reportedly successful in seven out of ten tests between 2015 and 2018. In the first year of the Trump administration, the MDA claimed that in its current operational configuration THAAD successfully intercepted a missile in fifteen out of fifteen tests. And Patriots, according to the manufacturer, successfully intercepted more than one hundred ballistic missiles in combat during 2016–2017 alone, primarily in the Middle East in the Yemen war.

Almost all of these missile defense components have been integrated into a tri-national network of early warning, tracking, identification, and command. That early-warning information, together with the intelligence system, feeds what the military calls a "counter-battery fire" network. It is designed to target short-range North Korean rockets, artillery, and mortars through triangulation of enemy fire. Part of this counter-battery system is being able to track the gun and rocket path in reverse to locate where projectiles are shot from, allowing American and South Korea artillery and aircraft to attack those locations before the launchers can be moved. The South Korean army alone possesses more than 5,900 modern artillery guns and rocket launchers to conduct counter-battery fire, almost a quarter of which are positioned to be able to reach North Korean firing sites. The United States adds its own multiple rocket launchers as well as a long-range more precise High Mobility Artillery Rocket System, both of them part of the counter-battery fire network.

The U.S. military well understands the value of counter-battery fire. In the March 2003 invasion of Iraq, rapidly advancing U.S. forces with their counter-battery radars were able to detect Iraqi artillery fire, resulting in almost one hundred successful counter-fire missions to destroy or disable Iraqi gun positions. As a result, no American soldier was killed by

Iraqi artillery, an area where Saddam Hussein's military was also thought to have an advantage. In the decade and a half since the Second Gulf War, the United States has further improved counter-battery integration, incorporating new radars, guns, rockets, and digital links to make the whole ever more efficient. To practice counter-battery fire on the peninsula, the United States and South Korea have set up "Rocket Valley," a live-fire training arena filled with targets in sharply defined mountainous terrain. When multiple rocket launchers deployed to the Korean Peninsula in 2015 to exercise just such a capability, Army major Jeremy F. Linney bragged that in less than sixty seconds, his unit could launch "576 rockets back at enemy artillery . . . utterly destroying that enemy's ability to [sustain] fire long-range."

And although American and South Korean artillery and rocket systems are the most immediate responders, because they are directly tied into on-the-ground radars, tactical aircraft and long-range bombers would also be relevant to the counter-fire battle once in the air and plugged into the same networks and receiving automated tip-offs. The United States and South Korea together have more than five hundred tactical aircraft on the ground, and the United States has even more on aircraft carriers and at bases in Japan. Starting in 2017, the United States began practicing B-1B bomber attacks from Guam to North Korea, some of those ten-hour flights culminating in dropping live ordnance on mock targets.

When one takes into consideration the hidden advantages associated with counter-battery fire, many of the so-called advantages of the North Korean arsenal begin to fade. Take, for instance, the North's 1,000-plus hardened artillery sites (HARTS), semiunderground shelters that are used to hide and protect guns, multiple-rocket launchers, and short-range missiles. The conventional wisdom is that the bunkers would force a ground invasion because they are so protective. But in fact war-gaming has shown that the heavily encased sites slow down the North's ability to mass forces and then engage in multiple volleys. Guns and launchers hidden at HARTS sites are even more vulnerable because their locations are already known and targeted. What is more, most of the longest-range systems are carried by multiton transporters, which, while "mobile," move at a snail's pace along limited paved roads. North Korea might get off a single salvo, but each launcher then becomes highly vulnerable—not just to counter-battery fire but also to direct attack.

Rather than some disaster that stacks Kim's fourth-largest army and his force of 21,000 guns and missiles against weaker American and South Korean counterparts, the actual arithmetic of modern warfare would pit North Korea's decades-old and largely lumbering industrial force against a sensing and maneuvering shield. It's a shield that is both defensive and offensive, both robust and expanding, and one that is undergoing significant enhancement at the very time that the North faces stringent sanctions and a declining economy.

Military planners accept that North Korea really could manage to fire hundreds if not thousands of projectiles, rockets, and missiles in the opening hours of any surprise attack. But sustaining military operations and a high rate of fire demands not just that the technology work but also that soldiers do their jobs. Yet in all human categories—everything from practice to skill level to soldier diets—North Korea is considered weak and getting even more so.

According to the latest intelligence assessments, including a national assessment done in early 2017, South Korea's ground forces now enjoy an indisputable qualitative advantage over their North Korean counterparts. In the air and at sea, South Korean forces operate highly advanced weapon systems

with capabilities that far exceed those of its northern counterparts. It is no wonder that Secretary Mattis and others in a
position to know speak about overmatching.

Here is another reason not to believe in the fearsomeness
of a North Korea surprise attack. North Korea hasn't practiced
a ground attack in decades. Army command sergeant major
John W. Troxell, who visited U.S. and South Korean troops at
and near the DMZ in 2017, said as much, also calling attention
to Kim Jung-un's hapless conscript force. "There's 750,000
North Korean troops on the DMZ, out of a more than 1.1
million man and woman force," Command Sergeant Major
Troxell said. "But we haven't seen them do a combined arms
maneuver in 20 years." In other words, moving to mass for a
surprise attack on Seoul is something North Korea has not
practiced and couldn't synchronize even if it wanted to do it.
Troxell pointed out that many of Kim's soldiers are medically
frail and, due to shortages and political control, are only allowed to fire about five to ten bullets out of their rifles *a year*.

Is my rendition of the situation on the Korean Peninsula
a lopsided depiction of all of the negatives about North Korea
contrasted against all of the positives for the United States and
the South? Isn't the lesson of Iraq in both 1991 and 2003
that even when you do win the battle, you can still lose the
larger war? In both cases I'd say yes. One shouldn't blindly
trust military claims any more than one should trust my own.
And one should be particularly skeptical about what the defense industry says about their own weapons, or politicians,
or former officials, or even many retired generals. These days
they all have axes to grind, and most aren't deep enough in the
weeds to understand how modern-day warfare really works
or how twenty years of fighting have so completely transformed things even from Desert Storm. Army generals largely
don't understand airpower and Air Force generals don't think

ground forces are relevant. And most of the time the very kind of officer who is a pleasant commentator in Washington is also largely out of touch with the realities, no matter how much experience in uniform they might have.

Remember too that for every instance of false optimism and excessive faith in American technology—about how great airpower is or how missile defenses "work"—the enemy has their own equivalent of exaggerated advantages. When I describe America and North Korea as a panther versus an elephant, that contest could just as much be a giraffe versus a hyena, the larger and more elegant getting killed by the pack, unprepared for brutality and defenseless against numbers. The other side of that argument is that superior American and South Korean military capability doesn't form a stable defense, particularly if the North feels threatened or behaves irrationally. The true danger, according to U.S. military intelligence analysts, is not North Korea attacking "out of the blue" or perceiving under any circumstances that it can win. It is that the North Korean leader may decide sometime in the future that his nation is approaching a military "cliff" where his capability, despite nuclear and missile investments, is about to disintegrate under the full effect of sanctions and isolation. In this scenario, there is a danger that the North might think its only option is to lash out—a "use-it-or-lose-it" mentality. Perhaps if we looked at the North's weaknesses more realistically, we would better position ourselves to avoid this eventuality.

chapter eight

THE POWER OF
THE NETWORK

In August 2018, neutral and nonaligned Sweden announced that it had struck a deal with the United States to buy Patriot air defense missiles. It was the largest and most politically important foreign arms purchase the country ever made. Although Stockholm divulged sparse facts, the State Department said that the Scandinavian country was going to purchase four firing units and three hundred missiles, each of the latest technology, all at a cost of $3.2 billion.

"Sweden will use the Patriot system to . . . promote regional stability," the State Department assured in its announcement, adding obligatory language that the "proposed sale" would not "alter the basic military balance in the region." It was straight out of some Cold War playbook, meaningless words for a country already increasingly aligned with NATO. Patriot missiles would "deter any potential aggression by Moscow," one commentator wrote to blandly describe the unprecedented move.

"Step by step," said Swedish defense minister Peter Hultqvist, "we are developing our military capability." Five years earlier Russia had dramatically rehearsed nuclear strikes against the country. Then a Russian submarine was supposedly detected operating in the Swedish archipelago. Some defense commentators argued that Moscow "might have designs on the Baltic Sea island of Gottland." Others said that Russian deployments to Kaliningrad—just 333 miles from Stockholm, the distance between New York City and Pittsburgh—directly threatened the country.

Faced with this threat, there was almost zero public debate about buying the American missile system. Practically every Swedish political party acquiesced without probing too deeply into either the justification or the consequences. And those who said anything mostly mentioned money. Opponents fretted about the $3 billion impact on Sweden's budget, while others questioned whether procurement of such a big-ticket item might weaken Sweden's other equally important military needs.

Perhaps the public debate was muted because most Swedes were already convinced that Russia demanded not only a direct Swedish response but also an international response, one that Sweden needed to be a part of. To stress the country's independence and neutrality, officials did not just stress the Patriot system's defensive mission in shooting down hypothetical Russian invaders but argued that the weapon would actually preserve Sweden's nonaligned status by enhancing the country's control of its airspace.

All of this was true on the surface. Sweden was not formally joining a military alliance against Russia. It would have national control of its Patriot air defenses—that is, it would decide when to fire them in response to an incursion. And yet, if one understands the nature of the modern perpetual war network, Sweden the nation-state was conforming to the new global network. To properly operate the Patriot system,

Sweden needs to be a part of a larger regional sensing organism of intelligence and early warning, independent on paper but part of, and dependent on the whole. And it is not only in its air defenses. Sweden's entire airspace needs to be integrated into the global network as well, to avoid shooting down friendly aircraft. And its military communications system needs to follow and be part of the security protocols of the whole; otherwise it cannot receive classified warnings or coordinate action. The country might officially only be labeled a "partner" nation to the NATO alliance, but in the modern world, where the network is everything, it was quietly joining a different kind of military alliance, one forged in having to be plugged into the whole. Membership has its benefits, for Sweden gets the intelligence information and even the common weapon systems that take advantage of American leadership. But the bald truth of perpetual war is that even a neutral and nonaligned country is forced to join a new kind of permanent war-fighting alliance, one that is ad hoc and has no charter and no physical headquarters.

The perpetual war network in many ways originated in the early 1990s, when a grand but wholly disharmonious coalition came together to fight Saddam's Iraq. The United States supplied the bulk of troops and aircraft, but incorporated into the same army, if only in name, were Afghanistan's mujahideen, Syria's Assad government, and even Senegal's soldiers. They all lined up together in the desert, these nations, to be part of the roll call that affirmed international law and the new world order. In adding their troops, though, they also all had to comply with the same rules, if for no other reason than not to shoot at each other by mistake. Another coalition formed in Somalia—international peacekeepers at first but eventually fighters—with the protocols and guidelines of cooperation and noninterference growing. Then Western

Europe banded together to use military force in the disintegrating former Yugoslavia. Intervention through the barrel of a gun was now accepted under a new humanitarian imperative that superseded national sovereignty. United nations—not *the* United Nations—would decide when a state's borders could be breached and when domestic affairs demanded external policing. It wasn't just the traditional U.S.-led coalitions with the usual allies; nor was it NATO or the European Union. And yet the common element was altogether part of a network, using and now increasingly obligated to use compatible technologies and doctrines that added to or at least didn't detract from the whole.

Sweden was there as well. Like other "neutral" nations, the country maintained its sovereignty and independence by staying away from conflicts that did not fall under UN mandate. And, befitting its neutrality, Stockholm specialized in being the go-to diplomatic leader in resolving the most difficult crises, such as Iraq and the long WMD standoff that preceded the second Gulf War. But then came 9/11, and Sweden, along with the rest of the civilized world, joined a new coalition that was wholly American and increasingly demanding of uniformity. The new uniformity and the even greater demand for network membership came with the emergence of the Internet and global appliances—satellite-guided navigation, precision weapons targeting, aerial refueling, even global transport—that increasingly constituted one system.

Sweden found itself in Afghanistan and Iraq, and later it joined the American-led coalition against ISIS. Officially the country was only on the ground to conduct training and to advise indigenous forces, continuing its traditional role as a high-end peacekeeping force in a world where there was no longer any peace to keep. Sweden deployed ships to Operation Atalanta, to fight pirates in the Gulf of Aden, off the

Somali coast. Sweden participated in the international action in Libya, airlifting supplies to those who bombed. During the ISIS campaign, Sweden even quietly dispatched spy planes to Cyprus in the eastern Mediterranean, the only function to spy on Russian forces in Syria and feed that intelligence back to the larger organism, a kind of dues paying that gave the neutral country access to secret information. And, at home, Sweden's security agencies worked closely with its European counterparts, exchanging intelligence information and vetting more than a million refugees from the Middle East, North Africa, and Somalia.

When Vladimir Putin's Russia began to back away from the post-9/11 international counter-terrorism partnership and when it began to build up its military forces as NATO expanded—first informally and then formally—into Eastern Europe, Sweden initially signed up for the eight-nation "Joint Expeditionary Force." It was a U.K.-led formation of Baltic and Northern European states (including neutral Finland) and described itself as "international by design," that is, operating on behalf of all, not dominated by either superpower. And yet at the same time, Sweden also increasingly conducted air, naval, and land operations with its partners and with NATO, eventually earning its special status as a "partner to the Allies."

"Security is built in solidarity with others," the Swedish Defense Ministry said about the country's 2018 participation of NATO's largest war game since the Cold War. "The capability of acting within the frame of a joint, multinational operation is fundamental for operating in Sweden, in Sweden's neighbouring region or in missions in more faraway locations. Our cooperation with NATO is key to the enhancement of our capabilities—both nationally and internationally."

Sweden might insist that its participation is merely a demonstration of the strength of its *national* security. And, yes,

Sweden can operate domestically on its own. But once it ventures an inch outside of its own borders, it is dependent on and a part of a larger network that is complex and fantastically expensive, one outside the reach of any one nation except the United States. We are talking here about a physical network, from satellites in space all the way down to radios that facilitate basic communications. It is the totality of bases or aircraft, ships and missiles, everything that allows foreign elements to occupy the same space within a larger organism. Just like the Internet with its open-source software, compatible protocols, and common specifications, the disparate pieces have to follow international standards to function. In the military sphere, this means open information, universal terminology, and common devices that can not only talk to each other and be supplied and resupplied by the whole but also cannot effectively work when disconnected.

Sweden still asserts that it is only "cooperating" and building national capability. It can choose not to participate in some operation and withdraw from some war game to assert independence. But there is something different about the Patriot missile system, about Sweden's own Patriot anti-air network and the larger network that also now makes the country inextricably a part of the whole. One could argue that no one owns this larger network—except that this network is dominated by one nation: the United States. Sweden's new Patriot missiles might someday shoot down an intruding Russian bomber or a threatening Russian missile. But if that happens, Sweden will do so informed by, and dependent on, early-warning data (and parallel action) from the larger network of synchronized countries. It's all an intellectual exercise, speculating on whether Sweden would *ever* shoot down a Russian object, but it's impossible to imagine, other than in an accident, how such an act could take place and not be part of the opening salvo of a larger war. And *that* war would mark Sweden as a soldier in the anti-Russian alliance, not just a global enabler of the larger body but a network node regardless of its insistence on its independence.

* *

The power of the network—how it binds together a perpetual war system that looks little different from a Cold War we seemingly left behind with the fall of the Soviet Union, and how it holds countries in its grip—can also be seen in the opposite of Sweden, in Saudi Arabia. Where Sweden is technologically advanced and progressive, a shining member of the international community, Saudi Arabia is backward and autocratic, an international lawbreaker and a covert supporter of terrorism. One is inextricably drawn into the network in the name of asserting internationalism and sovereignty. The other is wholly dependent, having the best military money can buy, seemingly a beneficiary but missing a certain something.

The Kingdom of Saudi Arabia spends more money on weapons than any other country in the world, its per capita spending on all things military putting it in the top ten. Despite this, the country has never been able to even defend itself. In 1990, when Saddam Hussein invaded neighboring Kuwait, Saudi Arabia was so frightened about a potential Iraqi invasion that it quickly agreed to American and then international military deployments on its soil. Although Saudi Arabia has never been neutral in the same way Sweden declares itself, it was a momentous move for a country at the center of the Islamic faith and that had never before invited foreign military forces to base themselves within its borders. It was a move, it could be argued, that was even the basis of Osama bin Laden's animus toward both the Saudi royal family and the United States.

After 9/11, even after Saddam was toppled, Saudi Arabia continued to host the American machine. And it has continued to buy arms like no other country. Between 2001 and 2019, the kingdom bought more than $151 billion worth of arms from the United States alone, including the most advanced smart weapons. Then, in 2014, perhaps heady from its participation in the various coalitions, perhaps convinced that its weapons equated to actual military capacity, Saudi Arabia formed its own alliance of countries to fight in Yemen, to support the fledgling Sunni government against a Shi'a Houthi insurgency.

What followed was a disaster in every way. On the ground, Saudi's "coalition" of forces—many paid mercenaries—were unable to seize or retain territory and unable to operate as a whole. In the air, Saudi aircraft were unable to properly utilize precision weapons. With rudimentary weapons, the opposing Houthis managed to attack Saudi forces and bases with artillery, rockets, and missiles, down Saudi coalition helicopters and reconnaissance drones, and even attack Saudi cities. As of this writing, the war drags on, with civilian casualties and damage reaching grotesque levels, and disease—even before Covid-19—ravaging the country. One U.S. general calls it "a man-made crisis of appalling proportions." Brookings Institution scholar Daniel Byman labels Saudi performance "incompetent and cruel." Former CIA analyst Ken Pollack, an expert on Arab armed forces, bluntly concluded that "the U.S.-trained Saudi military fell flat on its face" in Yemen.

U.S. trained, perhaps, but not endowed of the network capabilities that make modern warfare possible. Although Saudi Arabia purchased hardware and even plugged into the network, the country is dependent on American contractors to even maintain and operate their systems. Saudi Arabia is dependent on the U.S. Air Force for aerial refueling. And it is dependent on U.S. intelligence for targeting information. In fact, it is unable to accrue any actual advantages of being part of a larger whole, as all of the attributes of networking—access to free-flowing information, decentralized decision-making, and execution—are inimical to the ruling monarchy's interests.

This is the flip side of the network. Saudi Arabia doesn't provide enough technical education to its citizens and discourages the kind of individual initiative that is necessary to operate in network terms. Like North Korea, the ruling family is not interested in having a competent military. "There's no automatic translation from those weapons into an operational capacity," one observer said. The defense blog *War Is Boring* stated matter-of-factly that "Saudi Arabia cannot win wars on its own." Even those elements that supposedly did perform— special operations forces and Saudi Arabia's own Patriot air defense missiles—were largely foreign or contractor operated, able to do what they did only with American assistance.

Saudi Arabia may pride itself as a member of the network, but to the United States it is just another Middle Eastern node, its bases and infrastructure out-of-the-box ready for American deployments and use, whether that is in support of America's many wars or in preparation for war against Iran. Although it may grate upon European sensibilities and the strategic pretensions of the national security establishment, Sweden is largely the same, a node in the worldwide network, its actual importance to the United States merely symbolic. Swedish geography is useful but not unique. Its defense industry offers boutique items, but no external nation needs Sweden to sustain its military. And to American war planners Sweden's actual combat experience with high-end war fighting is near zero. Yet, through Sweden's alliance status and being plugged into the bigger network, the United States not only gets to have Patriot missiles closer to the Russian north but it also gets Sweden to keep its mouth shut about the broad outlines of perpetual war. That contrasts starkly with the pre-9/11 era, when Sweden virtually led the international opposition to the Vietnam War and the nuclear arms race and worked mightily to prevent conflict between the United States and Iraq.

In wiring the world together for perpetual war, and for a certain type of high-tech precision war that has become the American way, there is perhaps a future silver lining, one revealed in both the Swedish and Saudi stories. Acquiring better network skills is not just about militarism; it is a feature of education and independent thinking and even democracy. We see that the first step of any autocratic regime crackdown is always directed at information. Conversely, the making of a modern military depends upon free flow of information and upon the ability of everyone, from the lowest ranking to the top, to operate with literacy, open systems, and initiative. A networked military can't guarantee that it will win wars, and in some ways, as we've seen in the past two decades, it becomes so unmanned and remote in the projection of power that it is able to soldier on with minimal interference from civil society. But if everyone aspired to hyper-precision like the United States—if Russia and China and North Korea and Iran struggled to incorporate modern weapons and networked forces in place of brute-force World War II models—then their societies would also have to change: first their militaries would have to professionalize in new ways, and then their education and information industries would have to follow. None of this can happen—or be sustained—in an autocratic state.

One might ask, especially in the realm of cyber weaponry, whether these four countries haven't already attained network strength—that is, in the ways that Russia or North Korea, or even China and Iran, have made forays into the American network, even into the American network of democracy. So far, it is mere mischief, carried out by special operations, able to do some damage and certainly threatening, but not the vanguard of some networked force lurking behind. And, yes, America, in being so heavily networked, is uniquely vulnerable. But part of that vulnerability results from spending too much national treasure and energy to strengthen military systems at the expense of civil needs. The effects of the imbalance were exposed by Covid-19, in the weakened public health system and the empty reserve, the ultimate cost of embracing perpetual war.

chapter nine

CONVERGENCE

Behind chain-link fences north of a government-controlled private beach in Key West, Florida, Joint Interagency Task Force South sits so blocked from sight that if you walked down Angela Street to the pre–Civil War installation Fort Zachary Taylor, you'd have no idea that JIATF (pronounced "j-eye-ate-if") South was there. This very obscure command, established in 1989 after President Reagan declared a war on drugs, is cited as the modern-day model for a "whole of government" effort and a "gold standard" for interagency cooperation that breaks down all post 9/11 walls and connects all dots.

JIATF South is a super–watch center, overseeing 42 million square miles of the Atlantic and eastern Pacific Oceans all the way down to Antarctica. Its official mission is "detection and monitoring of illicit trafficking across all domains." It is a frightening example of how perpetual war has found its way back into infiltrating our domestic lives, "illicit trafficking" representing an ever-expanding enemy, "all domains" perfectly embodying the network, encompassing everything from land to sea, air to cyberspace, undersea and underground.

From its Key West hub, the task force says it "enables the disruption and dismantlement of . . . converging threat networks." "Convergence" is perhaps the most important perpetual war buzzword you've never heard. It is a nexus—sometimes called a hybrid super-threat—where terrorist and criminal threat networks collaborate, sharing and utilizing illicit pathways to move everything from people to drugs to bomb-making materials to money.

The idea of *threat networks*—those of the enemy—came out of all the frustrations of Iraq after the fall of Saddam Hussein. Former regime elements, as the military dubbed rejected Ba'ath Party members, *converged* with other opponents of the United States military occupation, who *converged* with Sunni tribal leaders, who *converged* with criminal elements, who *converged* with smugglers and bomb makers, who *converged* with Al Qaeda and new terrorist groups, who *converged* with Shi'a militias and Iranian agents, who *converged* with corrupt officials, who crossed borders into Iran, Kuwait, Syria, Jordan, Saudi Arabia, and Turkey, recruiting still new members, forging relations with each other, creating organized syndicates, and then fighting the occupiers. The convergence of all created one super-network that government officials simply labeled "the insurgency." It encompassed layers upon layers of nodes and cells, some so powerful that they grew stronger than the official government.

Understanding this enemy network growing in Iraq, and then defeating the network, became the U.S. government's top priority. All of a sudden the military had to shift itself to operating more akin to police work than traditional combat. American military leaders dipped into the experiences of people who had spent their lives fighting drug-trafficking organizations and organized crime.

"September 11 demonstrated the dangers that arise when

these threats converge . . . ," CIA director George Tenet, one of the first high-level officials to articulate these growing connections, said in February 2002. "This convergence of threats has created a world . . . in which dangers exist not only in those places we have most often focused our attention, but also in other areas . . ."

Washington's recognition of this cross fertilization—and the pivot to a singular focus on terrorism—wasn't lost on people working in Latin America. "A top priority for SOUTH-COM," said the commander of U.S. Southern Command in 2002, was going to be to "foster regional support" for the war on terrorism. "The nexus of guerrillas, terrorists, drug traffickers, and illegal self-defense forces," he said, opened the way for future Al Qaedas. When the Bush administration expanded the mission of Plan Colombia from drugs to terrorism, drug traffickers morphed into being called narco-terrorists overnight. The convergence theory was that, whether they were in Colombia or Afghanistan, terrorist organizations financed terrorism by selling drugs, and drug-smuggling organizations were resorting to terror. A "new" war against those super-networks became the opportunity to rebrand and become relevant in the post 9/11 world, connecting terrorism to drug smuggling, either in their cooperation or merely because the violence of the drug cartels was now relabeled "terrorism."

John Arquilla and David Ronfeldt famously wrote at the beginning of the information age that "it takes a network to defeat a network." That became the fighting banner not just in Iraq and Afghanistan but also around the world. Interagency cooperation—"whole of government"—emerged as the way to tear down the proverbial wall between agencies. U.S. intelligence completed a new comprehensive assessment, concluding that networks were not only proliferating but that they were converging, "striking new and powerful alliances." By the time Barack Obama became president, "converging threat networks" were accepted as the very design of all non-state enemies. In July 2011, Obama signed the *Strategy to Combat Transnational Organized Crime*, which identified nearly half of the sixty-three top drug-trafficking organizations as having ties to terrorist groups. Smuggling networks were now so sophisticated, the intelligence community concluded, that they were newly concerned that these converged networks might even facilitate the transfer of weapons of mass destruction into the United States.

Although the Key West command never used the words "It takes a network to defeat a network," it turned out the task force embodied that concept precisely. The six-hundred-person organization combines all four services and the Coast Guard—not just military and law enforcement but also homeland security and intelligence—and even includes officers and liaisons from more than twenty partner nations. The original premise was a "friendly network" to interdict the flow of drugs from Central and South America. Although it might be a bit of revisionist history, the Joint Chiefs of Staff later wrote: "From the onset, it became readily apparent that traditional approaches and processes used to address drug cartels and their associated threat networks were going to be ineffective."

Over its thirty years in existence, JIATF South has expanded its geographic operations and increased its workforce sixfold. Meanwhile, the focus has decidedly shifted from stopping drugs one airplane or one speedboat at a time to understanding and pursuing the broader networks behind them. That's why JIATF South says today that it seeks to identify and interdict—that is, stop—everything that's going on related to so-called illicit trafficking. That means everything from drugs to cash to people. The task force commander in 2017 stated: "We are an interagency and international coalition . . . working to facilitate the eventual dismantlement of large criminal enterprises aimed at undermining stability and security in the Western Hemisphere."

To do its outsize job, the task force says it seeks to achieve "100% domain awareness." In English this means that the task force tries to see everything that is happening in its area of operations. It can make such a boast because all possible types of intelligence flow into Key West with what its commander calls "an unprecedented degree of information coordination." Analysts screen communication intercepts, look at satellite images, scrutinize drone footage, interpret and annotate surveillance and reconnaissance data from aircraft and ships, process foreign government information, exploit CIA agent and FBI informant reports—even tap into law enforcement and homeland security databases—all in real time, to create a picture of a mind-boggling array of dynamic movements over a gigantic area. Working with the latest analytical software and employing sophisticated data mining and artificial intelligence, they pick out potential threats and distribute their results as "tactical data" to a myriad of international forces out on patrol.

At JIATF South's thirtieth anniversary celebration in February 2019, Lieutenant General Michael T. Plehn, deputy commander of SOUTHCOM, cited the task force's "record setting achievements year after year after year" in pulling all of this information together. He said that JIATF South now interdicts in a single day twice what it interdicted in its entire first year of operations in the 1980s. Plehn and other Pentagon leaders brag that, with less than 2 percent of the U.S. counter-drug budget, the task force accounts for "more than 40 percent of global cocaine interdiction," seizing more than five times as much cocaine as the rest of the U.S. government combined. Testifying before Congress in 2019, SOUTHCOM commander Admiral Craig S. Faller credited the task force with delivering "steady returns." Their take was the equivalent, he said, "of 600 mini-vans full of cocaine off U.S. streets" every year.

Effective. Working together. Mission driven. Sharing information. You'd almost think we were talking about the rarest of government birds: an agency that applies all of the lessons of 9/11 and really works. And yet none of this happy talk stacks up against actual results. In fact, the military concludes that even with all of the information known to mankind, even with the epitome of cooperation, it is only interdicting some 6 percent of the total of drugs being trafficked in the Latin America and Caribbean region. Despite the military's hyperbole, that 6 percent figure shouldn't be that surprising. After all the "war" on drugs is a war in name only, and only so many resources are applied. In a way, though, it is also a metaphor for the war on terror, where the activity becomes as important as the results.

It gets even worse when we look at how the joint task force counts its own success. In fiscal year 2017, the latest year for which there are complete numbers, JIATF South said that it achieved 71 percent interdiction "success." This is officially defined as the "percentage of detected events successfully handed-off to interdiction and apprehension resources." It's the bottom line, and if we didn't already think of the organization as the gold standard, this number would indicate a government best of the best. But then comes the fine print: How exactly is that 71 percent success rate calculated? What are this seven out of every ten "illicit traffickers" being caught? That same year the Key West task force logged 8,008 "Critical Movement Alerts," its term for intelligence reports referring to "events"—that is, smuggler preparations, aircraft taking off, drug-related boat and submarine sightings, truck movements, and so on. After analysts double-checked those 8,008 events, they elevated exactly 6,489 of them into "Drug Movement Alerts," whereby the Task Force tipped off naval ships, police boats, standby commando units, and SWAT teams of an impending or ongoing illicit drug movement. The analysts' qualifying criteria was that they needed to have a location, date, and time. Of those 6,489 Drug Movement Alerts, a total of 4,567 were further validated as meeting the even stricter criteria to enter them into the Consolidated Counterdrug Database (CCDB). Of those 4,567 CCDB validated events, the analysts at JIATF South were able to send aircraft, drones, helicopters, and ships to check out only a total of 1,186 to "try to find or search for the illicit conveyance . . . highly mobile, asymmetric, non-communicative targets." They didn't target the other 3,381 events primarily because they ran out of planes and boats to send.

Of the 1,186 pursued targets, 449 were "detected" on the ground, at sea, or in the air. That is, someone put eyes on the actual movement or activity. A third of these 449 eyes-on cases got away. The other 318 were successfully handed off to an appropriate law enforcement agency—be that the Coast Guard or the DEA or Customs and Border Protection or even a foreign police or military force—for apprehension. *This* is a "success rate of 71 percent for seizures or disruptions."

It took a little digging to find the fine print, but any way you count it, 318 out of 4,567 valid targets or 6,489 alerts or 8,008 raw reports is a very strange 71 percent success rate. It's statistical success without an actual result, the very epitome of not just the drug war but of perpetual war. In the Caribbean and Central America, the combined forces fighting threat networks are working hard and fighting something—"in the fight," as they say—countering threats to America and trumpeting success while also knowing well that America's actual longest war, the war on drugs, is a losing battle. Admiral Faller told Congress in early 2019 that the effort "isn't enough to keep pace with the increasing demand" or the volume of drug movements. The *best* the military and the task force could do, he said, was "improving efficiency." In thirty years of America's first perpetual "war," the enemy has never been defeated, nor has the outcome of fighting—or all the effort—been greater security at home. In fact, today it is estimated that 9.4 percent of the entire American population (or almost 25 million people) are illicit drug users. They collectively provide drug producers and traffickers with $19 billion to $29 billion in annual revenue.

This numbers game is repeated in so many other areas, not just the drug war. That's because, despite all of the effort and the many billions spent, results in the drug war or border control or even the war against terror do not produce conclusive results. One obvious starting point to estimate what resources were needed to devote to counter-terrorism might be to know how many terrorists the United States and its partners are killing or taking off the battlefield in comparison with the total number of terrorists.

So how many terrorists are there in the world? And how many is the United States fighting? Astoundingly, not even the intelligence community knows—not just because it doesn't track them centrally, not even despite having a National Counterterrorism Center and a multibillion-dollar watchlisting system that records individuals down to their birthmarks. It is also because *who* is a terrorist has become so vague, largely as a result of convergence, that there is just no clear answer. Counter-terrorism is precisely like the drug war, or a kid's Little League participation award. *Effort*, not results, is all that is really being counted.

Thus, estimates of membership in different terrorist groups range from dozens to tens of thousands. From the State Department, which produces the annual *Country Reports on Terrorism*, to the Department of Homeland Security–funded

National Consortium for the Study of Terrorism and Responses to Terrorism (known as START), to the State Department's list of foreign terrorist organizations, most organizations track incidents or individuals but not the total. Even when it comes to Al Qaeda, there is no comprehensive official number. Bruce Hoffman, one of the world's leading experts on terrorism, offered an estimate in 2018, saying that the organization had about 40,000 fighters. It is an astounding number after two decades of perpetual war, especially since, after Osama bin Laden's death in 2011, CIA director Leon Panetta said that the organization was "on the path to defeat."

Then there is ISIS. A UN Security Council document estimated in 2018 that ISIS had about 20,000 to 30,000 fighters in Syria and Iraq. The State Department pegged the number at only 6,000 to 10,000, while the Pentagon said they thought it was more like 13,100 to 14,500, but cautioned that the numbers were "in flux." And yet, former White House special envoy for the counter-ISIS coalition Brett McGurk estimated in 2017 that some 40,000 foreign fighters alone had traveled to Syria to join ISIS. The Defense Department inspector general said they thought 15,500 to 17,100 remained in Iraq as of mid-2018, with another 14,000 in Syria. An estimated 5,600 ISIS fighters were estimated to have returned to their home countries. An additional 1,000 to 3,000 ISIS fighters were estimated in Afghanistan, plus 6,000 more across the African continent. So, was the total number of 6,000 to 13,000 ISIS fighters on the low side or was some 40,000 on the high side? And how many had been killed? How many had given up the cause? How many cycled through both Syria and Iraq and were double-counted elsewhere? How many more were lying in wait in Europe or the United States, never having traveled to the Middle East in the first place?

This dizzying pattern of vagueness and hedging extends

around the globe, everywhere that perpetual war has itself migrated. Al Shabaab in Somalia? The best estimate seems to be 7,000 to 9,000. Boko Haram in Nigeria and West Africa? "Several thousand," almost every source says. The Taliban in Afghanistan? The estimate is "several thousand," and yet more than half of the country is held by them and their reach extends into major parts of Pakistan. And Hizballah in Lebanon? The best sources cited "tens of thousands," but this seems to be hard-core fighters rather than the entire movement. It is almost as if the question of how many exist is avoided so as to not have to answer whether the war on terror has been a success. But it is also affirmation that nobody really knows, because the reality of our war against terrorism is that countless terrorists are being added every day.

At a conference between the U.S. military and their Caribbean counterparts in March 2017, a sort of marketing meeting to sell convergence, American officials told their neighbors to the south that ISIS was the best example of the terror-crime nexus. It had risen to power, they said, by committing crimes and terrorist activities. "ISIS is considered the richest terrorist group in the world engaged in widespread extortion, oil smuggling, human trafficking, bank robbery, and antiquities looting," the conference report read. The Los Zetas cartel in Mexico, conference-goers were told, used similar tactics to control their operating areas. Illicit networks consisting of criminals, terrorists, proliferators, and their facilitators were operating in a "grey zone between war and peace," looking for new products and markets. Movement of drugs, weapons, and other contraband, and even people, was the new challenge for the war on terror, American officials said, and the Caribbean had better take notice.

The Joint Chiefs of Staff affirmed this worldview in a 2016 manual entitled *Countering Threat Networks*, saying that "in a world increasingly characterized by volatility, uncertainty, complexity, and ambiguity, a wide range of local, national, and transnational irregular challenges to the stability of the international system have emerged." Although the manual stated that insurgencies and criminal gangs had been exploiting weak or corrupt governments for years, what was new was how "transnational extremists" teamed up with "traditional threats." Convergence.

Countering threat networks is the new perpetual-war mantra, broad enough and vague enough to encompass everything. It took years of wordplay, and many fits and starts, but bureaucrats representing the military, the intelligence community, homeland security, and law enforcement finally, themselves, converged on a single all-purpose mission that didn't even need terrorism anymore to keep fighting. Counter-threat networks consolidated and, in some cases, eliminated nineteen different "counter-campaigns" that existed in various agencies of the national security establishment. Of course, the granddaddy of them all was the Nixon-era counter-drug campaign, which evolved into counter-narcotics and then counter–narco terrorism (CNT) after 9/11. Counter-proliferation—an active military program—was another early joiner, one that pursues to destroy the building blocks of WMD before they become weapons. That program shifted to Countering WMD (CWMD), a mission set like Counter-IED (C-IED)—for improvised explosive devices—that assigned tasks to actual multi-billion-dollar agencies: the Defense Threat Reduction Agency for WMD and the Joint Improvised-Threat Defeat Organization (JIDO) for IEDs. Counter-terrorism for a while became Countering Violent Extremism (CVE) when soft power was favored in the Obama years. Although no one thinks that CVE competes or will supplant counter-terrorism in a military sense, the survival of the term gives the State Department and the civilian agencies a role to play in perpetual war. Then there is Counter Threat Finance (CTF), the government campaign to chase bad money, an effort that even extends into the private sector. Counter Corruption (CC) describes a specific campaign in Afghanistan and later Iraq, and Counter Malign Foreign Influence was invented to refer to Iran, later shortened to Counter Malign Influence, and even renamed Counter Iran Threat Networks. Counter Human Trafficking became Combating Trafficking in Persons (CTIP) in the Obama administration, "Human" perhaps being . . . well, too human. And then, as terrorists started to use their own drones in Syria, Counter–Unmanned Aerial Systems (C-UAS) emerged as the newest counter-campaign, spawning a billion-dollar slush fund similar to the earlier Counter-IED campaign when roadside bombers were the threat du jour.

The Defense Department admits that its decades-long focus on illicit commodities—cocaine, heroin, methamphetamines, and precursor chemicals for WMD—hasn't really slowed illicit trafficking. U.S. and international efforts are just forcing the traffickers to "change the mix of products," it says. As a result of U.S. and international counter-efforts, the threat networks transporting drugs shifted to transporting people (including migrants and terrorists), money, weapons, and anything else that paid or could find a market. "These converging criminal and extremist networks" are also recruiting new participants using a combination of social media, popular culture, and violence to further their ends, the Pentagon warns. That has spawned counter–social media, the State Department running an overt arm, the clandestine agencies operating increasingly undercover.

Does it ever end? Pentagon marketers noted in their Caribbean presentation that proceeds from cybercrime already outstripped the illegal drug trade and were "growing exponentially." And so counter-cybercrime, something that affects everyone, becomes another battle in perpetual war. Other "counter" campaigns that bubble up in government documents and military manuals include countering trafficking in wildlife, countering illegal timber, countering "illegal, unregulated, and unreported (IUU) fishing," countering the spread of infectious diseases, countering counterfeit medicines, countering epidemics, countering hazardous wastes and resource exploitation, countering counterfeit consumer goods, and countering illicit travel for child exploitation.

In convergence, the national security establishment has perhaps reached its highest pinnacle, policing anything and everything. The expansive focus to trace movement pathways—global, regional, and country-based—makes each criminal activity the equivalent of terrorism, mission creep at its worst. Each piece of this battle might make sense if it is seen in isolation. But the ultimate convergence of perpetual war is not only how it turns activities on the entire planet into one networked enemy but how at the same time it further obscures the dividing line between what is military and what is civilian.

While convergence provides justification to fight an expansive enemy, "persistence" is the latest concept that ensures that perpetual war will maintain its worldwide footprint. "The strategic environment is uncertain, contested, complex, and can change rapidly, requiring military leaders to maintain persistent military engagement," the Joint Chiefs of Staff said in a new 2018 manual. In other words, uncertainty and change doesn't demand that we constantly rethink what we do and how we do it; the military instead needs to be everywhere and in every domain—including the virtual domain—if it is to be ready to instantly counter any enemy movement or action.

These days the military believes warfare will unfold so quickly that striking the enemy requires the next natural modification of the 9/11 prevention mindset. Rapid military action—they don't call it "preemption"—has to be able to move ever faster to anticipate and even head off whatever the enemy might do. "Through persistent presence, persistent innovation, and persistent engagement, we can impose costs, neutralize adversary efforts, and change their decision calculus," Army general Paul M. Nakasone, commander of the new worldwide Cyber Command, said in May 2019. He noted that his cyber warriors are "fully engaged with adversaries in the cyber domain, full-time." In English that means that the military is already fighting a frontless cyber war every day. They are not the only warriors who stay engaged. So too are thousands of others: special operations teams and individual fighter and drone pilots, ship captains and platoon leaders on the ground. Whether they are in the Middle East or in the African Maghreb, their task is to stay in contact with the enemy like a blind person with an outstretched cane, sensing the presence and motion of any possible threat.

Persistent engagement particularly means the national security establishment now operates in so many places, in so many different ways, with so many different organizations, that—like the big mystery of how many terrorists there are— no one really has a holistic view of all of the counter-activities. The Pentagon recognizes that this is a problem, saying in its *Summary of the 2018 National Defense Strategy* that one of its top priorities is to create better tools to track enemy *and* friendly forces. Ever since the digital era began, this has been the dream: transparency that allows the United States to sense and see the enemy wherever it may hide—on the ground, in the air, in space, and even in cyberspace. It should perhaps not be surprising that such transparency is impossible, or at least that no human will be able to assimilate all of the data—that the tools being created increasingly rely on artificial intelligence to keep track of everything in real time. Convergence is the dangerous wedge that inserts all of this into American domestic life. As the theory of convergence and the threats that it poses plays out, never-ending clandestine networks extending into and operating in American society will have to be sensed and characterized in real time. American society will be like the nations of the Caribbean and Central America, with supra-organizations logging activities and movements, endeavoring to distinguish that which is potentially unlawful and threatening amidst the entire universe of communications, movements, and activities. We are years if not decades away from such government capability—to ingest everything in an effort to find illicit activity—but expanding the search for terrorists into a search for a myriad of suspected lawbreakers is the justification to attempt the feat.

chapter ten

A GLOBAL
SECURITY INDEX

L ike Barack Obama, Donald Trump came into office with
perpetual war in full bloom but also with the national security establishment in revolt. As a candidate, Trump called the
military leadership "embarrassing" and said that he would fire
Obama's generals. He said that Washington insiders had made
the U.S. "a mess" and called the nation's capital a "swamp." He
insulted national security leaders by name, including Robert
Gates. He questioned the competence of U.S. intelligence and
said that he would approve of the use of torture.

Initially seeming to pick a fight with North Korea when
he came into office, with military moves to match, a narrative
unfolded that the country, perhaps even the planet, needed to
be saved from the new president: he was a man with neither
the competence nor the temperament to be commander in
chief. "The worst security risk in U.S. history," wrote George
W. Bush speechwriter David Frum. "A clear and present danger to the national security of the United States," said a former Justice Department counterintelligence chief. Members
of Congress introduced legislation that would prevent the

president from pushing the nuclear button without their approval—even if under attack by Russia.

Has the world become more dangerous because of Donald Trump? Chaos seemed to follow him into office and the headlines have certainly been alarming. He declared a Muslim ban, insulted long-standing allies, unilaterally withdrew from treaties and agreements, waged war at the Southern border, picked fights with North Korea, blamed China for Covid-19. Even before he muddled his way through a coronavirus response, exclaiming hoaxes and erratically flip-flopping on the federal government's response and responsibility, instances of his erratic pronouncements and behavior were legion. *Wired* magazine declared the tweeting president the world's most dangerous online persona: worse than ISIS, worse than Russian hackers who may have even helped get him elected.

Could things get worse? On October 19, 2018, a United States Navy battle group entered the Arctic Circle for the first time since the fall of the Berlin Wall and the breakup of the Soviet Union, beginning two weeks of intense operations. Navy captain Nick Dienna, commanding officer of the aircraft carrier USS *Harry S. Truman*, said, "It has been over three decades since carrier aviation has been tested by this environment, and, despite the arduous weather and sea conditions, these men and women are demonstrating this ship can bring a full-spectrum of capabilities to bear anywhere in the world." The *Truman* was at the center of Carrier Strike Group Eight, a powerful armada of ships and attack submarines sent into the Norwegian Sea to conduct mock air strikes against an unnamed Russia, all in freezing weather and extremely rough seas.

Six days later, the *Truman* and its full strike group joined twenty-nine other nations for Trident Juncture, a monthlong NATO war game, the largest in almost three decades. Simulating mobilization out of its Norfolk, Virginia, homeport, the

Truman practiced moving north against mock Russian submarines, "fighting" its way past Iceland and into the Arctic. There
it played first chair in the giant war game, leading an orchestra
of 50,000 sailors, soldiers, airmen, and marines on board a total
of sixty-five ships: aircraft carriers, destroyers, frigates, and patrol boats. The exercise included a U.S. Marine Corps amphibious invasion of northern Norway. And a total of 250 fighter
and intelligence collection aircraft took to the skies, operating
from the deck of the *Truman* and from land bases. "Neutral"
Sweden was there, and the exercise made use of Finnish airspace as well. Submarines swarmed north. Other ships entered
the Baltic Sea sailing toward Russia. Carrier Strike Group
Eight commander Rear Admiral Eugene H. Black called it "a
global network of navies capable of uniting against any potential threat."

If Western countries were really going to war—"big
war"—against Russia, NATO says this is what the battle
would look like. Of course, Russia responded. Vladimir Putin
told participants of a business conference going on at the time
that "Russia doesn't threaten anyone," pledging that Moscow
would continue to modernize its own armed forces, adding
hypersonic weapons and long-range missiles to counter what
he called NATO's ever more provocative behavior. Russian
defense minister Sergei Shoigu decried NATO military activity so near to Russia and at the highest level of intensity since
the Cold War, saying that the war games were indeed "simulating offensive military action" against his country.

U.S. Navy leaders, however, continued to publicly down-
play any Russian connection. They had even invited the Krem-
lin to send observers, they said. Moscow instead announced
that it would conduct its own simultaneous live-missile drill
off the coast of Norway. And then, in a show of force, they sent
two Tu-160 long-range bombers on their own mock-attack

runs over the Barents and Norwegian Seas. The Russian "play" was happily welcomed into the game—American and NATO intelligence collectors going to work, Norwegian air force fighters scrambling to intercept the Russian attackers.

Ten days into the exercise, the "at-sea" portion of the Trident Juncture war game was suspended after the NATO fleet struggled in a storm that thrust waves more than thirty feet into the air. To finish, war planners from all twenty-nine participating nations gathered with their American counterparts to "play" out the rest of the game over computer networks, working out the kinks of an alliance that was shifting focus from the Middle East to Russia.

The *Truman* and its sister ships returned to their homeports just before Christmas. Donald Trump never said anything about the war game. Washington hardly noticed. But when the Trump administration released its new budget three months later, to everyone's surprise, the budget declared that the aircraft carrier USS *Harry S. Truman*, star of the previous year and at the prime of capabilities, would be retired rather than undergo its midlife nuclear refueling and overhaul. Such a decision, the budget said, would cut off nineteen years from its forty-year projected life span, making way for building new ships instead.

"A ridiculous idea," said Elaine Luria, a former Navy officer who represented Norfolk in the House of Representatives. Others questioned the math presented by the budget makers who suggested that the savings from not overhauling the *Truman* would allow two new aircraft carriers to be built and other futuristic projects like unmanned ships and laser weapons to be funded.

"The strategic choice is to take more risk with day-to-day presence so investments can be made to develop the ability to defeat the Chinese Navy if war breaks out," wrote one Navy captain in defending the cut, arguing that present capability could be sacrificed to purchase more for tomorrow. He called the habit of sending aircraft carriers on peacetime missions like those that threatened Russia "faith-based," adding that there was "little hard evidence that deployed naval forces have actually deterred anything or coerced anyone," an argument that could be used to describe almost any aspect of the automatic system but one now used to justify a purely bureaucratic decision.

"The U.S. needs both enough ships to meet its global commitments *and* advanced technology to equip them," wrote another bureaucratic fighter from the other side of the argument. "Cutting either to fund the other is like giving up your health insurance to replace a leaking roof."

A classic Washington budget war commenced: more versus even more, supposed future threats and vulnerabilities filling the air. Then President Donald Trump intervened, sending Vice President Mike Pence to Norfolk to stand on the *Truman*'s deck and announce that the retirement of the aircraft carrier had been canceled. "[Retiring the *Truman*] would have been an awful decision," Congresswoman Luria sighed.

As Trump countermanded his own budget request to Congress—when he realized what the machine was doing—it became clear that the demonstrations of the *Truman*'s efficacy the previous year were never part of his decision. In fact, sources say, they have no reason to believe that President Trump knew about the NATO exercise or the aircraft carrier's voyage to Russia's doorstep. Indeed, in Mike Pence's remarks in Norfolk, he merely congratulated the *Truman* for dropping 1,600 smart weapons on ISIS fighters in the Mediterranean phase of their voyage. He never mentioned Russia or suggested the military usefulness of the aircraft carrier beyond perpetual war.

Like the jigsaw puzzle that arranges unit and personnel schedules, the decision to scrap the *Truman* was based more on how long it would take to build a new aircraft carrier—fifteen years—than on any assessment of actual threats. That's how most resource decisions are made: with an eye on the distant future under perpetual war while schedules are jiggered around to accommodate competing communities and even corporations. And yet, there was the *Truman*, and a three-years-in-the making military exercise with real-world implications, being pushed into the background. Donald Trump knew nothing about the war game, and so, it raised the question of whether this new, erratic, and seemingly dangerous president was indeed making us less safe. And, by extension, it raises a bigger question: Are we any safer today than we were on that cloudless Tuesday morning two decades ago? And is there any way to assess whether events build on or detract from our basic security?

The answer is that there is no way, no methodical way. What we need is an index to measure security—some impartial meter. We have numerous "indexes" that track the state of the world: economic indexes, terrorism indexes, human rights indexes, democracy indexes. But none of them provides a holistic measure of security, nor are they configured for the challenges we face today. We can track military activity—for example, war games, drone strikes, missile launches, aircraft sorties. It is possible to count numbers of soldiers, terrorists, or civilians killed, and we can observe events—exercises like the Trident Juncture war games, and incidents that occur between countries—but whether any of it adds to or detracts from greater security is a big mystery.

In 2016, when Director of National Intelligence James Clapper presented his annual threat assessment to Congress, he warned that "unpredictable instability has become the new normal and will continue for the foreseeable future." When

Oklahoma senator James Inhofe quipped that Clapper was just delivering his annual "litany of doom," Clapper didn't disagree. "In my 50 plus years in the intelligence business," he said, "I cannot recall a more diverse array of challenges and crises that we confront as we do today." *But*, he then admitted, "I've said something like that virtually every year."

Certainly one question emerged in 2017 and that was whether Donald Trump, with all of his bluster and unpredictability, had actually made the world a more dangerous place. Is it possible to determine, year over year, from 2016 (the last year of the Obama administration) through the end of 2017 (the first year of Trump), whether security increased or declined? It isn't an easy exercise. One can stack up the facts of two years—for instance, about direct violence—and make a comparison. By that measure, the world *seemed* to have gotten safer in Donald Trump's first year in office:

- In 2017 there were fewer terrorist attacks and fewer people were killed by terrorism than in 2016. There were fewer countries experiencing terrorism and fewer hostage takings. A total of ninety-four countries became safer (while forty-six became less safe) in terms of bloody violence, according to one index.
- In 2017 there were fewer wars fought in the world between nation-states, the number decreasing slightly from the previous year. On the other hand, conflicts involving terrorists, rebels, and other "non-state" actors increased significantly, and 2017 was labeled "one of the most violent years since the end of the Cold War."
- In 2017, primarily because of increased (and probably temporary) stability in Iraq and Syria, civilian casualties from warfare and terrorism also declined.

- In 2017, for the second year in a row, the "Global Peace Index" said that security declined in North America more than any other region in the world, based on their methodology of domestic conflict and "higher perceptions of criminality."
- And, contrary to what I previously assumed, in 2017, violence cost the world less money.

None of this definitively answers the bigger question. There are trends involved but there's also no indication that any of these statistics changed because of the Trump administration's policies. And there are longer-term trends to consider. Raw violence, including terrorism, has generally been trending down since 2014. That year a record 104,000 civilians were killed as a direct result of armed conflict. That year also witnessed a spike in drug trafficking into the United States as well as unprecedented drug overdoses from opioids and heroin. A record number of undocumented minors crossed the U.S.-Mexico border that year. And, worldwide, millions were driven out of their homes to seek asylum, more than at any other point since World War II.

Other events could be added to the 2014 list during the Obama administration: Russia invaded Crimea and Russian forces shot down Malaysia Airlines flight MH17 over eastern Ukraine, killing everyone on board. North Korea hacked Sony Pictures, ushering in a new era of state-sponsored attacks by an otherwise minor power. China's military started to claim territory by force in the South China Sea. Civil wars started in Libya and Yemen and Gaza. In Africa, an outbreak of Ebola virus, the "invisible enemy," killed more than 10,000.

So which is it? Safer or less safe? And how would we know? This data—events, terrorist attacks, casualties, and the record violence—can help. But there are other, blurrier factors to weigh in: military activity and cat-and-mouse games that can lead to potentially dangerous incidents between the great powers, and even recklessness on the part of hostile parties— for instance, between India and Pakistan, or the United States and Iran.

On the other hand, sending an aircraft carrier above the Arctic Circle and conducting the largest exercise in decades did not trigger any real crisis. Yes, Russia complained and conducted its own drill in response, but that was it. Perhaps the reason that the situation did not escalate was that NATO and Russia were doing exactly the same thing. Although one was being offensive and the other defensive, maybe what they were doing was routine to each of them, perpetual war evolving in the background noise of the planet, invisible to the international public but not out of character with whatever the norm of the day was when seen from military command centers.

As part of this security-measuring experiment, then, I prepared a 2,000-page timeline logging military activities for the years 2016 and 2017 to see whether the machine had actually built up to Trident Juncture and whether it had indeed shifted from the Middle East to "great power competition" as the administrations had changed. The data show that during those two years there were four significant encounters between the United States and Russia every month. These military confrontations— aircraft incursions into foreign airspace, incidents involving ship and aircraft operations—increased from forty-four in 2016 to fifty in 2017.

Of course, there were probably many incidents that are not publicly known. So it isn't clear whether the 10 percent increase was the beginning of a long-term trend or a steady state. And if it was an increase, what did it mean? Could it even be said that the world was safer or more dangerous from one year to another? And what would one look for to assess whether security declined after that, in 2018 and 2019? Did the metrics that might answer this question go up or down over previous years or decades, and what can be learned from history? Is the national security establishment even accurate when it says that the world keeps getting ever more dangerous? The demand for some kind of measure goes beyond Donald Trump. Precisely because we are in a state of perpetual war, and because the national security establishment has grown increasingly impervious to outside direction, some kind of tool is needed.

Although 2,000 pages of timelines for two years endeavors to track the big picture, what if we had the security equivalent of a Dow Jones Industrial Average? Such an index would measure national and international events in real time. It would methodically track and calculate a broad set of data—not just military activity and what is traditionally the domain of national security, but also the economy, demographics, levels of human health, and the physical environment—to determine simply (and not so simply) whether "security" is improving or getting worse. Every event around the world—the combined wire services move approximately 3,000 new stories daily—would be categorized and scored as to the parties involved and the effect.

I call this a global security index (GSX), a methodology and an algorithm to collect and then process an enormous amount of event data to create an integer (and a set of numbers) that would measure change, country by country and then in various regions and finally for the globe as a whole. Put simply, an event-driven engine would establish baseline states of security for every country (an integer)—based on demographic, environmental, military, and economic data—and that baseline would be "adjusted" by events. The algorithm would score the importance of events based upon the baseline status of the participants and based on the judgment of country and subject matter experts. There would be an absolute number created by big data analytics, but analysts could and would also input their judgment and sentiments to supplement the automated process, much in the same way that Wall Street analysts influence stock prices with their insights and projections.

Even warfare could be subject to some scoring that would create the GSX. For instance, does bombing some country—Syria or Somalia—make the country safer, based upon the target, the collateral effects, an analysis of overall campaign, year over year and decade over decade comparison? In other words, can we consider all of the factors embedded within events such as these to determine whether they weigh down or elevate security—that is, move a numerical index?

The GSX would serve two immediate purposes. With the national security establishment constantly questioning America's safety, we need a public reckoning to determine and compare national strength and security, both for the United States and across other nations. We need it especially because—even though the United States is clearly the most powerful nation on earth, with the most powerful military and the world's largest economy—it is now in dispute whether it is a leading source of higher education and innovation, and that means we may not be equipped to assess how our military-dominated world impacts a broader future. The power of a GSX might be that some measurements indicate improved security, suggest hidden benefits to certain policies or trends. Or if events and factors prove to be negative, these data might tell us to consider other policies or approaches. In other words, we would be empowered to hold decision-makers accountable based on facts instead of forming opinions and casting votes based on fear and spin.

And then there's just the mental exercise involved in thinking through the problem. The first step to creating a GSX would be to define "security"—and not just as being safe.

Security is a holistic representation of war and peace and how they measure up, so it's necessary to figure out how to assign values to events. Hopefully, even if the GSX were imperfect, its very existence would provoke a practical debate about what constitutes security and how it might be measured. There are many efforts underway that use financial data and computing power to determine risk, but what if similar means were applied to problems other than investments?

In my conception of the GSX, data from every country would be measured along a set of categories that, on balance, would assign a single value to quantify each nation's base "strength," or security. Once determined, a comparison between country base strength would also determine the weight given to each event as it occurs—how it does or doesn't change the index. The values assigned to base strength wouldn't remain static; rather, they would work like a stock price, whose value, in theory, is based on economic data (profitability, potential, etc.) but is also subject to analysts' expert adjustments. Infant mortality plummets in one country? Poverty increases across a set of countries? The strength indices would change accordingly.

Once these security factors are determined in the strength indexes, the GSX would churn real-time activity—the news, social media sentiment, shifting data—measuring individual events against the baseline. By sorting thousands of events that happen around the world minute by minute, the GSX would then isolate what impacts security. By measuring the importance of events against an analytical baseline, the process would provide pointers—and early warnings—about what's important and what's trending based upon what's actually happening. The aggregate, based on a series of weighted strength factors, would create the security index for individual countries, for the Americas, for Europe, for the Middle East, and so on—even a single GSX for the entire world, the product of shifts in security at the micro level measured against a common baseline. Index ratings would drop if a country is at war, if it experiences a terrorist attack, even if there is a destructive hurricane or tsunami. But ratings would also go up with positive developments: improvements in public health or basic infrastructure, if the country does "well" in responding to some weather event—that is, better than the norm. From day to day, week to week, and eventually year to year, we would start to see trend lines: not just more or less terrorism and war but other markers, like increased GNP or per capita income or even levels of incarceration—the products of practices and policies, each assessed in terms of creating or detracting from security for the civilian population.

Consider terrorism in terms of understanding how the GSX would put events into perspective. Government and nongovernmental organizations meticulously track terrorist incidents. We already know how many occur daily by country, by region. But if we tracked terrorist events over time, paying attention to a country or region's trend line, maybe the GSX would tell a different story. GSX "analysts" could "smooth" the numbers just like Wall Street analysts do. Yes, a set of Easter bombings in Sri Lanka makes it into the news no matter what, as it did in 2019. But in analyzing this one event, wouldn't it be helpful to know how many attacks routinely target Christians worldwide? Or the average number of terrorist attacks in Bangladesh? Wouldn't context help us to put events into their proper perspective?

By searching for events that move the security needle, the GSX would sort through the news based on quantitative measurements and facts rather than habit, sentiment, personal judgment, clickability, or TV ratings potential. The common enemy today, whether in the newsroom, the situation room, or your living room, is information overload. The GSX would help, beyond the immediate triage of early warning, to identify and isolate events because of their effects. The news might not be transformed by this qualitative exercise, but I can see a day when a GSX, like the stock market report, will be reported in the news, an authoritative data point on something—the question of are we or are we not more safe—that we can all agree neither gets enough attention nor is it handled methodically.

Finally, the idea of a GSX challenges the venture capitalists and Silicon Valley to engage in national security. For the charities and nonprofits, this isn't completely new. During the Cold War, major foundations spent tens of millions of dollars to build a cadre of civilian experts on the nuclear arms race. These civilian experts were able to offer alternate strategies and push arms control over the arms race. That cadre, of which I myself was part, played a major role in guiding and ending the Cold War. Now, almost two decades after 9/11, the need for another set of civilian experts could not be greater to take on the permanency of perpetual war.

The GSX concept may not be perfect, but as it stands, we make assumptions about the state of our security based on very few actual facts. It must be clear that there is so much we don't and cannot know. But if we were empowered with a system, could we then measure continuing policies against what the alternatives might be? Do we not have need to make such a measurement? That is the GSX challenge. And maybe it's folly to imagine that a mere integer—and a global index— would attract the same attention that the stock market averages or sports scores do. But I can also see how the GSX might captivate the public, particularly in these days when most people think that the news media is biased or they feel overwhelmed by how much information there is.

In 2018, when the Pentagon issued its new *National Defense Strategy* directing a return to "great power competition," decisions like the retirement of the USS *Harry S. Truman* were the natural outcomes. Or were they? In the ways of these strategy statements, the potential losers in a bureaucratic battle between concentrating on big war or the ongoing wars against terrorism fought to hold on to as many resources as they could. But what if, instead of the military's knee-jerk reactions and the bureaucracies' games, the GSX said Russia is weak and getting weaker, and that the long term isn't as important as the short. Or vice versa. What if a true measure showed that the combined power of Europe and the United States over Russia is so ridiculously lopsided that "threat" is purely a fundraising instrument and a psychological weapon? Every special interest and claimant to money and attention loves the Pentagon's shift to Russia and China, but what if our decisions were more than just a feeling on the part of the national security establishment?

When the Trident Juncture exercise was held, Admiral James Foggo III, the exercise's commander, said that his force was "rebuilding muscle memory" reorienting aircraft carrier operations from sitting offshore, bombing ISIS, to fighting in contested waters against a peer adversary. But that's also the muscle memory of fighting big wars in a particular way, in the ways that might have once been imagined but also made obsolete by the developments of long-range strike. Muscle memory imagines that aircraft carriers can move into Russia's waters to "restore" some balance. But maybe such a capability isn't even what is really needed. If the GSX showed that, for all of Russia's meddling and mischief, it is a dying nation, wouldn't we and shouldn't we pursue different policies or approaches? That is the question.

When Secretary Mattis signed the 2018 *National Defense Strategy*, calling for a refocus of the military away from unconventional to conventional war, he communicated to awaiting commands—to the entire bureaucracy and defense industry—that he thought that America's "competitive edge" was eroding in every domain of warfare. But is such a proposition even true? And when we ponder the story of the aborted retirement of the USS *Harry S. Truman,* some battle between military readiness today and supposedly greater readiness fifteen years from today, what are we left with in supporting or opposing such choices except for power politics and a sense of only vaguely understanding the issues? In truth, the national security establishment is charged with making an impossible set of choices. But one thing is clear: except for occasional influence that local politics (or industry or institutional lobbying) might exert, these decisions are made based on internal factors that have more to do with bargaining among competing entities, accommodating schedules and resources, and even running at deficits, than on building greater security.

A global security index would not only help to highlight activities like Trident Juncture but also might serve to clarify whether claims of America losing this or that edge are even valid. One would think that the implication that the United States is getting weaker, if true, would surely have some effect on American politics and the psyche of the country, not just on the tinkering of inside strategists. But, as the former director of national intelligence said, the national security establishment repeats the same thing all the time, almost ensuring that the people stop listening. Who are these people? They are both retired military men who have spent their entire lives inside a system that is increasingly cut off from society. And that brings me to the second proposal I would make for ending perpetual war: that we develop a civilian class of experts who have the historical knowledge and authority as scholars to challenge the ways of the military and the national security establishment, going toe-to-toe with its leaders.

chapter eleven

CIVILIAN CONTROL
OF THE MILITARY

Barack Obama's lack of national security credentials and his absence of military experience didn't seem to be a factor with the voting public in the 2008 election. Like Bill Clinton, who had defeated two World War II veterans in 1992 and 1996, Obama handily beat a war hero, retired Navy captain John McCain, to become president. Still, ongoing terrorist threats to the United States, and the ascendancy of the national security establishment itself, made the new president feel he needed to prove that, despite his lack of personal knowledge of combat, he had national security covered.

Obama chose retired Marine Corps general James L. Jones to be his national security advisor. "Gentleman Jim," as Jones was nicknamed, was in some ways a perfect match for the rookie president: wonky and understated, with a reputation for being respectful to everyone. But Obama hadn't even met Jones until two weeks before he was elected. According to the account by journalist Bob Woodward, Jones "was astounded that the president-elect would give such a position of responsibility and trust to someone he hardly knew."

Then came retired Navy admiral Dennis C. Blair, a former Rhodes Scholar, described by some as one of the smartest men ever to wear the uniform. Obama asked Blair to be his director of national intelligence. Blair had met Obama only once, and he too was "astonished" that the president-elect would select him to lead the entire intelligence community.

For Secretary of Defense, Obama implored Robert Gates, the very epitome of the national security establishment, to stay on from the Bush administration. Gates had been telling everyone who would listen that wartime was no time for a learning curve, opining that the first presidential transition in war since 1968 augured grave threats. But he also wrote that he had only met the young Illinois senator once and, being a Republican, had barely "crossed paths" with most Obama insiders. Consequently he thought himself an odd choice to join the new president's cabinet.

Leon Panetta, whom Obama asked to be CIA director, also didn't know the president. But he was a Washington fixture and an experienced manager, and Obama told him that only a savvy insider like him would be able to "restore" the credibility of an agency that he thought had "badly damaged America's standing in the world" through its post-9/11 pursuits of torture and secret prisons.

With perhaps the exception of Panetta, who had served as Bill Clinton's White House chief of staff, all of the appointments represented defensive moves. Obama reasoned that his quartet of heavy hitters would show America's enemies that there would be no major disruption but also that he could be trusted on national security. Obama told Gates that he wanted "continuity and stability" on national security, particularly so that he could focus on economic recovery from the 2008 market collapse. The president thought that retired general Jones would "give him someone outside the Pentagon to deal with the secretary of defense and the generals on a more or less equal footing." Panetta would "secure the support of . . . agency veterans." And Obama tapped John Brennan, a career CIA operative, to be his counter-terrorism czar, someone who was additionally described as a "heat shield against the agency."

Granted, the economic crisis was paramount—and perpetual war seemed to be running itself—but none of these men ended up being champions for Obama's core promises: the withdrawal from Iraq and Afghanistan, the closing of Guantánamo, greater transparency and openness. Although Obama had a coterie of aides who represented a "dovish" mindset and anchored a vaguely "anti-military" wing against the national security juggernaut, Obama's titans in the end prevailed, dismissing the Obama people as politicos and idealists and decidedly junior varsity, amateurs to be avoided and cut out. The titans complained that the Obama people lacked experience in the real world, that they had never managed anything, and of course, as every bureaucrat complains, that they micromanaged from 1600 Pennsylvania Avenue.

Eight years after 9/11, the national security establishment had become so busy in the *doing* of perpetual war, their main concern was that whatever President Obama might decide, they wanted to make sure that the situation in Iraq, or Afghanistan, or the Middle East, or America, didn't get worse than it already was. The physical demands of perpetual war—the *doing*—didn't leave much room for flexibility, let alone radical alternatives. As I have already said, the national security establishment prioritized the continuation of perpetual war, especially in regard to the Iraq withdrawal. Obama's vision of change seemed an impossible dream.

Maybe there was little more to expect, given who occupied almost all of the national security leadership positions. But there's no question that Obama's selections to staff his national security team undermined his own goals. And when Obama's two retired military officers, Jones and Blair, left—Blair after sixteen months and Jones after less than two years—Obama chose more of the same to replace them. Some of this can be ascribed to the young senator's newness to Washington—that he just didn't know who his ideological allies were in the national security establishment. And once he was in the White House, he became even more isolated, his "people" constantly at war with those who could either implement his personal objectives or stymie them.

Much of the problem Obama faced was also just the nature of Washington. The capital had transformed since the end of the Cold War, where no one left after an administration went out of office. Former officials went on to work for consultancies or populate think tanks and increasingly the information age defense industry that clustered around the Beltway. Retired generals and admirals also cashed in. Even Congress people stayed after being voted out or retiring, taking up lucrative Washington jobs as lobbyists. Washington, D.C., was not only where the action was in national security; the wages were astronomical, the D.C. metropolitan area boasting the highest median household income in the entire country. And although there are significant nuances between the two parties when it comes to nuclear weapons and the balance between security and civil liberties, perpetual war narrowed the policy.

What Barack Obama in fact lacked was a set of civilian national security experts that he could call upon who weren't a part of the Washington mindset. I don't just mean experts as Washington defines them: wonks who know how to work the bureaucratic system and can recite the details of every program. I also mean business leaders or academics, even people from other walks of life—people known for their management skills or their ideas about the world, not merely their Washington credentials. In other words, I mean true outsiders, people of knowledge or stature who had independent views and who were not steeped in the singular Washington perspective.

The reason why President Obama wasn't able to fulfill his agenda and, more importantly, the reason why perpetual war doesn't end is that we have too few choices. Retired generals and admirals may be straight talking and knowledgeable, and even good and evenhanded managers, but their entire careers have been about fighting. And in the current environment they are also creatures of the ways of Washington. The current generation of *civilian* national security experts has similarly spent their careers fighting America's many wars and are successful in and out of government precisely because they hew to the narrow spectrum in the center. Those who espouse another way—whether it be "soft power" or, God forbid, peace—are marginalized and assumed to be not even fit to oversee warriors. Somehow after 9/11, because we never admitted the possibility that there was any other way—not just about whether to go to war in Iraq but fundamentally about how to fight terrorism or even how to understand it— the idea that there could be a set of alternative experts never emerged. There are outliers, but the perpetual-war equivalent of Cold War arms controllers, academics, and scientists who can challenge the conventional military mindset just doesn't exist.

Civilian control of the military is such a sacrosanct and assumed part of the American experience, we seem to have missed a subtle yet perilous shift that happened as we transitioned from Cold War to perpetual war. No great "statesmen" of this era have emerged, but more importantly non-Washington-dipped civilians have largely disappeared

from the most important government advisory and decision-making positions. This subtle takeover by a singular
national security establishment leaves no place for any real
change, let alone for peace. And when we put all aspects of
national security policy and war making into the hands of a
single establishment, there is another consequence. Everything
begins to revolve around the *doing*, around the decisions and
the processes of immediate action, so much so that it drowns
out any fundamental questions like stopping to ask *why* we are
doing things in the first place.

None of what I'm suggesting—a new cadre of civilian experts conversant on military affairs—is possible as long as the
delineation between hard power and soft power is maintained.
There are few independent academic programs that teach
military affairs, and there are very few experts in Washington
think tanks and pressure groups who are focused on conventional war-making, not in the same way that there were abundant nuclear physicists and others in the arms control field
who were truly independent of government influence and
dependence. Obama did get some of his own people, such as
Samantha Power at the UN, but they occupied his personal
political postings and the soft-power jobs, those dealing with
diplomacy and global matters, not the nitty-gritty of perpetual
war. The truth is that after 9/11 no such civilian expert cadre
similar to the arms controllers of yesteryear emerged to deal
with terrorism. Perhaps it was because Al Qaeda was considered so undeniably evil and fighting in Afghanistan initially
seemed a simple in-and-out operation. The idea, let alone the
necessity, to fund a new generation of experts to bring alternate military views into government never took hold. When
muted voices questioned whether terrorism shouldn't be a law
enforcement issue, when they pointed that we were just playing whack-a-mole—when they questioned whether terror

was even an existential threat demanding so much effort and resources—they were shouted down or politely ignored.

The vital need for such a new set of civilian experts was demonstrated in 2002 as war with Iraq neared. Weapons of mass destruction dominated as the main question of why the United States should attack, because WMDs fit with the Cold War skill set of Bush administration senior officials. The saga has its own sad history, but the assumptions about how easy war would be dominated because there were few civilian experts—independent experts—on actual warfare. All of the claims being championed as to why the United States should depose Saddam Hussein—that it would all be a cakewalk, that the United States would be greeted as liberators, that everyone wanted democracy—were challenged mostly by people in uniform, many of whom, such as Army chief of staff General Eric Shinseki, tried to speak up, only to surrender and follow orders or have their careers ruined. There were muted debates about how many troops would be needed, and there were rumblings from Middle East experts that Iraqi society might not be as welcoming or compliant as some were saying. But true experts challenging the military and the government and even the news media to look deeper into all the justifications for war? There were very few. Most were drowned out as left-wing or "alternative."

Finally, to make positive outcomes even more complex, civilian control is no magic bullet. In the modern era, civilian leaders like Robert McNamara and Donald Rumsfeld have been disasters, McNamara playing a major role in escalating U.S. military involvement in Vietnam, Rumsfeld in framing the challenge of terrorism as brutal war in which the enemy had no standing. Civilian control, then, is so important not because civilians will make the right choices but because it is important to maintain the distinction between what is military and what is civilian. In a way, I want the military to be pro-war and uncomfortably ruthless in its belief regarding the use of force. I don't want those in uniform to have to be pro and con, to end up as pseudo-diplomats or Washington operators. Conversely, I envision civilian experts as not just national security parrots out of uniform but true students of the humanities, conversant about the material and spiritual needs of our society. Civilians out of the high-tech world, for example, might have a better understanding of the network and the allure of information. Civilians with a deep understanding of history—even the history of our own nation—might be able to resist the allure of convergence and our era of total warfare. Certainly, after coronavirus, health experts will get more attention and opportunities. Hopefully they will argue that dealing with pandemics is not just another convergence threat to be subsumed under the rubric of "national security."

A clear distinction between military and civilian, moreover, would also inherently produce more decisive and conclusive uses of force when the decision to go to war is chosen. "Just war" doctrine in its broadest articulation should be the only true objective in the wars we pursue. That means that the purpose of war is to restore peaceful relations as rapidly as possible, the law of armed conflict providing abundant and sufficient guidelines for how we should fight so that the use of military force doesn't undermine the prospects of peace. Fighting terrorism doesn't fit into this centuries-old model. What happened after 9/11 is that the national security experts merely bent the rules, arguing that terrorism is different but still insisting on the warfare paradigm. Then they sought to manage conflict, not attacking the enemy to achieve some eventual peace, but putting America on a treadmill that is essentially an effort to kill individual perpetrators who aren't soldiers. Along the way, the establishment gauged public and

Washington opinion, modulating to get away with whatever they could, pursuing false war, unable to bring any conflict to an end. Now, two decades later, we neither seem to have the military appetite to annihilate our enemies nor do we have the humanity and insight to figure out how to restore peace. On national security, Obama never stood a chance.

chapter twelve

AN ALTERNATIVE

At the end of 2018, when President Trump said he was going to withdraw from Syria, Secretary of Defense James Mattis resigned in protest. "We cannot protect our interests," the retired general wrote, "without maintaining strong alliances and showing respect to those allies." Seventy-four nations, he said, had lined up with the United States in what he called the "Defeat-ISIS coalition." Although he never mentioned Syria by name, Mattis admonished the president on this and "other subjects," telling him that he had the right to have a Pentagon chief whose views were better aligned with his.

For two years, Donald Trump had campaigned against the national security "blob" and the "swamp" in Washington, pushing an "America First" agenda and complaining about endless war. On the campaign trail and then in office, he offended the intelligence community and insulted the military brass. In one closed meeting with his war council just six months after becoming commander in chief, he is said to have called the generals and admirals "a bunch of dopes and babies," railing that they were unable to win any wars. "We've spent $7 trillion," the impetuous baby himself is quoted as saying, remarking that "everybody else got the oil."

Donald Trump is easy to dismiss, with his ineptness and his ignorance of the world. But he isn't wrong. The American military hasn't been able to win, as it has misunderstood its adversaries and stumbled in its war making. The intelligence community has also faltered, because it is unable to forecast the future and is even incapable of safeguarding its own secrets. Whether it was predicting 9/11 itself or responding to the gathering cyclone of Russian interference, those with the so-called intelligence have consistently failed. The list of those the national security establishment blames is unending: fickle politicians, an intrusive press, a weak public, the laws of the United States, even the evils of the world. Somehow the national security establishment has evaded public accountability while growing ever larger and collecting more funds. It's not an exaggeration to say that this kingdom has orchestrated a multi-administration program of failure, acquiring as many enemies and battlefields as it has partners in arms.

What the national security establishment excels at is continuing, portraying whatever it is that it wants as judicious and necessary while attacking anything that challenges it as dangerous and naïve. Thus "America First"—the desire to tend to American interests—is dismissed as selfish or isolationist, too blunt and too ideological for our globalized world. And yet the singular pursuit of stopping another 9/11 is "America First" in its essence. "America First" has been used to justify kidnapping and secret surveillance and protection against weapons of mass destruction—even the summary execution of American citizens by drones. When the national security establishment finds it convenient, "America First" justifies unilateral operations that disregard our allies. When it comes to the armed forces, "America First" is the doctrine that they can never operate under foreign command. And now "America First" is the close to $1 trillion we've spent on homeland security.

Donald Trump isn't wrong to question America's endless war, not the general trend nor the specific fights in Afghanistan or Syria. Slogans like "our interests" are vague and indeterminate, hiding ever expanding missions beyond terrorism. The term "ally" is equally maddeningly hollow, encompassing every country from Great Britain to Kyrgyzstan, from Israel to Saudi Arabia. And Donald Trump isn't and was never wrong on the specifics when it came to Syria. If his desire to bring American troops home was based on anything, it came from listening to what the national security establishment itself advertised. The yearlong battle to liberate Mosul from ISIS was concluded as his administration was getting underway. Or so the Pentagon said. Then ISIS was reportedly pushed out of western Iraq. Then the ISIS capital of Raqqa in Syria was reportedly taken. Every month, military maps showed ISIS territory shrinking to isolated pockets. ISIS leaders and fighters were reportedly being killed and captured by the thousands. By the end of Donald Trump's first year in office, Secretary Mattis himself was saying that the organization was broken and "on the run."

The president was oblivious to process and diplomacy, and did not seem to care about consequences, but it was the national security establishment that blithely ignored the contradictions between declared success and an end to the fighting. Then came the new set of imperatives, an endless list of conditions that needed to be achieved before the United States could ever leave Syria. Not only did ISIS have to be eradicated, they said, but civilians had to be protected and the United States had to defend the Kurds. Then they added that fighting couldn't end as long as Syrian leader Bashar al-Assad was still in power, or as long as Damascus had chemical weapons, or as long as Russia and Iran were present in the country. Then national security advisor John Bolton went as far as to say that the United States wasn't going to leave Syria "as long as Iranian troops are outside Iranian borders."

Variants of all of these same requirements are applied to the fighting in other countries as well. The establishment's claim, and the picture most in the public have, is that perpetual war is stopping the next 9/11—that if we stop fighting, Al Qaeda or some other terrorist organization will coalesce and successfully perpetrate a new mega plot. It's an effective argument, as no one wants to be the person responsible for such an outcome. But it is another huge contradiction. Even though we've been promised that fighting "over there" means that we won't have to fight at home, the Pentagon itself says that "the homeland" is no longer a sanctuary. This isn't some post 9/11 philosophical lament, nor is it an ass-covering pretext just in case there's a future attack and they can say they predicted it. It's a policy statement, contained in the *National Defense Strategy* authored by Secretary Mattis. The professional military, not Donald Trump, says that during *any* future conflict "attacks against our critical defense, government, and economic infrastructure must be anticipated," surely one of the most damning condemnations of the entire enterprise.

Unable to end any of America's wars and unable to provide domestic guarantees of safety, the establishment falls back on the argument that we are building foreign capacity to fight terrorism so that at least our wars will eventually end. With our money and trained by our forces, we are told that local governments will eventually be able to defeat terrorists and ensure that ungoverned spaces don't reemerge. That's the multitrillion-dollar plan. But after two decades, not one of the governments we supply holds firm control over its own territory, not even where we've declared an end to combat. In

Afghanistan, the Taliban control large swaths of the country, and so much of the territory is a sanctuary that opium poppy cultivation is at its highest level *ever*. In Iraq, borders are porous and ISIS and other extremist groups, Iranian-linked militias—even the Kurds—control their own domains. The same can be said about Yemen, Somalia, Libya, Niger, Mali, Nigeria, and on and on.

America keeps fighting and the national security establishment continues to fight any decisive withdrawal anywhere while at the same time it tacitly accepts that the reason for the fight is no longer what was originally intended. Nowhere is this shift clearer than in Afghanistan, America's longest war *ever*, where the military persists even while the United States negotiates "peace" with the Taliban. It's an inconclusive (and wholly "America First") solution that not very long ago would have seemed inconceivable: peace with a group that we also label as terrorists, withdrawal without the eradication of Al Qaeda. Still, exhaustion with Afghanistan has been long coming. Mattis himself said as secretary of defense that the role of the military was merely "to keep the peace, to keep the peace for one more year, one more month, one more week, [and] one more day." Military forces, he said, were just holding the line to provide diplomats a position of strength from which to negotiate. In other words, the armed forces were not seeking to eradicate terrorism—not anymore.

In Afghanistan, the military is reconciled to withdrawal, accepting the fact that the United States can only achieve so much on the ground. And yet in Syria they insist that we fight on. However, the terrorist threats are practically synonymous, the reverberating impact of stopping equally ominous. I'd argue that the reason the American military seems willing to accept accommodation in Afghanistan but not in Syria is no more profound than the fact that there is exhaustion in one country and new energy in another. The military command responsible for Syria, and the patchwork alliance that operates there, exudes hope merely because it is new. And so it chases the ball around the field, doing so to merely hold the line, neither applying the resources needed—by its own standards—to "defeat ISIS" nor willing to stop.

How much goes into the fight, which country gets the resources and the attention, is decided today based on how skillful and assertive commanders and diplomats are, even by powerful lobbies. The migration of perpetual war to so many countries in Africa, in reality, is as much fueled by the creation of an African Command and the consequent need for it to do something as it is by any analysis of either sheer threat or American interest. These institutional players—in what I earlier called the bargaining process—all work in isolation from each other, and all compete. Rarely is perpetual war seen in a broader or more holistic context. And yet, the greatest effects of perpetual war extend well beyond the countries or regions where military actions are performed. Not in killing terrorists but in manufacturing them. Here, I'm talking about the hidden infrastructure of war making.

Consider this: between August 2014, when the fight against ISIS began, and the end of October 2019, when ISIS was declared to have lost the last remnants of its "physical" caliphate, almost 35,000 American air strikes were conducted, with airplanes and drones dropping more than 60,000 munitions. Ignore for a moment the military impact and the destruction involved. These bombers, fighter planes, and drones all demand weapons and fuel and operate from bases near and far—in Kuwait and the Gulf States, in Jordan and Turkey, in Djibouti and Bulgaria. Thousands of people sustain these aircraft and supply the intelligence information to them. The war support infrastructure is made up of additional thousands who need to eat and drink and be protected. We may exclusively focus on a couple of thousand troops on the ground in places like Syria, but for those people who live in the Middle East, for the citizens of those countries, it's the perpetual war infrastructure that they see. So while we find some comfort in our seemingly small footprint, it is the giant machine that others see. The visible actions of the war on ISIS belie an enormous amount of hidden infrastructural activity that is its own stimulus, exuding negative effects not just where it operates but throughout the region. It is bluntly an American occupation, one that spawned Al Qaeda in the first place and one that today triggers young men and women to take up arms against us.

Little is reported on this hidden infrastructure, and even less is explained or contemplated about what impact it has. But we shouldn't just blame our inattention. When Donald Trump started to question the U.S. war effort, the Pentagon decided that it would no longer report how many troops were physically located in individual Middle Eastern countries. Then it decided that it would make the details of air strikes an official secret as well. In Afghanistan, while the Pentagon negotiated "peace" and withdrawal, it also made certain that secret American intelligence collection and high-value targeting by special operations forces would continue.

It is an inscrutable state, this combination of clandestine force plus airpower and information gathering. Part of the problem is in that we lack the right vocabulary to even describe what is going on. Much of the heroic narrative so common throughout our history of warfare just doesn't easily apply to this world. What we mostly get are industrial statistics: this number of aircraft sorties flown, that number of bombs dropped, these many hours accumulated, the bookkeeping of a war factory operating so many days without an accident. Then, when we do hear news, it is because some machine doesn't work as advertised, resulting in a crash or accidental civilian deaths. Not only does this convey the wrong impression, to ourselves and our adversaries, but the need for "success"—that is, the continuation of the enterprise without bad news—subtly influences how the Pentagon fights.

I submit that few possess an understanding of this big picture, and those who do see it prefer to take measures to protect soldiers and operators on the ground, to take precautions to minimize external interference—even to leverage fewer resources with ever greater efficiency rather than to openly push for more. This streamlined machine employs more and more artificial intelligence techniques that are able to prioritize which target is most important and which is closest to the top, thus tilting toward leadership attack. I know it seems jarring that we expend such resources and wrap up what we are doing in such grand and grave terms, but in the end we are not protecting civilians, not seeking regime change, not even relentlessly going after terrorists. And yet, we are also doing all of those things, just less wholeheartedly than is necessary to be successful while applying different rules for different countries.

Terrorist and extremist groups growing and dispersing. Instability and weak governments are everywhere. Russian and Iranian meddling. China rising. The laundry list of consequences and dangers subtly creates the distinct impression not just that we're not winning and can't stop fighting but also that we have to do more. The news media feeds this narrative, communicating a subtle message of constant menace, one that supports the argument that nothing can change or even more needs to be done. So then two final questions emerge: Can we do less? And how do we get there?

Doing less is key. The true measure of American military supremacy is the global capacity of the wider warfare network that has been built, one that neither Russia nor China comes anywhere close to possessing. The network is invisible strength, a fabric of military capacity derived from common outlook, doctrine, and training, one that is also a physical chain of connecting lines and nodes. The American military isn't flawless, nor has it won its many wars, but it is more experienced and has built a more powerful and unrivaled network, one that is not inferior or falling behind. What is more, over the past twenty years, even if terrorism hasn't been eliminated and nations haven't been rebuilt, the actual security measures taken to protect the United States have equally improved. If we stop fighting in the Middle East and Africa and bring our forces home, we will not revert to what existed before September 2001. A homeland security apparatus has been created and there are modernized and expanded law enforcement and intelligence capacities. Foreign forces have been trained. Everyone is focused on terrorism.

All of the disasters that the national security establishment argues will come with change—that there will be another 9/11, that Afghanistan will fall again under hostile rule, that Iraq will join Iran's camp, that ISIS will flourish, and radical Islam will spread into Africa—are actually the products of perpetual war, of continuing to fight for fighting's sake. Terrorists have already struck in America and will likely do so again. Another 9/11 hasn't occurred, but that's not to say that another one couldn't. What we *can* say is that the actual risks to America of continuing to wage perpetual war are greater than those involved in stopping and focusing inward. We should stop fighting not just because *where* we are fighting and *how* we are fighting is ineffective but also because we are making things worse. We should bring our forces home and eliminate as many overseas bases as we can. We should rebalance our counter-terrorism efforts away from the military and back to law enforcement. We should stress even stricter controls on foreign travelers and on movements. We should withdraw our military support for corrupt and authoritarian governments, forcing nations to repair their own domestic injustices and tend to their own security.

It's a bitter pill to admit that we will never win, and there will undoubtedly be great suffering when we stop fighting and withdraw. But we deceive ourselves if we really think we are alleviating suffering today. We aren't. And if ever there were a strategy behind perpetual war—to eliminate Al Qaeda or to bring governance and the rule of law to ungoverned places where terrorism gestated—today it is a distant and failed goal. Whatever happens in Syria, under Trump or his successor, ISIS isn't being defeated worldwide. Whatever we do in Afghanistan, we are not eliminating Al Qaeda. Whatever we do against the Houthis in Yemen or Al Shabaab in Somalia or so many other extremist groups in other places in the world, the trends are that such groups are transforming into conventional armies and territorial dwellers. If we are to defeat them, we need a different approach.

In early 2020, just before coronavirus hit, the Trump administration decided to kill General Qassim Soleimani, the commander of Iran's Revolutionary Guards. With that, it looked like the two countries were headed toward war. Critics argued that the crisis was one solely of Donald Trump's making, lamenting that the White House's unilateral decision meant that America was moving forward without its allies. Others claimed that Iran would speed up its efforts to build a nuclear weapon. Although I doubt that anyone in the U.S. military wants war, I started hearing from people in the Pentagon that there was something about Donald Trump, about his willingness to choose the most audacious option, about his recklessness, that worried them.

There was something about what I was hearing that

reminded me that I'd heard it before: the same fretting when Barack Obama became president—that there was something about his dreaminess and his pledges that were reckless and worrisome. As I hope I've demonstrated, the national security establishment ultimately sabotaged virtually everything the young president wanted to do—and a decade later we're still in Iraq and Afghanistan, Guantánamo hums along, and nuclear disarmament is so far in the rearview mirror as to be nonexistent. Donald Trump may have made things worse by killing Soleimani, but it wasn't his idea; it was presented by the system. Iran's infiltration into Syria and Yemen, its buildup of ballistic missiles, its increased meddling in the region, its cyberattacks—they all happened under Obama and they all set in motion not just an eventual clash but the automated processes of leadership targeting, that very spearhead of perpetual war. That system is so powerful, I can't help but think that in a different administration and under the same circumstances another president wouldn't have done the same thing. Nor can I help thinking how much less criticism there would have been if the paperwork had been immaculate and there had been better consultation.

North Korea is similar. As a result of the failed policies of four administrations, Pyongyang developed nuclear weapons and long-range missiles. When Donald Trump woke up and decided that "fire and fury" and "rocket man" insults weren't working, then announced that he was ready to negotiate complete denuclearization face-to-face, critics argued not only that it wouldn't work but that it wasn't even worth trying. The experts called for excruciatingly prepared talks to reach a technical arms control agreement, the same old playbook of lessened sanctions in exchange for incremental progress. No doubt that is a more judicious approach, but it is visionless in terms of bringing conflict to an end. If Donald Trump were more competent, if we focused more on outcomes and less on processes, I could see a package of concessions—ending war games, withdrawing U.S. troops, lifting sanctions in exchange for verified progress toward disarmament—that could be offered to North Korea in exchange for a lasting peace. But I doubt that the system can conceive of or consent to such a radical move.

I realize I've seen this before too: how the national security establishment reacted to Ronald Reagan when he said he wanted to get rid of nuclear weapons, and how they worried that the fact-free Reagan would end up giving up the store. And give up Reagan did: his Star Wars scheme, the MX missile, long-range nuclear weapons in Europe—all concessions that ultimately helped to halt the nuclear arms race and defeat the Soviet Union. We might argue about what influenced Russia to later become so belligerent, but I'd say that perpetual war and the national security establishment helped turn sparring systems into open conflict. NATO had an almost institutional need to justify its existence with the end of the Cold War, expanding into the former Soviet states and "defending" Europe—necessary, perhaps, but I'd say a bureaucratic and self-interested course. That's the problem with a worldwide machine running itself: the objectives are always seemingly reasonable, the other side always portrayed as the problem and the aggressor. I'm not making an excuse for Russia. I'm just arguing that we should be more honest about what our own systems do.

There is nothing isolationist in what I'm proposing, and I'm not suggesting a general withdrawal from the world or that we should turn our back on our friends. The pursuit of real American security and vitality—as a center of something more than just national security and then as an enlightened leader—will surely serve to create a sounder and more sustainable global ecology. And finally it's time to close the 9/11 chapter of our history. This means not just to stop warring but also to stop letting a couple of hundred thousand terrorists have so much influence. We need to step back and rethink what our interests are and then, through our leadership, exert new pressures and influences to enhance our security and then enhance global security.

In ending perpetual war, I'd argue that "America First" should be turned on its head: that in a globalized world what's best for the world's sole superpower is indeed what's best for the world. This doesn't mean cutting off the country from the rest or recklessly imposing our will. Nor does it mean grabbing all the world's resources—as if oil were even relevant or important anymore in ensuring our happy future. Once we stop the perpetual-war machine, I believe we should focus inward and spend our energies improving the state of civic life, strengthening our systems of balanced governance, building up our public health apparatus, making America a more diverse and law-abiding beacon for the rest of the world, and spending more money and applying more brainpower to resolve our own problems.

EPILOGUE: CORONAVIRUS

On February 1, 2020, the United States declared a public health emergency due to the spreading coronavirus. Defense Secretary Mark Esper signed the first "execute order" of the Covid-19 era, a five-hundred-page, six-stage pandemic war plan to "protect the force and its health, while preserving readiness to conduct our many missions." Esper's order was first to shape—i.e., prepare—then prevent, then contain, then interdict, then stabilize, then recover.

As the virus raged across Asia and into Europe, and as the first cases were reported in California, Washington State, and then New York—and the first case in the U.S. military was reported in South Korea—the Defense Department canceled exercises with Seoul and other countries, cut back on movements, and tightened up security and access to its domestic bases. Covid-19 crisis management teams were set up, and an apparatus started to be assembled to provide military support to civil authorities.

On March 9, as confirmed U.S. cases passed the 500 mark, the military's top doctor, Air Force brigadier general Paul Friedrichs, reassured the public in the Pentagon's first Covid-19 press conference that the military had been doing pandemic planning for more than twenty years and knew what to do.

Halfway around the world, the U.S. military continued its global reach. The USS *Theodore Roosevelt* departed the port of Da Nang, only the second visit by an aircraft carrier to Vietnam in forty years. For four days, hundreds of sailors had gone ashore for volunteer projects and cultural exchanges in a country already reporting coronavirus cases. They visited an orphanage and a vocational school for Agent Orange victims, painted a mural of friendship, and attended a dance at Dong A University.

Elsewhere, U.S. Navy ships were visiting Thailand, Singapore, and Japan, and B-2 bombers forward deployed to the Portuguese Azores on the way to Europe for anti-Russia probes. Cold Response 20, an amphibious-assault war game, opened in Norway. Valiant Liberty, an air and special operations deployment, finished in Great Britain. Bersama Warrior, a joint U.S.-Malaysian military exchange, got underway. The destroyer USS *McCampbell* conducted a routine "freedom-of-navigation" patrol into disputed waters near the Paracel Islands in the South China Sea.

Without mentioning the coronavirus, Kenneth Rapuano, assistant secretary of defense for homeland defense and global security, told the House Armed Services Committee that the United States continued to be "a target in a complex global security environment." That included Russian and Chinese nuclear, cyber, and space forces as well as an ongoing and aggressive psychological warfare campaign the two countries were waging against the American people. "We continue to improve our ability to defend the U.S. homeland in all domains and develop capabilities to defend the nation's interests globally," he said.

"We've got fighters, bombers, maintainers deployed working to keep America safe," Air Force chief of staff General David L. Goldfein would say at the Pentagon on March 18.

"We're still flying global mobility missions and conducting global space operations." Conducting the mission, keeping the armed forces ready for warfare, he said, was "priority one."

On March 15, two days after President Trump declared a national emergency, the CDC advised Americans not to gather in groups larger than fifty people. Behind the scenes, the national security establishment and the military were taking unprecedented measures to prepare for the possibility of Washington being crippled and for there to be a complete breakdown of civil rule throughout America. "Continuity-of-government" plans were dusted off just in case. A special military task force was activated to take over in Washington. Military forces throughout the country were prepared for stage one of "civil disturbance operations," domestic war plans that were indeed implemented after the killing of George Floyd.

On the same day that the White House was acknowledging a national emergency at home, the USS *Roosevelt* began its own three-day "show of force" in the South China Sea. The aircraft carrier was accompanied by three U.S. destroyers, including the USS *McCampbell*, plus amphibious ships of the USS *America* expeditionary strike group, which were packed with marines.

But behind this business-as-usual front, back in the United States, cases spread onto military bases, and National Guard formations were activated. The Pentagon announced that two hospital ships, the USNS *Comfort* and the USNS *Mercy*, would be sent to New York and Los Angeles. In Colorado, the underground early-warning bunker in Cheyenne Mountain shifted to Phase 3—"Respond"—of the pandemic war plan, sequestering a shadow staff that mirrored the one working aboveground.

For the first time in decades, the blast doors of the mountain were closed and the staff was "buttoned up" in nuclear-hardened isolation and placed on alert to scan the planet for incoming missiles or bombers. In the basement of Strategic Command headquarters in Omaha, the nuclear command center created separate "blue" and "silver" teams that would never interact, separating decision-making cells for extended 24/7 operations. Command-equipped aircraft were dispersed to alternate bases. Even a secret ground unit in Wyoming, with a half dozen eighteen-wheel armored trucks filled with all of the gear needed to act as a "survivable mobile command center," was placed on alert. At individual missile and bomber bases, alert duties were extended and staggered. New crews didn't come on alert until they had been quarantined for fourteen days.

On March 22, the day Covid-19 cases surpassed 1 million globally and more than 33,000 in the United States, the *Roosevelt*, still on its Pacific cruise, publicly reported its first coronavirus case, eleven days after it had left Vietnam. Several other U.S. ships, all of them in the Pacific region, were also reporting cases. Although major exercises were now being routinely canceled and a worldwide "stop movement" was instituted for nonessential travel, the Pentagon leadership continued to insist that it had things under control. "This is not the first war we've ever been in," chairman of the Joint Chiefs General Mark Milley said at the Pentagon, again stressing that the military could maintain mission readiness while also looking after the health of soldiers, sailors, marines, and airmen.

Two days later, three more sailors on the *Roosevelt* tested positive. Admiral Michael Gilday, the chief of naval operations, said he didn't necessarily tie the cases to the Da Nang port call. "We've identified all the folks they've had contact with, and we're quarantining them," acting Secretary of the Navy Thomas B. Modly said. Gilday said the force would remain on watch, continuing to execute "the national defense strategy"—the shift to great power competition against Russia and China—"even with active COVID-19 cases." The next day, five more *Roosevelt* sailors were diagnosed and airlifted off the ship. The Navy said it would no longer give out specifics on individual units or locations, not wanting to give information on American military readiness to its enemies. And the next day, adhering to its secrecy policy, all the Navy would say was that "17 sailors assigned to a ship underway in the Pacific" had tested positive.

"No Sailors have been hospitalized or are seriously ill," Admiral Gilday wrote in an open letter to the force as rumors started to swirl that coronavirus had arrived. He concluded the letter by saying, "We are confident that our aggressive response will keep USS *Theodore Roosevelt* able to respond to any crisis in the region."

But the reality was very different. The aircraft carrier pulled into Guam on March 27 and sailors that were showing symptoms started to be moved ashore. On March 30 the ship's commanding officer, Captain Brett E. Crozier, frustrated with the Navy's dogged insistence that he maintain ship wartime readiness despite almost one hundred crew members already diagnosed with Covid-19, wrote a confidential memo to his superiors pleading that the aircraft carrier be relieved of its combat duties, saying that the close quarters aboard the ship were endangering people's lives.

On March 31, the plight of the *Roosevelt* became public when the *San Francisco Chronicle* published Captain Crozier's memo. A native of Santa Rosa, California, Crozier had argued in his memo to Pacific Fleet and Navy leadership that evacuating his 4,800-strong crew was obviously a tough "political solution" but was also "the right thing to do."

"We are not at war," he wrote in his now-famous memo. "Sailors do not need to die. If we do not act now, we are failing

to properly take care of our most trusted asset—our Sailors."
Three days later he was relieved of his command, having committed the cardinal sin of causing public embarrassment. The
media furor that followed—including the widespread distribu-
tion of a purloined video taken by a sailor showing hundreds of
crew members cheering Crozier as he left the ship—reached
the White House, and Navy Secretary Modly rushed to Guam
to settle the crew. When an audio recording of his insincere
and expletive-laced address was also leaked, it only made matters worse. Less than seventy-two hours after Crozier's departure, Secretary Modly resigned in disgrace, his handling of the
entire affair now a national embarrassment.

By this time, the New York State death toll from coronavirus
topped 3,500, more than the number of people killed on 9/11.
And less than a week later, across the United States, the number of deaths surpassed 20,000—more than the number killed
on 9/11 *plus* all of the American soldiers and marines killed
in two decades of perpetual war. The deaths mounted rapidly:
40,000 by April 19; 60,000 ten days later; exceeding 200,000
before the end of September. It was clear that the world would
never go back to what it had been. Michael Chertoff, one of
the architects of the post-9/11 world and a Bush administration secretary of homeland security, said coronavirus exceeded
September 11 "in terms of its profound effect on our society."
John Negroponte, the first director of national intelligence—a
position created because of those terrorist attacks—said coronavirus "marks the final nail in the coffin of the post-9/11 era."

It was also clear—regardless of how policy makers had divided the country and how much Donald Trump had failed to
lead—that no one had quite anticipated the gravity of coronavirus, how virulent it would be, how quickly and extensively
it would spread, and how it would spare no one, not even
the young and healthy. "Having an enemy that you don't fully

understand is always a little bit frustrating," said U.S. Northern Command's General Terrence J. O'Shaughnessy. Yes, the Pentagon had a plan for combating a pandemic, he told *60 Minutes*, but, like so many other well-thought-out war plans, his pandemic response "did not survive contact with the enemy."

Enemy. War. This characterization of the coronavirus and the challenge of pandemics is not just the bluster of generals in uniform. "The crisis we face from coronavirus is on the scale of a major war, and we must act accordingly," Senator Bernie Sanders said in describing the coronavirus in its early stage. "We need to . . . call out the military—now," urged then presidential candidate Joe Biden, criticizing the administration for acting too slowly. Donald Trump wouldn't disagree; he started to label himself a "wartime president" in mid-March. "Every generation of Americans has been called to make shared sacrifices for the good of the nation," he told reporters.

In a crisis, political and military leaders are tempted to invoke a "state of war." It conjures up images of bold leadership and top-down commands and society all pulling together against a common enemy. And in this case, with patriotic flyovers by the Blue Angels and the Air Force Thunderbirds, and then dozens of other fighters and bombers taking to the skies to salute America, it seemed that the armed forces were everywhere. But with this coronavirus pandemic, the analogy is wrong and dangerous. It is not only that the core function of national defense is and should be strictly military—that is, against military threats to the United States—but what is shown in the military's response, as laudable as it might have been once the *Theodore Roosevelt* served as a wake-up call, is an institution that indeed has a priority mission that conflicts with public health. And it is an institution that has practices, particularly secrecy, that makes it inherently unsuitable for domestic duties because it so undermines public confidence.

The real heroes of the coronavirus pandemic are not the men and women in uniform; they are the doctors and nurses who stayed at their posts. And although it may look as if the military was a standout institution in mobilizing the National Guard and the Army Corps of Engineers, in sending two hospital ships, in transporting matériel to assist communities in trouble, the military response to coronavirus, despite all of the attention lavished on those in uniform, was tiny.

At the end of April, *three months* after Secretary Esper's initial order to implement the pandemic war plan, the Pentagon tallied a total of 62,300 people supporting coronavirus relief, an impressive-enough-sounding number except when you look at the fine print. Three-quarters were National Guardsmen and women mobilized by the states and another 5,000 were reservists, most of them civilians who volunteered for active duty. The truth was that out of a pool of almost 1.3 million active duty soldiers, sailors, airmen, and marines, only about 12,000—less than 1 percent—were actually supporting the national effort.

Even in the case of the National Guard, by the end of April, barely 10 percent of the 450,000 strong organization was mobilized. More Guardsmen and women were mobilized for the 9/11 response in 2001; more were mobilized for Hurricane Katrina in 2005. The medical, transportation, and engineering ranks of the Guard were fully engaged, as were the many thousands who had been trained post-9/11 for weapons-of-mass-destruction response, their biohazard skills now applied to coronavirus isolation and testing. But the Guard is also mostly made up of combat units, forces that are expected to be synonymous and interchangeable with those on active duty, and most of them have few skills that are directly applicable.

That limitation of the military in a public health crisis is further seen in the story of the hospital ships sent to New York and Los Angeles. The white-painted, 1,000-bed USNS *Comfort*, emblazed with gigantic red crosses, deployed with much fanfare to New York on March 31. But the mission of the military hospital ship, with twelve operating rooms, is built around trauma care. It was never meant to treat patients with a highly contagious virus. It was sent to New York to provide comfort, and the additional hospital capacity was meant to alleviate local facilities overwhelmed by coronavirus patients. That was the plan. But five days after its arrival in New York, the *Comfort* received a change of orders. It would be reconfigured to receive coronavirus patients after all. That entailed moving 80 percent of the ship's Navy staff to New York hotels to protect their health. And that demanded changes on board the ship to prevent the spread of infection. While the changes were instituted, the *Comfort* shifted the bulk of its medical staff to work at the Javits Center, where a makeshift hospital had been built. On April 29 the Navy announced that the *Comfort* would depart New York, mission accomplished. In twenty-eight days of operations, the ship treated a total of 161 patients.

None of this is to impugn those who did come out and performed well, nor do I mean to dismiss the thousands in uniform—including more than 1,100 aboard the USS *Roosevelt* itself—who eventually contracted the virus. But what the numbers actually suggest is that the military, despite a gung ho willingness, isn't the right institution to look to in the event of a pandemic. Partly it is just the reality that the vast majority of those in uniform are young men and women with guns. Yes, the military reached deep into its ranks to offer up some 5,000 doctors and nurses to civil society. In the fields of medical care, transportation, and engineering, the existing skill sets of those in uniform were even relevant. But, overall, *any* organized federal reserve force—say, for instance, a bolstered U.S. Public Health Service—could have done the job better and quicker. And that is what is truly needed in America if we are to reconfigure for a post-coronavirus era: a robust civilian reserve focused on public health, one that might be able to call upon the military if it needed to, but one that at its core is singularly focused and organized for civil response.

This is not to say that some parts of the military, particularly the National Guard, couldn't be reorganized to focus more on civil needs. The so-called total force organization of the Guard today is a far cry from its origin as a militia in the hands of state governors "to execute the Laws of the Union, suppress Insurrections and repel Invasions," as spelled out in Article I of the Constitution. But since 1933—in the modern military era—Guardsmen and women have been required to take dual enlistments and commissions into the federal armed forces, conforming with the warfare needs of the nation overall; therefore, we must go back to a stricter Constitution role, and reapplying "repel Invasions" to mean repelling viruses as well. Such a reorientation would mean staffing the Guard with civil response capabilities rather than military ones, getting rid of armored brigade combat teams and fighter interceptor aircraft in favor of first responders, and instilling a civilian mindset of disaster response.

Organizational changes in the armed forces such as these now seem ever more likely as a consensus is jelling across the political spectrum that, post-coronavirus, American policy priorities need to change. Before the coronavirus, many of the same people who are arguing that Covid-19 has transformed everything were arguing that climate change was the existential threat that should reorient America. Both might be right. It is more important to point out that this kind of apocalyptic vision is almost needed to bring about changes in the power of the military and the national security juggernaut. More observers will undoubtedly now argue that perpetual war took

America's eye off the ball in terms of more important threats, but—in anticipation of the funding battle that is to come between guns versus ventilators—no one seems to dare argue that the military can do with less. The true story behind the USS *Theodore Roosevelt* and the military's response should make it clear not only that the military is the wrong institution to look to for public health and civil response but also how, even in pursuit of its many missions, it has too much discretionary capability and excess capacity.

The coronavirus did force the military to make one especially important decision, one that no president has managed to do in the twenty years since 9/11, which should be instructive in thinking about a post-pandemic future. As the nuclear force stayed on alert and as "essential" combat missions continued through the spring of 2020, the coronavirus forced the Pentagon to determine what was really essential. As testing for the virus became more readily available at the end of April, the Pentagon established a four-tiered hierarchy. Secretary Esper designated nuclear forces, the apparatus of early warning and decision-making, the disaster response force itself, and certain nationally committed special operations as the first tier to receive testing. The enormous force posted overseas—in Europe, the Middle East, and even on the Korean Peninsula—was formally designated Tier 2, or less essential. Tier 3 was those conventional ground, air, and naval forces slated for movement and war plans once coronavirus restrictions were lifted. And Tier 4 was everybody else.

Specific hints of excess capacity were also offered by Defense Secretary Esper when he reassured the public about the impact of the sidelining of the USS *Theodore Roosevelt*, saying, "We have more than two carriers in the inventory." And indeed those other aircraft carriers were readied for the next cycle of overseas deployments, with crews quarantined and schedules intentionally delayed, the sizes of battle groups reduced, port calls restricted, and missions limited—a presence in the world, to be sure, but a lesser one, a less aggressive one. Even with the stop movement, the military continued to hold the fort in the Middle East and Africa. And despite canceled training and exercises, slowed operations, and hundreds of thousands sent home just like the rest of America to wait it out, so much continued to get done with far fewer resources and at a slower pace.

True, America's "enemies" were equally weakened by Covid-19. But reducing the physical presence and slowing the machine revealed how resilient the global network was. To be sure, an important political message was also conveyed. In Afghanistan, the Taliban was put on notice that they shouldn't delay peace negotiations in the false hope that the coronavirus would create an artificial withdrawal. And so, when the Army announced that seven brigades would be ready to deploy as soon as the stop movement was lifted, two were earmarked to deploy to Afghanistan.

In the Persian Gulf region, similar messages were conveyed to Iran, itself one of the countries hardest hit by the virus. In late-March, two aircraft carriers operated together in an anti-Iran patrol. Iran was put on notice that one of the seven brigades was designated to take up the Spartan Shield banner and deploy to Kuwait, a mission that now openly embraced an anti-Iran focus, even the defense of Saudi Arabia.

In North Korea, there was speculation that Kim Jung-un was sick or even dead. South Korea is generally thought to have mounted an effective response, and though U.S. forces were initially hit hard there, the message conveyed was that the allies were ready for anything. In the most volatile place on the planet, the commander of U.S. forces assured the North that readiness hadn't declined. He had already made changes to sustain preparedness of his force months before the coronavirus, adjusting to White House orders to cancel major exercises, part of Trump's overtures to the North, those directives having no impact on his ability to wage war.

In the China theater, "freedom-of-navigation" ship forays continued through May. Strategic bombers were sent forward to Europe and the Pacific to signal readiness to Moscow.

At the beginning of April, amidst all of this sensible prioritizing, the Pentagon surprisingly announced that it was *doubling* the counter-narcotics missions in Latin America. It was one of those showcase missions undertaken largely in response to a White House order. Despite big talk that the cartels wouldn't be allowed to take advantage of the coronavirus to increase the flow of drugs, the effect on the supply of illicit drugs inside the country was as meaningless as ever. For the Navy, "doubling" actually meant four instead of two ships. And it proved to be another disaster. More than 80 members of the 380-person crew of the USS *Kidd*—assigned to the "surge" campaign—came down with the virus, and the warship was sent retreating back to its homeport, quietly signaling, as in pandemic response, that the opioid crisis and drug problem wasn't a military one.

America has a magnificent military. When the history of coronavirus is written, they will be shown to have been a ray of hope for a country yearning for any hero. Any talk of slow response has to be tempered by everyone's surprise, disbelief, and underestimation of the crisis. As we begin to process what happened and set new priorities, hopefully we will be honest enough to remember that major media outlets ran *plenty* of their own stories in the beginning of 2020 questioning the severity of the coronavirus. Donald Trump will of course be a magnet for blame in the political arena. But, in the long term, what was missing wasn't just a more rapid federal response;

it was a credible and well-financed government entity with the capability—intelligence and early warning, excess capacity to respond to civilian needs, ability to take command when needed—to compensate in the face of nonmilitary threats.

In talking about the impact of Covid-19 and the future for the armed forces, Vice Chairman of the Joint Chiefs of Staff General John Hyten said that "2019 normal will never exist again." The military, he said, will "have to figure out how to operate and fight through a world where coronavirus exists." As the military adjusts, we have a new opportunity. The trauma of 9/11 in fact has been eclipsed. Now comes the hard work of dismantling the machinery to rebalance the nation more toward a civilian world and away from perpetual war.

ACKNOWLEDGMENTS

Jonathan Karp first contacted me after he read my letter to NBC colleagues, asking me to expand on my thoughts about perpetual war. I thank him for his faith and support. Priscilla Painton proved to be a tough and diligent editor. Hana Park served as valuable back up. Thanks too to the Simon & Schuster marketing and production folks for shepherding this book through difficult times. Thanks to Erin Cauchi for all her hard work and Peter Pringle for his close reading of many drafts of the manuscript.

I rarely mention my sources in my writing, and they prefer it that way, but I could not continue to understand what's going on in this world without their help, particularly "Source 1," a friend and guide now for well over thirty years. I have found inspiration (and ideas to steal) in the writings of Andy Bacevich and Michael Klare and, yes, even in the writings of conservatives, particularly my old pal Eliot Cohen. I have depended on the "citizen journalism" of electrospaces.net, bellingcat, airwars.com, and The Bureau of Investigative Journalism amongst others to keep a watch on the details. These exemplary organizations don't always get it right, and I don't always agree with their interpretations, but more like them are needed.

This book could not have been written, nor could my life of writing and solitude be sustained, without the support of Peter and Eleanor, Cynthia, Jacques and Christine, Nancy S., Lena and Tove, Barbara, Luciana, and Julia and Reed. A special thanks to Suzanne. Sultana, Alexa, Kevin, Kenzi, Bob, Eric, David C., and Steve S. were good and consistent friends and supporters, as were my social media friends who encouraged my work and perseverance. For most of the writing of this book I found refuge playing tournament poker at The Club, and my pals there kept my mind sharp. Thanks to *The Guardian* for reaching out even if I wasn't what they were looking for. Nancy Cooper gave me a great opportunity at *Newsweek*, one that became ever more important as Covid-19 descended. And thanks especially to Ben Cohen for supporting my work. All my love as always goes out to Rikki and Hannah.

From E. D. Cauchi: Foremost thanks go to Bill who, on a brisk January afternoon in 2019, in the bowels of New York's Grand Central Station, asked me to help him on the journey to create this book; for all the spreadsheeting, timelining, and heated debates that followed, his militant devotion to empirical analysis, and for teaching me how to see the secrets hidden in plain sight.

I owe a debt of gratitude to Investigative Reporters and Editors, who fiscally sponsored this endeavor and without whom months-worth of digging would not have happened. To Steve Aftergood, for pointing me in several right directions; to Hugh Handeyside and his colleagues at the ACLU's National Security Project, for always making time to talk documents and law; to the Electronic Frontier Foundation, Electronic Privacy Information Center, National Consortium for the Study of Terrorism and Responses to Terrorism, Brown

University's Cost of War Project, and NBC News which, in many ways, was the reason this book came about. To Michael D'Souza and Christine Haughney, for their constant support and mentorship. To the nervous civil servant who called me on a blocked number, demanded anonymity, and then, in hushed tones, urged me to stop sending questions to their office because, "The government doesn't want you to know this information," thanks for the intrigue.

I am especially grateful to Leslie Shvemar, for telling me my first classified war stories; the remarkable Bertha, who imparted upon me the importance of books, public service, and setting the record straight; Suzanne Dennison and Peter Cauchi, for my foundation without which I, quite literally, would not be here. And to my husband Frank—my North Star, who makes it possible—for every day, and all our 'gatoring ahead.

NOTES

chapter one PERPETUAL WAR

6 "*at least* ten different countries": Afghanistan, Iraq, Libya, Mali, Niger, Pakistan, Philippines, Somalia, Syria, and Yemen.

6 "the so-called global war on terror engaged the U.S. military in fifty-five different countries": These are the officially recognized countries engaged in the GWOT: Afghanistan, Algeria, Azerbaijan, Bahrain, Bosnia-Herzegovina, Bulgaria, Burkina Faso, Chad, Colombia, Crete, Cyprus, Diego Garcia, Djibouti, Egypt, Eritrea, France, Georgia, Greece, Hungary, Iran, Iraq, Israel, Italy, Jordan, Kazakhstan, Kenya, Kosovo, Kuwait, Kyrgyzstan, Lebanon, Mali, Mauritania, Morocco, Niger, Nigeria, Oman, Pakistan, Philippines, Qatar, Romania, Saudi Arabia, Senegal, Sierra Leone, Somalia, Syria, Spain, Tajikistan, Tanzania, Tunisia, Turkey, Turkmenistan, Uganda, the United Arab Emirates, Uzbekistan, and Yemen. See "Global War on Terrorism Expeditionary Medal GWOTEM and Global War on Terrorism Service Medal GWOTSM" as of May 1, 2019, https://www.hrc.army.mil/content/6043.

6 "our 'allies'": Allied countries actively engaged in the wars against Al Qaeda, ISIS, and the Taliban include at least Afghanistan, Australia, Bahrain, Belgium, Canada, Denmark, Egypt, France, Iraq, Israel, Italy, Jordan, Kenya, Kuwait, Lebanon, Morocco, the Netherlands, Niger, Pakistan, Qatar, Saudi Arabia, Somalia, Sudan, Turkey, Uganda, the United Arab Emirates, the United Kingdom, and Yemen.

The U.S.-led Coalition Against ISIS/Daesh at its peak included seventy-nine countries as of February 2019.

6 "only a quarter of those countries were officially acknowledged": U.S. Special Operations Command (SOCOM) says that

as of February 2018, special operations forces were deployed to ninety-two countries. See also the comparison of Leo Shane III, "SOCOM Head: We Can't Do Everything," *Military Times*, May 4, 2017, https://www.militarytimes.com/news/pentagon-congress /2017/05/04/socom-head-we-can-t-do-everything/; and Briefing by Mark Peterson, USSOCOM, "Ready for the Current Fight: Preparing for the Future," PowerPoint presentation, 2018.

9   "'countering violent extremism'": See *Empowering Local Partners to Prevent Violent Extremism in the United States*, The White House, August 2011, https://www.dhs.gov/sites/default/files/publications/ empowering_local_partners.pdf; and "FACT SHEET: The White House Summit on Countering Violent Extremism," The White House, February 18, 2015, https://obamawhitehouse.archives .gov/the-press-office/2015/02/18/fact-sheet-white-house -summit-countering-violent-extremism.

9   "by President Obama": Although the Obama administration made much of stopping use of the term Global War on Terror (or Terrorism), it persisted in the military. An Internet search in the military domain in May 2019 revealed 52,500 results for "global war on terrorism" and 907 for "countering violent extremism." The military also still confers the Global War on Terrorism Medal to those who participate: "The GWOTEM was established by Executive Order 13289, 12 March 2003. It is authorized for award to members of the Armed Forces of the United States who deployed abroad for service in the GWOT Operations on or after 11 September 2001 to a date to be determined." See "Global War on Terrorism Expeditionary Medal GWOTEM and Global War on Terrorism Service Medal GWOTSM" as of May 1, 2019, https:// www.hrc.army.mil/content/6043.

9   "nearly 11,000 Americans have died fighting": As of July 2019, the estimated number is 10,798 American deaths. It includes 22 civilians working for the Defense Department, plus 6,983 soldiers and an estimated 3,800 U.S. private contractors. See Department of Defense, Casualty Status as of 10 a.m. EDT July 19, 2019, https://dod.defense.gov/News/Casualty-Status/; and Neta C. Crawford, Brown University, Watson Institute for International & Public Affairs, *Human Cost of the Post-9/11 Wars: Lethality and the Need for Transparency*, November 2018, https://watson.brown.edu /costsofwar/files/cow/imce/papers/2018/Human%20Costs,%20 Nov%208%202018%20CoW.pdf.

The Watson Institute says that between October 2001 and

October 2018 (the most recently available numbers through Fiscal Year 2019), 7,820 private U.S. contractors were killed. That includes 3,937 in Afghanistan, 90 in Pakistan, 3,793 in Iraq. They calculate that number according to "Office of Workers' Compensation Program (OWCP): Defense Base Act Case Summary by Nation," Department of Labor, https://www.dol.gov/owcp dlhwc/dballnation.htm (data through March 31, 2020). Department of Labor (DOL) data for U.S. contractor deaths are 3,630: at least 1,675 in Iraq; at least 1,784 in Afghanistan; and at least 42 in Pakistan. These DOL figures do not include other DOL reported deaths (as of March 31, 2020) likely connected to the named military operations in Iraq and Afghanistan, including contractor deaths in Kuwait (105), Jordan (36), Qatar (21), Saudi Arabia (24), Syria (8), the United Arab Emirates (13). Note that these deaths are not complete data, as there are many unassigned country-related deaths and classified deaths. The Watson Institute estimates an additional number of unreported deaths, totaling 7,820, based upon their estimates. The number does not include non-U.S. contractor deaths.

9   "53,000 have been physically broken": As of February 2019, there were 53,244 wounded in action, according to "Casualty Status as of 10 a.m. EDT Aug. 31, 2020," Department of Defense, https://dod.defense.gov/News/Casualty-Status/.

10   "number of contractors killed began to exceed the number of soldiers": See T. Christian Miller, "Disposable Army—This Year, Contractor Deaths Exceed Military Ones in Iraq and Afghanistan," ProPublica, September 23, 2010, https://www.propublica .org/article/this-year-contractor-deaths-exceed-military-ones -in-iraq-and-afgh-100923.

10   "double standard": This phenomenon of contractor deaths and of ignoring contractors was documented in Dana Priest and William M. Arkin in the "Top Secret America" series, *Washington Post*, July 2010, http://projects.washingtonpost.com/top-secret-america/.

10   "worst since World War II": "Refugee Crisis in Europe," USA for UNHCR: The UN Refugee Agency, accessed on April 26, 2019, https://www.unrefugees.org/emergencies/refugee-crisis-in-europe/.

10   "there are probably a couple of hundred thousand": There is no official number of terrorists fighting against the United States, and it is difficult to calculate, as seen in the discussion in Chapter 10.

10   "8.5 million troops": The total number is 8,451,987. This is based on a grand total in the U.S. military including reservists and DOD civilian employees as 2,882,061. As of 2020, that

includes 1,361,097 active duty personnel stationed both state-side (1,190,072) and overseas (171,025). See "Military and Ci-vilian Personnel by Service/Agency by State/Country," DOD Defense Manpower Data Center, June 30, 2020, and Jennie W. Wenger, Caolionn O'Connell, and Linda Cottrell, "Examination of Recent Deployment Experience Across the Services and Com-ponents," RAND Corporation, March 2018; https://www.rand.org/pubs/research_reports/RR1928.html.

The total NATO military manpower is an estimated 5.57 million. See "Member countries," North Atlantic Treaty Orga-nization, May 14, 2019, https://www.nato.int/cps/en/natohq/topics_52044.htm; "2019 Military Strength Ranking," Global Firepower Index, accessed on July 10, 2019, https://www.global firepower.com/countries-listing.asp; and "Armed Forces Person-nel, Total," The World Bank, 2017, https://data.worldbank.org/indicator/MS.MIL.TOTL.P1.

11 "more than $6.5 trillion": See "Summary of War Spending, in Billions of Current Dollars (Rounded to the Nearest Billion), FY 2001–FY 2020, Brown University," Watson Institute for In-ternational & Public Affairs, November 13, 2019, https://watson.brown.edu/costsofwar/figures/2019/budgetary-costs-post-911-wars-through-fy2020-64-trillion.

The Pentagon calculates, according to its budget protocols, that the global war on terror cost $1.5 trillion as of 2019: "COST OF WAR Through September 30, 2019," Department of Defense, https://fas.org/man/eprint/cow/fy2019q4.pdf. This number ex-cludes much, as the Brown University accounting explains.

11 "more than the defense budget of all the other nations combined, *over six years of spending*": The total military spending not including the United States was approximately $1 trillion in 2017 accord-ing to "Global Military Spending Remains High at $1.7 trillion," Stockholm International Peace Research Institute (SIPRI), May 2, 2018, https://www.sipri.org/media/press-release/2018/global-military-spending-remains-high-17-trillion.

11 "cost of annual health care for all Americans": This is based upon the total cost estimate of $6.5 trillion. As of February 2019, the United States currently spends $3.5 trillion annually on health care, according to the U.S. Centers for Medicare and Medicaid Ser-vices, https://www.cms.gov/research-statistics-data-and-systems/statistics-trends-and-reports/nationalhealthexpenddata/national healthaccountshistorical.html.

11 "ten times the annual budget of the entire American public school system": Total education spending is estimated to be $668 billion annually, one-tenth of the $6.5 trillion total, according to the National Center for Education Statistics. See "Public School Expenditures," NCES: National Center for Education Statistics, April 11, 2018, https://nces.ed.gov/programs/coe/indicator _cmb.asp.

11 "'We face the most diverse and complex set of threats we have ever seen'": Dan Coats, Director of National Intelligence, "Remarks as Prepared for Delivery by The Honorable Dan Coats Director of National Intelligence Presentation of the 2019 National Intelligence Strategy," Office of the Director of National Intelligence, January 22, 2019, https://www.dni.gov/index.php/newsroom /speeches-interviews/item/1942-remarks-as-prepared-for-delivery -by-the-honorable-dan-coats-director-of-national-intelligence -presentation-of-the-2019-national-intelligence-strategy.

11 "'unpredictable instability' had become 'the new normal'": Director of National Intelligence (DNI) James Clapper, "Global Threats," Testimony Before the Senate Armed Services Committee, C-Span, February 9, 2016, https://www.c-span.org/video /?404436-1/james-clapper-testimony-global-threats.

12 "its most uncertain time since the Second World War": As quoted in Jim Garamone, "Dunford Details Implications of Today's Threats on Tomorrow's Strategy," U.S. Dept. of Defense, August 23, 2016, https://www.defense.gov/Explore/News/Article/Article/923685 /dunford-details-implications-of-todays-threats-on-tomorrows -strategy/.

12 "the most unpredictable I have seen in 40 years of service": As stated in the Department of Defense, *National Military Strategy of the United States of America*, June 2015, I.

Dempsey also said: "I will personally attest to the fact that it [the world] is more dangerous than it has ever been." See General Martin Dempsey, Chairman of the Joint Chiefs of Staff, *Hearing to Receive Testimony on the Impacts of Sequestration and/or a Full-Year Continuing Resolution on the Department of Defense*, hearing before the U.S. Senate Armed Services Committee, 113th Congress, 1st Session, February 12, 2013, 22, https://www.armed-services .senate.gov/imo/media/doc/13-03%20-%202-12-13.pdf.

16 "to protect the American people and to make a safer world for our children": This is the mission as precisely laid down by former secretary of defense Ashton Carter. See Ash Carter, *Inside the*

Five-Sided Box: Lessons for a Lifetime of Leadership in the Pentagon (New York: Dutton, 2019), 433–34.

chapter two THE NATIONAL SECURITY ESTABLISHMENT

18 "a beacon of light for those in dark places": See *National Defense Strategy*, U.S. Dept. of Defense, June 2008, https://dod.defense.gov /Portals/1/Documents/pubs/2008NationalDefenseStrategy.pdf.

22 "military-industrial complex": Still the most powerful image of the military and national security establishment. See Dwight D. Eisenhower, "President Dwight D. Eisenhower's Farewell Address (1961)," Our Documents, January 17, 1961, https://www.our documents.gov/doc.php?flash=false&doc=90.

25 "'staggered'": Leon Panetta, *Worthy Fights: A Memoir of Leadership in War and Peace* (New York: Penguin Press, 2014), 205.

25 "virtually disappeared from the President's Daily Brief": Obama deputy national security advisor Ben Rhodes wrote this of the Presidential Daily Brief (PDB): "I was always struck by the exclusion of large global trends—climate, governance, food, health—in favor of an intricate level of detail about terrorist plots." See Ben Rhodes, *The World as It Is: A Memoir of the Obama White House* (New York: Random House, 2018), 88.

25 "never came to understand the complexities of Iraqi society": When Panetta took over the CIA at the beginning of the Obama administration, he tells the story of outgoing director Michael Hayden telling him that "he thought Iraq was on track and wouldn't require much attention." That, after an invasion and insurgency, with an implosion soon to come. See Panetta, *Worthy Fights*, 205.

25 "'completely by surprise'": See Rick Brennan, "Withdrawal Symptoms," *Foreign Affairs*, November/December 2014, https://www .foreignaffairs.com/articles/united-states/withdrawal-symptoms.

25 "'We didn't get a warning?'": Rhodes, *The World as It Is*, 291.

25 "The intelligence community also didn't anticipate": Panetta, *Worthy Fights*, 301.

26 "would empower his son to be his successor": Ibid., 276.

26 "We have never once gotten it right": Robert M. Gates, "Secretary of Defense Speech: United States Military Academy (West Point, NY)," delivered on February 25, 2011, U.S. Dept. of Defense, https://archive.defense.gov/speeches/speech.aspx?speechid =1539.

27 "admitted they didn't even know that the United States had people in that country": See Daniella Diaz, "Key Senators Say They Didn't Know the US Had Troops in Niger," CNN, October 23, 2017, https://www.cnn.com/2017/10/23/politics/niger -troops-lawmakers/index.html.

27 "Gates later remarked": Robert M. Gates, *Duty: Memoirs of a Secretary at War* (New York: Knopf, 2014), 360, 501.

27 "$50 billion-a-year": The FY 2019 budget for Department of Homeland Security was $47.5 billion, according to *Budget-in-Brief, FY 2019*, Department of Homeland Security, https://www.dhs .gov/sites/default/files/publications/DHS%20BIB%202019.pdf.

27 "almost unlimited in scope": See Janet Napolitano, *How Safe Are We? Homeland Security Since 9/11* (New York: PublicAffairs, 2019), 55.

28 "60,000 domestic people with badges": The total in 2019 was some 57,500 (combining 12,466 ICE and nearly 45,000 Customs and Border Protection law enforcement officers), plus thousands of federal air marshals under the TSA, as well as another 43,877 TSA officers (who, despite their appearance as such, are *not* law enforcement officers).

As of FY 2019, ICE has a total of 6,347 Homeland Security investigation special agents and another 6,119 deportation officers and immigration enforcement agents. Email to author from Britney L. Walker, Office of Public Affairs, Immigration and Customs Enforcement (ICE), March 15, 2019; phone interview with ICE Public Affairs Officer Britney L. Walker on Friday, March 15, 2019.

Under the umbrella of ICE, Homeland Security Investigations (HSI) has "8,500 employees, including nearly 6,500 special agents (law enforcement officers) and 700 intelligence analysts who are assigned to more than 200 cities throughout the U.S. and more than 60 offices in more than 45 countries." See "Who We Are," Immigration and Customs Enforcement (ICE), https:// www.ice.gov/about (accessed on March 12, 2019).

For Customs and Border Protection (CBP) numbers, see Rebecca Gambler, "U.S. Customs and Border Protection Progress and Challenges in Recruiting, Hiring, and Retaining Law Enforcement Personnel," Government Accountability Office, June 27, 2018, https://www.gao.gov/assets/700/692832.pdf.

The precise number of federal air marshals is classified. The public total number is "in the thousands," according to TSA press secretary Jenny Burke, who declined to be any more precise, saying she didn't want "the bad guys" to know. Phone interview with TSA press secretary Jenny Burke on Tuesday, March 12, 2019.

For total number of transportation security officers, see: "FY 2019 Budget in Brief," Department of Homeland Security, 6, https://www.dhs.gov/sites/default/files/publications/DHS%20 BIB%202019.pdf.

28 "four times the size of the entire FBI": As of March 2019, the FBI had 13,513 special agents. This is the total number of law enforcement agents. See email from FBI Public Affairs Specialist Linda Wilkins, Federal Bureau of Investigation, "Media Request About Law Enforcement Totals," March 25, 2019, https://drive.google .com/open?id=1r3y2cdu17o37KhUCiHpfX_03aTO8c01E.

28 "and it is growing": As of the end of 2019, President Trump has signed two executive orders to hire an additional 15,000 border patrol officers and another 10,000 ICE agents. Hiring an additional 10,000 enforcement agents and officers was directed by DHS secretary John Kelly. See DHS, "Secretary of Homeland Security Memorandum: Enforcement of the Immigration Laws to Serve the National Interest," February 20, 2017, https://www.dhs.gov /sites/default/files/publications/17_0220_S1_Enforcement-of-the -Immigration-Laws-to-Serve-the-National-Interest.pdf.

29 "Obama lacked the necessary familiarity with 'American military culture'": Gates, *Duty*, 383.

29 "neither major candidate for the presidency has any military experience": John Nagl, "Does Military Service Still Matter for the Presidency?," *Washington Post*, May 25, 2012, https://www.washing tonpost.com/opinions/does-military-service-still-matter-for -the-presidency/2012/05/25/gJQAAAMupU_story.html.

30 "establishment accuses Congress": Rhodes, *The World as It Is*, 49.

30 "'huge cash cow'": Gates, *Duty*, 315.

30 "'nearly paralyzing direction, micromanagement, restrictions, and demands for reports'": Gates, *Duty*, 454.

chapter three CLOSING THE CHAPTER ON 9/11

33 "Dean later explained": Diana Dean interview with *60 Minutes*, "The Millennium Plot: It Almost Happened Once Before," *60 Minutes* (CBS News), October 3, 2001, https://www.cbsnews .com/news/i60-minutes-ii-ithe-millennium-plot/.

33 "they found what they first thought was drugs": Ahmed Ressam court testimony in the case of his coconspirator, *United States of*

America v. Mokhtar Haouari (United States District Court, Southern District of New York), July 5, 2001, https://web.archive.org/web/20051014025142/http://news.findlaw.com/hdocs/docs/haouari/ushaouari070501rassamtt.pdf.

33 "The goal was to kill hundreds": Brent L. Smith, Kelly R. Damphousse, and Paxton Roberts, "Pre-Incident Indicators of Terrorist Incidents: The Identification of Behavioral, Geographic, and Temporal Patterns of Preparatory Conduct," University of Arkansas, Terrorism Research Center in Fulbright College, May 2006, https://www.ncjrs.gov/pdffiles1/nij/grants/214217.pdf.

33 "on numerous occasions": The story of Ressam making it all the way to the U.S. border with a bomb was the result of intelligence and law enforcement's failure to stop him despite ten distinct opportunities over the course of six years in France, Canada, and the United States. Ressam was arrested four times for immigration fraud and theft and was under surveillance by intelligence authorities as part of a terrorist cell for four years leading up to the attempted Y2K attack.

The Canadian Central Intelligence Service (CSIS) was monitoring Ressam from the time he was recruited through his journey to Al Qaeda training in Afghanistan and every stage of the plot, though how many specifics they gleaned is unclear. CSIS was acting on a tip from Italian and French authorities to monitor what they suspected was a growing terrorist cell in Montreal. Among his regular associates, Ressam interacted with a known Al Qaeda recruiter in Canada who was under investigation by authorities in France.

CSIS built up a four-hundred-page dossier on the Montreal cell, but the threat didn't seem to be taken too seriously by the Canadian intelligence agents, who nicknamed their suspects "BOG" (Bunch of Guys) and the gatherings "Tupperware parties," and who considered Ressam the least likely security risk among them. CSIS put the suspects' names on a watch list, but the men assumed fake identities, which shouldn't have been a surprise since Ressam had been arrested multiple times for doing exactly that. The Canadian failure to catch the fake names or fake passports or to share intelligence with the U.S. authorities meant that an American immigration agent did not register anything wrong when Ressam returned from Al Qaeda training and presented himself during a layover at LAX on February 7, 1999, carrying bomb-making supplies—although several of his coconspirators were arrested on their own version of that same journey, and his recruiter was extradited to France to face terrorism charges. Eight months later, when the RCMP finally raided the apartment where Ressam and his coconspirators were working, Ressam snuck out the back. After the raid, Ressam was not stopped from recruiting three new collaborators or from flying to the West Coast en route to their target. A tired fifty-four-year-old customs officer was the only thing that stood in their way.

34 "the deadliest terrorist attack on American soil": Death toll calculated as 2,749 at the World Trade Center, 184 at the Pentagon, and 40 on United Airlines Flight 93 in Pennsylvania, according to "The 9/11 Commission Report," Final National Commission on Terrorist Attacks Upon the United States, July, 22 2004, https://www.govinfo.gov/app/details/GPO-911REPORT.

35 "Six of the nineteen hijackers had lived in the United States for more than a year": The intent here is not to adjudicate the intelligence failures but merely to point out that, as of September 11, 2001, the State Department watch list called TIPOFF had the names of two 9/11 hijackers on it. See "Three 9/11 Hijackers: Identification, Watchlisting, and Tracking: Staff Statement No. 2," National Commission on Terrorist Attacks Upon the United States, 2004, http://condor.wesleyan.edu/mcrenshaw/govt327/staff_statement_2.pdf.

35 "even if they had tried": Transcript of Condoleezza Rice's 9/11 Commission statement, May 19, 2004, https://www.9-11commission.gov/archive/hearing9/9-11Commission_Hearing_2004-04-08.pdf.

35 "trumpeting their success": In a Fox News interview at the end of September 2006, former President Bill Clinton got very testy on the subject of how much his administration had done. "I tried and I failed to get bin Laden. I regret it. But I did try," he said, saying as well that in eight months in office, the Bush White House had done little in comparison. See transcript of *Fox News Sunday* in the *New York Times*, September 24, 2006, https://www.nytimes.com/2006/09/24/us/24cnd-transcript.html.

35 "would later tell NBC": Lisa Myers, "Foiling Millennium Attack Was Mostly Luck," *NBC Nightly News*, April 29, 2004, http://www.nbcnews.com/id/4864792/ns/nbc_nightly_news_with_brian_williams/t/foiling-millennium-attack-was-mostly-luck/.

36 "because of the 'wall'": Admiral J. Michael "Mike" McConnell (USN, Ret.), Director of National Intelligence, testifying

before the House Judiciary Committee Hearing on Warrantless Surveillance and the Foreign Intelligence Surveillance Act: The Role of Checks and Balances in Protecting Americans' Privacy Rights, 110th Congress, September 18, 2007, https://www.gov info.gov/content/pkg/CHRG-110hhrg37844/html/CHRG -110hhrg37844.htm.

37 "a reluctant government": It is important to remind ourselves that the idea of a commission was not accepted as necessary or even desirable by many in Washington, not just the Bush administration. See "9/11 Commission: Opposition and Obfuscation," Center for American Progress, April 7, 2004, https://www.americanprogress .org/issues/security/news/2004/04/07/715/911-commission -opposition-and-obfuscation/.

37 "until he had to withdraw his name due to personal scandals": President George W Bush nominated former New York City po- lice commissioner Bernard Kerik to become the second White House director of homeland security. Just eight days later, amidst scandal about his personal life, Kerik withdrew his name from consideration. Calling his nomination "the honor of a lifetime," Kerik said withdrawing "was the right thing to do" after a barrage of scandals emerged. As the *New York Times* summarized Kerik's transgressions, he had been outed for "an undisclosed marriage, clandestine love affairs, unsavory business ties and unreported gifts," not to mention "Nannygate," in which it was revealed that Kerik's housekeeper and children's nanny was working for him illegally because she was an undocumented immigrant.

See Eric Lipton and William K. Rashbaum, "Kerik Pulls Out as Bush Nominee for Homeland Security Job," *New York Times*, December 11, 2004, https://www.nytimes.com/2004/12/11 /politics/kerik-pulls-out-as-bush-nominee-for-homeland-security -job.html; Bernard Kerik, "Prison Is Like 'Dying with Your Eyes open,'" CNBC, April 29, 2015, https://www.cnbc.com /2015/04/29/bernard-kerik-prison-is-like-dying-with-your -eyes-open-commentary.html; Nina Bernstein and Robin Stein, "Mystery Woman in Kerik Case: Nanny," *New York Times*, De- cember 16, 2004, https://www.nytimes.com/2004/12/16/us /mystery-woman-in-kerik-case-nanny.html; and Jeff VanDamm, "Bernie Kerik's Tumble," *New York Magazine*, October 25, 2009, http://nymag.com/news/intelligencer/topic/60293/.

38 "public support for military conflict reached all-time highs": Dina Smeltz et al., "America Engaged 2018: American Public Opinion

and US Foreign Policy," Chicago Council Survey, October 2, 2018, https://www.thechicagocouncil.org/sites/default/files/report _ccs18_america-engaged_181002.pdf.

In 2018, three-quarters of Americans thought that the United States held a special responsibility to act as a world leader. See "U.S. Position in the World," Gallup, November 12, 2018.

38   "two-thirds of the public still": "Military and National Defense," Gallup, January 8, 2010; and Frank Newport, "Americans See U.S. Military as No. 1 Now, but Not in 20 Yrs.," Gallup, January 8, 2010, https://news.gallup.com/poll/126218/americans-military -no-not-yrs.aspx.

38   "precipitous loss of confidence": "Record Number Favors Removing U.S. Troops from Afghanistan," Pew Research Center, June 21, 2011, http://www.people-press.org/2011/06/21/record-number -favors-removing-u-s-troops-from-afghanistan/; Public Attitudes Toward the War in Iraq: 2003–2008," Pew Research Center, March 19, 2008, http://www.pewresearch.org/2008/03/19/public -attitudes-toward-the-war-in-iraq-20032008/; Eric V. Larson and Bogdan Savych, *American Public Support for U.S. Military Operations from Mogadishu to Baghdad*, RAND Corporation, 2005.

38   "a decline that has persisted to this day": John Mueller and Mark G. Stewart, "Public Opinion and Counterterrorism Policy," Cato Institute, February 20, 2018, https://www.cato.org/publications /white-paper/public-opinion-counterterrorism-policy.

38   "to near-historic lows": "Public Trust in Government: 1958– 2017," Pew Research Center, December 14, 2017, http://www .people-press.org/2017/12/14/public-trust-in-government-1958 -2017/.

38   "one-quarter to one-half of all Americans even believe": A Chapman University study in 2016 found that more than half (54.3 percent) of Americans believed the U.S. government was concealing information about 9/11. See "What Aren't They Telling Us? Chapman University Survey of American Fears," Chapman University, October 11, 2016, https://blogs.chapman.edu/wilkinson /2016/10/11/what-arent-they-telling-us/.

One quarter (25 percent) of people thought the U.S. government helped plan the attacks on 9/11. See Economist/YouGov poll, December 17–20, 2016, https://d25d2506sfb94s.cloudfront .net/cumulus_uploads/document/ljv2ohxmzj/econTabReport.pdf.

Approximately 60 percent of Americans believed that the U.S. government was withholding information about what happened on 9/11. "Americans Want Government to Tell All About 9/11," Rasmussen Reports, April 25, 2016, http://www.rasmussen reports.com/public_content/politics/general_politics /april_2016/americans_want_government_to_tell_all_about_9_11.

In 2015, one quarter (24 percent) of people thought what happened on 9/11 was "likely to have a different explanation." See "Conspiracy Theories," *60 Minutes/Vanity Fair*, May 2015, https:// www.cbsnews.com/news/60-minutes-vanity-fair-poll-conspiracy/.

In 2013, 78 percent of Americans did not accept government explanations. See "Democrats and Republicans Differ on Conspiracy Theory Beliefs," Public Policy Polling, April 2, 2013, https:// www.publicpolicypolling.com/wp-content/uploads/2017/09 /PPP_Release_National_ConspiracyTheories_040213.pdf.

In 2006, 36 percent of Americans polled said it was either very or somewhat likely that the "people in the federal government either assisted in the 9/11 attacks or took no action to stop the attacks because they wanted to United States to go to war in the Middle East." See Thomas Hargrove and Guido H. Stempel III, "Anti-Government Anger Spawns 9/11 Conspiracy Belief," Scripps Survey Research Center, August 2, 2006, https://web .archive.org/web/20060815124458/http://www.newspolls.org /story.php?story_id=55.

In 2006, 53 percent of Americans thought President Bush was hiding something about 9/11 and an additional 28 percent believed he was mostly lying about it. See "Americans Question Bush on 9/11 Intelligence," *New York Times*/CBS News, October 14, 2006, https://web.archive.org/web/20061112105223/http:// www.angus-reid.com/polls/index.cfm/fuseaction/viewItem /itemID/13469.

In 2004, immediately following the publication of the 9/11 Commission Report, half (49.3 percent) of New York City residents and 41 percent of New Yorkers overall said that some government leaders "knew in advance that attacks were planned on or around September 11, 2001, and that they consciously failed to act." See "Half of New Yorkers Believe US Leaders Had Foreknowledge of Impending 9-11 Attacks and 'Consciously Failed' to Act," Zogby International, August 30, 2004, https://web.archive .org/web/20041018213016/http://www.zogby.com/search /ReadNews.dbm?ID=855.

39 "Donald Trump floated 9/11 conspiracy theories": Tim Hains, "Donald Trump on 9/11: 'You Will Find Out Who Really Knocked

Down the World Trade Center,'" RealClearPolitics, February 17, 2016, https://www.realclearpolitics.com/video/2016/02/17 /trump_you_will_find_out_who_really_knocked_down_the_world_ trade_center_secret_papers_may_blame_saudis.html.

39 "Americans have generally been willing to make sacrifices": "Illegal or Not, Voters Are More Supportive Than Ever of NSA," Rasmussen Reports, May 11, 2015, http://www.rasmussenre ports.com/public_content/politics/general_politics/may_2015 /illegal_or_not_voters_are_more_supportive_than_ever_of_nsa; "Terrorism," Gallup, July 22–24, 2005, https://news.gallup.com /poll/4909/terrorism-united-states.aspx.

39 "eight out of ten": "How Americans Have Viewed Government Surveillance and Privacy Since Snowden Leaks," Pew Research Center, June 4, 2018, http://www.pewresearch.org /fact-tank/2018/06/04/how-americans-have-viewed-government -surveillance-and-privacy-since-snowden-leaks/.

39 "one-fifth of Americans supported active military engagement abroad": Gregory Holyk and Dina Smeltz, *Background Brief for Final Presidential Debate: What Kind of Foreign Policy Do Americans Want?*, Chicago Council on Global Affairs, October 19, 2012, https://www.thechicagocouncil.org/sites/default/files/2012 _CCS_FPBrief.pdf.

39 "would 'most likely' vote for a candidate who supported withdrawal from foreign conflicts": J. Wallin Opinion Research and Gunster Strategies Worldwide, *Nationwide Voter Survey: Report on Results*, Committee for Responsive Foreign Policy, January 28, 2018, http://www.responsibleforeignpolicy.org/wp-content /uploads/2018/02/J-Wallin_Nationwide-Voter-Survey_Gunster -Worldwide-Strategies_Committee-for-Responsible-Foreign %E2%80%93Policy_Presentation.pdf.

39 "Most Americans said": Dina Smeltz et al., "America Engaged 2018: American Public Opinion and US Foreign Policy," Chicago Council Survey, October 2, 2018, https://www.thechicagocouncil .org/sites/default/files/report_ccs18_america-engaged_181002 .pdf.

39 "Today the public puts more value on": Ibid.

39 "the lowest it has been since before 9/11": Justin McCarthy, "Seven in 10 Trust U.S. Government to Protect Against Terrorism," Gallup Organization, June 19, 2017, https://news.gallup .com/poll/212558/seven-trust-government-protect-against -terrorism.aspx.

40   "public opinion didn't move": As noted in *Unclassified Summary of Information Handling and Sharing Prior to the April 15, 2013 Boston Marathon Bombings, Prepared by the Inspectors General of the: Intelligence Community, Central Intelligence Agency, Department of Justice, Department of Homeland Security*, April 10, 2014, https://www .oig.dhs.gov/assets/Mgmt/2014/OIG_Bos_Marathon_Bom_Rev _Apr14.pdf.

40   "Since at least the late 1980s.": The American public has consistently held the military in increasingly higher esteem than any other institution since 1988. See "War and Sacrifice in the Post-9/11 Era—Chapter 5: The Public and the Military," Pew Research Center, October 5, 2011, http://www.pewsocialtrends.org /2011/10/05/chapter-5-the-public-and-the-military/.

40   "a higher approval rating than any other American institution": "Confidence in Institutions," Gallup, 2018, https://news.gallup .com/poll/1597/Confidence-Institutions.aspx.

40   "'rally-round-the-flag' effect": James M. Lindsay, "Rally 'Round the Flag," Brookings Institution, March 25, 2003, https://www .brookings.edu/opinions/rally-round-the-flag/. See also Shoon Murray, "The 'Rally-'Round-the-Flag' Phenomenon and the Diversionary Use of Force," American University, June 2017, https://oxfordre.com/politics/view/10.1093/acrefore/978019 0228637.001.0001/acrefore-9780190228637-e-518.

40   "overwhelmingly supported mounting a retaliation": Eric V. Larson and Bogdan Savych, "American Public Support for U.S. Military Operations from Mogadishu to Baghdad," RAND Corporation, 2005, https://www.rand.org/content/dam/rand /pubs/monographs/2005/RAND_MG231.pdf.

40   "Most in the public supported": In November 2001, President George W. Bush had an 87 percent approval rating for military action fighting terrorism abroad. See "Presidential Ratings—Issues Approval," Gallup, June 1–4, 2013, https://news.gallup.com/poll /1726/presidential-ratings-issues-approval.aspx.

In 2001–2002, only a slim majority of Americans supported the Afghanistan war; between 52 and 74 percent of the public. See Lydia Saad, "Top Ten Findings About Public Opinion and Iraq," Gallup, October 22, 2002, https://news.gallup.com/poll/6964 /top-ten-findings-about-public-opinion-iraq.aspx.

In January 2003, consistent polling showed approximately 50 to 60 percent support for a possible Iraq war. See "Public Struggles with Possible War in Iraq," Pew Research Center, January 30, 2003,

http://www.people-press.org/2003/01/30/public-struggles
-with-possible-war-in-iraq/.

In March 2003, just weeks after President Bush declared war on Iraq, 72 to 76 percent of Americans supported the war. See Frank Newport, "Seventy-Two Percent of Americans Support War Against Iraq," Gallup, March 24, 2003, https://news .gallup.com/poll/8038/seventytwo-percent-americans-support -war-against-iraq.aspx.

In September 2003, Bush's approval rating was overwhelming, at 90 percent. See Jeffrey Jones, "Sept. 11 Effects, Though Largely Faded, Persist," Gallup, September 9, 2003, https://news.gallup .com/poll/9208/sept-effects-though-largely-faded-persist.aspx.

40   "remained as great in 2018 as it was in 2001": John Gramlich, "Defending Against Terrorism Has Remained a Top Policy Priority for Americans Since 9/11," Pew Research Center, September 11, 2018, http://www.pewresearch.org/fact-tank/2018/09/11 /defending-against-terrorism-has-remained-a-top-policy-priority -for-americans-since-9-11/.

40   "they did not know enough to engage in the complex and tangled national security debate": As an example, a quarter of Americans said they "don't know" whether they approve or disapprove of government surveillance. This is a common response. When questioned by pollsters, "don't know" is a more popular reply than any one specific answer, even when people are asked about their knowledge of basic constitutional rights and amendments. In another poll, a third of Americans said they "don't know" any branches of government and 37 percent didn't know what rights the First Amendment protects. See "Americans Are Poorly Informed About Basic Constitutional Provisions," Annenberg Public Policy Center, September 12, 2017, https://www.annenbergpublic policycenter.org/americans-are-poorly-informed-about-basic -constitutional-provisions/.

See also Mary Madden and Lee Rainie, "Americans' Views About Data Collection and Security," Pew Research Center, May 20, 2105, https://www.pewinternet.org/2015/05/20/americans -views-about-data-collection-and-security/.

Nearly 20 percent of young Americans said they weren't going to vote in the 2018 federal election because they didn't think they knew enough to be able to. See Julia Manchester, "Young People Vote in Lower Numbers Because They Don't Think They Know Enough About the Process, Says Pollster,"

The Hill, October 30, 2018, https://thehill.com/hilltv/what-americas
-thinking/413938-young-people-vote-in-lower-numbers
-because-they-dont-think-they. See also Asma Khalid, Don Gon-
yea, and Leila Fadel, "On the Sidelines of Democracy: Ex-
ploring Why So Many Americans Don't Vote," NPR, September
10, 2018, https://www.npr.org/2018/09/10/645223716/on
-the-sidelines-of-democracy-exploring-why-so-many-americans
-dont-vote.

chapter four WHAT HAPPENED TO OBAMA

42 "bellies full with hot dogs and ribs": Joseph Logan, "Last U.S.
Troops Leave Iraq, Ending war," Reuters, December 17, 2011,
https://www.reuters.com/article/us-iraq-withdrawal/last-u-s
-troops-leave-iraq-ending-war-idUSTRE7BH03320111218.

42 "the sandy air was filled by the humming sound": "Last Convoy of
U.S. Soldiers Rolled out of Iraq Sunday Morning," Associated Press,
December 18, 2011, https://www.syracuse.com/news/2011/12
/last_convoy_of_us_soldiers_rol.html. See also Joseph Logan,
"Last U.S. Troops Leave Iraq, Ending War," Reuters, December 17,
2011, https://www.reuters.com/article/us-iraq-withdrawal/last
-u-s-troops-leave-iraq-ending-war-idUSTRE7BH03320111218.

42 "the *last* American convoy in Iraq": Tim Arango and Michael S.
Schmidt, "Last Convoy of American Troops Leaves Iraq," *New
York Times*, December 18, 2011, https://www.nytimes.com
/2011/12/19/world/middleeast/last-convoy-of-american-troops
-leaves-iraq.html; and Greg Jaffe, "Last U.S. Troops Cross Iraqi
Border into Kuwait," *Washington Post*, December 18, 2011, https://
www.washingtonpost.com/world/national-security/last-us
-troops-cross-iraqi-border-into-kuwait/2011/12/17/gIQArEy
X1O_story.html.

42 "the most difficult undertaking in our lifetime": Kelly McEvers,
"Last U.S. Troops Make Quiet Exit out of Iraq," NPR, December
18, 2011, https://www.npr.org/2011/12/18/143914052/time-to
-heal-as-u-s-troops-leave-iraq. See also "Raw Video: Last US
Troops Roll Out of Iraq," Associated Press, December 18, 2011,
https://www.youtube.com/watch?v=vyef___pB5o.

42 "U.S. drones kept a watchful eye from the skies overhead": U.S.
AFCENT, "Last Crossing Out of Iraq—USAFCENT News,"
YouTube, December 18, 2011, https://www.youtube.com/watch
?v=zVLN5H8VFNs. See also Spencer Ackerman, "Video: Drone

Watches Last U.S. Convoy Leave Iraq," *Wired*, December 18, 2011, https://www.wired.com/2011/12/predator-convoy-iraq/.

43 "chest bumps, and embraced in enthusiastic bear hugs": Associated Press, "Last Convoy of U.S. Soldiers Rolled out of Iraq Sunday morning," December 18, 2011, https://www.syracuse.com /news/2011/12/last_convoy_of_us_soldiers_rol.html.

43 "It's all smooth sailing from here": Associated Press, "Last American Troops Leave Iraq Marking End of War," Fox News, December 18, 2011, https://www.foxnews.com/world/last-american-troops -leave-iraq-marking-end-of-war.

43 "taken nearly 4,500 American military lives": Iraq war U.S. Department of Defense deaths totaled 4,496. Operation Iraqi Freedom casualties, including both U.S. military and Department of Defense civilians, totaled 4,431 people killed, plus Operation New Dawn added an additional 74 U.S. military personnel deaths. See "Casualty Status as of 10 a.m. EDT Aug. 31, 2020," Department of Defense, https://dod.defense.gov/News/Casualty-Status/.

43 "cost $1 trillion": Even by the Pentagon's accounting, Operations Iraqi Freedom and New Dawn cost $815 billion, totaling 51 percent of the budget for war operations following 9/11. See Amy Belasco, "The Cost of Iraq, Afghanistan, and Other Global War on Terror Operations Since 9/11," Congressional Research Service, December 8, 2014, https://fas.org/sgp/crs/natsec/RL33110.pdf.

43 "left behind 'a sovereign, stable and self-reliant' country": "Remarks by the President and First Lady on the End of the War in Iraq, Fort Bragg, North Carolina," The White House, December 14, 2011, https://obamawhitehouse.archives.gov/the-press-office /2011/12/14/remarks-president-and-first-lady-end-war-iraq.

43 "he told Barbara Walters": Devin Dwyer, "President Obama Faults Republican 'Lurch into Extremes' for DC Gridlock," ABC News, December 15, 2011, https://abcnews.go.com/Politics/president -obama-faults-republican-lurch-extremes-divisiveness-dc/story ?id=15163372.

43 "the previous administration had also agreed": President George W. Bush signed the Strategic Framework Agreement with Iraq in December 2008. "President Bush and Iraq Prime Minister Maliki Sign the Strategic Framework Agreement and Security Agreement, Prime Minister's Palace, Baghdad, Iraq," The White House, December 14, 2008, https://georgewbush-whitehouse.archives .gov/news/releases/2008/12/20081214-2.html.

The 2008 Framework ended Operation Iraqi Freedom and

initiated Operation New Dawn, stipulating that combat forces would be withdrawn from Iraqi population centers by the end of 2009 and out of Iraq completely by the end of 2011. In February 2009, President Obama announced that he would reduce force levels from 160,000 to 50,000 by August 2010. He promised that the remainder would be withdrawn by the end of 2011.

43 "he promised that troops would be gone by mid-2008": Barack Obama, "Renewing American Leadership," *Foreign Affairs*, July/August 2007, https://www.foreignaffairs.com/articles/2007-07-01/renewing-american-leadership.

Obama further amplified his goal in July 2008 in the *New York Times*, promising the summer of 2010 as his timetable. See Barack Obama, "My Plan for Iraq," *New York Times*, July 14, 2008, https://www.nytimes.com/2008/07/14/opinion/14obama.html.

43 "insisted on a 'responsible drawdown of troops'": Leon Panetta, *Worthy Fights: A Memoir of Leadership in War and Peace* (New York: Penguin Press, 2014), 382.

43 "three prominent Iraqis penned an op-ed": Ayad Allawi, Osama Al-Nujaifi, and Rafe Al-Essawi, "How to Save Iraq from Civil War," *New York Times*, December 27, 2011, https://www.nytimes.com/2011/12/28/opinion/how-to-save-iraq-from-civil-war.html.

44 "rounding them up to be arrested as soon as U.S. forces were gone": See Dexter Filkins, "What We Left Behind," *New Yorker*, April 28, 2014, https://www.newyorker.com/magazine/2014/04/28/what-we-left-behind; Harith Hasan Al-Qarawee, "Iraq's Sectarian Crisis: A Legacy of Exclusion," Carnegie Middle East Center, April 30, 2014, https://carnegieendowment.org/files/iraq_sectarian_crisis.pdf; and "Renewed Violence in Iraq," Council on Foreign Relations, August 9, 2012, https://www.cfr.org/report/renewed-violence-iraq.

44 "Sectarian violence and then terrorism escalated": Prashant Rao, "Increase in Iraq Executions Draws International Ire," Agence France-Presse, December 31, 2013.

44 "some wanted as many as 55,000 American troops": Robert M. Gates, *Duty: Memoirs of a Secretary at War* (New York: Knopf, 2014), 324–25.

44 "to hold the country together": A former assistant to Vice President Biden writes: "It was not for lack of trying. I worked for Vice President Biden at the time; he had Iraqi political leaders on speed-dial and traveled to Iraq multiple times in the first Obama term. For his part, President Obama spoke or met with Prime Minister

Maliki three times in 2011. The politics were just too hard for the
leaders in Baghdad, who were highly sensitive to sovereignty concerns after eight years of a sizable American presence." See Brian P.
McKeon, "False Comparisons: Obama's Military Withdrawal from
Iraq and Trump's Syria Disengagement," Just Security, December
21, 2018, https://www.justsecurity.org/61991/false-comparisons
-obamas-military-withdrawal-iraq-trumps-syria-disengagement/.

44 "Leon Panetta would later write": Panetta, *Worthy Fights*, 393–94.

44 "Obama's fault for leaving too soon": "U.S. Presidential Hope-
fuls Bush, Clinton Spar over Iraq," RFE/RL, August 12, 2015,
https://www.rferl.org/a/us-presidential-hopefuls-bush-clinton
-spar-over-iraq/27184366.html.

44 "Candidate Obama had said": Barack Obama cited then chairman
of the Joint Chiefs Admiral Mike Mullen, saying that "sufficient
resources" wouldn't be available to "finish the job" in Afghanistan until the United States reduced its "commitment to Iraq."
See "Obama's Remarks on Iraq and Afghanistan," *New York Times*,
July 15, 2008, https://www.nytimes.com/2008/07/15/us/politics
/15text-obama.html.

44 "committing himself to Afghanistan over Iraq": "Obama's Remarks
on Iraq and Afghanistan," *New York Times*, July 15, 2008, https://
www.nytimes.com/2008/07/15/us/politics/15text-obama.html.

44 "was 'Bush's war'": Obama's Deputy National Security Advisor
Ben Rhodes wrote that Iraq "was a marker of a different era." See
Ben Rhodes, *The World as It Is: A Memoir of the Obama White House*
(New York: Random House, 2018), 171.

44 "the greatest strategic blunder in recent foreign policy": Barack
Obama, "My Plan for Iraq," *New York Times*, July 14, 2008, https://
www.nytimes.com/2008/07/14/opinion/14obama.html. See also
Rhodes, *The World as It Is*, 171–72.

44 "Obama agreed to two packages of an additional 30,000 troops":
The comprehensive "New Strategy for Afghanistan and Pakistan,"
released in March 2009, promised that the area would never again
become "a base for terrorists who want to kill as many of our
people as they possibly can." See "Remarks by the President on
a New Strategy for Afghanistan and Pakistan," The White House
March 27, 2009.

44 "Obama pressured a reluctant NATO": "Almost none of the
[NATO] leaders want to do this . . . ," Ben Rhodes writes of
Obama's discussions with NATO leaders. And Obama told him
on his first trip to Europe that he felt like he was "spending all

of my political capital just to keep things going," not seeing any change in policy. See Rhodes, *The World as It Is*, 41.

45 "2,200 soldiers in this first fight": Total U.S. military casualties in Afghanistan for Operation Enduring Freedom and Freedom's Sentinel totaled 2,448 people killed. An additional 131 military personnel were killed in this operation outside Afghanistan. See "Casualty Status as of 10 a.m. EDT Aug. 31, 2020," Department of Defense, https://dod.defense.gov/News/Casualty-Status/.

45 "spent close to $700 million": Even by the Pentagon's accounting, Operation Enduring Freedom cost $686 billion, totaling 43 percent of the budget for war operations following 9/11. See Amy Belasco, "The Cost of Iraq, Afghanistan, and Other Global War on Terror Operations Since 9/11," Congressional Research Service, December 8, 2014.

45 "Obama promised": "Remarks by the President on the Way Forward in Afghanistan," The White House, June 22, 2011, https://obamawhitehouse.archives.gov/the-press-office/2011/06/22/remarks-president-way-forward-afghanistan.

45 "the Obama administration watched": "Gaddafi Vows to Crush Protesters," Al Jazeera, February 26, 2011, https://www.aljazeera.com/news/africa/2011/02/2011225165641323716.html.

45 "'the last thing that President Obama wanted to do'": Panetta, *Worthy Fights*, 381.

45 "under Arab League and United Nations cover": Martin S. Indyk, Kenneth G. Lieberthal, and Michael E. O'Hanlon, "Obama's Foreign Policy: Progressive Pragmatist," Brookings Institution, March 9, 2012, https://www.brookings.edu/opinions/obamas-foreign-policy-progressive-pragmatist/; and Panetta, *Worthy Fights*, 380.

45 "Fighting was limited to airpower alone": Panetta, *Worthy Fights*, 381.

45 "'Everything went right,'" Obama said": Rhodes, *The World as It Is*, 159, 239; and Panetta, *Worthy Fights*, 380.

45 "the usual fretting in the Obama camp": Rhodes, *The World as It Is*, 198.

45 "'it's a question of when'": The White House, "Press Conference by the President," The White House, March 6, 2012, https://obamawhitehouse.archives.gov/the-press-office/2012/03/06/press-conference-president.

46 "said General Martin Dempsey, chairman of the Joint Chiefs": Rhodes, *The World as It Is*, 197, 223–26, 229.

46 "by then spent $35 billion 'training and assisting' the Iraqi armed forces": William D. Hartung, Arms and Security Project

at the Center for International Policy, "Arming Iraq: From Aid
to Sales 2005 to 2012," n.d. (2012), https://watson.brown.edu
/costsofwar/files/cow/imce/papers/2013/Arming%20Iraq-%20
From%20Aid%20to%20Sales%2C%202005%20to%202012.pdf.

46 "obliged and again sent forces back": Tim Arango, "U.S. Troops,
Back in Iraq, Train a Force to Fight ISIS," *New York Times*, December 31, 2014, https://www.nytimes.com/2014/12/31/world/
us-troops-back-in-iraq-train-a-force-to-fight-isis.html.

46 "'We will degrade'": "President Obama: "We Will Degrade and
Ultimately Destroy ISIL," The White House, September 10, 2014,
https://obamawhitehouse.archives.gov/blog/2014/09/10/president
-obama-we-will-degrade-and-ultimately-destroy-isil.

46 "Obama took pains to declare": The White House, September 10,
2014, https://obamawhitehouse.archives.gov/the-press-office
/2014/09/10/statement-president-isil-1.

48 "Obama wrote to Congress": "Letter from the President—War
Powers Resolution," The White House, June 12, 2014, https://
obamawhitehouse.archives.gov/the-press-office/2014/06/12
/letter-president-war-powers-resolution.

48 "in ten countries": Afghanistan, Cameroon, Djibouti, Iraq, Jordan,
Libya, Niger, Somalia, Syria, and Turkey.

Not named were Azerbaijan, Ethiopia, Kuwait, Lebanon,
Oman, Saudi Arabia, or any of the Gulf States (Bahrain, Qatar, and
the United Arab Emirates) from which air and special operations
were also being mounted. U.S. military forces were also known to
be operating at that time in Chad, Kenya, Mali, and Mauritania.
Forces deployed to Uganda, Obama said in his December 2016
letter, had been redeployed to Djibouti.

48 "Obama wrote to Congress in his last month in office": "Letter
from the President—Supplemental 6-month War Powers Letter;
Text of a Letter from the President to the Speaker of the House
of Representatives and the President Pro Tempore of the Senate,"
The White House, December 5, 2016, https://obamawhitehouse
.archives.gov/the-press-office/2016/12/05/letter-president-supp
lemental-6-month-war-powers-letter.

48 "doing didn't rise to the legal definition of 'war'": "Authority to
Order Targeted Airstrikes Against the Islamic State of Iraq and the
Levant," Department of Justice, Office of Legal Counsel, December 30, 2014, https://www.justice.gov/olc/opinion/authority
-order-targeted-airstrikes-against-islamic-state-iraq-and-levant.

49 "CIA divulged that it had undertaken": Director of National

Intelligence, "Summary of Information Regarding U.S. Counter-terrorism Strikes Outside Areas of Active Hostilities," n.d. (2017), between January 20, 2009 and January 19, 2017.

49 "'that we have successfully pursued'": "Statement by the President on ISIL," The White House, September 10, 2014, https://obamawhitehouse.archives.gov/the-press-office/2014/09/10/statement-president-isil-1.

49 "hopeful Obama of 2007 promised five goals": "Obama's Remarks on Iraq and Afghanistan," *New York Times*, July 15, 2008, https://www.nytimes.com/2008/07/15/us/politics/15text-obama.html.

50 "he would address global challenges from poverty to climate change": Barack Obama, "Renewing American Leadership," *Foreign Affairs*, July/August 2007, https://www.foreignaffairs.com/articles/2007-07-01/renewing-american-leadership.

51 "'We cannot use force everywhere'": "Remarks by the President at the National Defense University," The White House, May 23, 2013, https://obamawhitehouse.archives.gov/the-press-office/2013/05/23/remarks-president-national-defense-university.

51 "strength was more than 'bellicose words and shows of military force'": "Remarks by President Obama to the United Nations General Assembly," The White House, September 28, 2015, https://obamawhitehouse.archives.gov/the-press-office/2015/09/28/remarks-president-obama-united-nations-general-assembly.

51 "Gates repeatedly complained": Gates, *Duty*, 282.

   The Pentagon bureaucracy is notorious. James Forrestal, who served as the first secretary of defense, once famously joked that "the peacetime mission of the Armed Services is to destroy the Secretary of Defense." Quoted in Charles A. Stevenson, *SECDEF: The Nearly Impossible Job of Secretary of Defense* (Dulles, VA: Potomac Books, 2006). Donald Rumsfeld, who returned to be secretary for a second time in the Bush administration, and who one might have thought would be a master at taming them, labeled the Pentagon "an adversary that poses a . . . serious threat to the security of the United States," adding that it was "the world's last bastion of central planning . . . that stifles free thought and crushes new ideas." See Donald Rumsfeld, *Known and Unknown* (New York: Sentinel, 2011), 333.

51 "just move forward on autopilot": Bob Woodward, *Obama's Wars* (New York: Simon & Schuster, 2010), 37.

51 "'We, the people'": "Inaugural Address by President Barack Obama," The White House, January 21, 2013; https://obama

whitehouse.archives.gov/the-press-office/2013/01/21
/inaugural-address-president-barack-obama.

chapter five SIPPING TEA AND SWAPPING T-SHIRTS

55 "like other reserve components": In the U.S. military of 2019–2020,
reservists constitute 38 percent. This is calculated based on 1,317,063
total active members of the armed service plus an additional 800,183
"selected" reservists as of March 31, 2019. The three components of
the Army are the active Army, the Army National Guard, and the
Army Reserve. See Defense Manpower Data Center, DOD Personnel, Workforce Reports & Publications, March 31, 2019, https://
www.dmdc.osd.mil/appj/dwp/dwp_reports.jsp. See also Department of Defense, "Defense Manpower Requirements Report, Fiscal
Year 2019," June 7, 2018; and Lawrence Kapp and Barbara Salazar
Torreon, "Reserve Component Personnel Issues: Questions and Answers," Congressional Research Service, October 4, 2018.

55 "make up just over 50 percent of all Army forces in the Middle East": Staff Sergeant Matthew Britton, "USARCENT Hosts
Operation Spartan Shield Community of Excellence," National
Guard News, February 15, 2019, https://www.nationalguard
.mil/News/Article/1758925/usarcent-hosts-operation-spartan
-shield-community-of-excellence/.

55 "'total force' policy": "Army Total Force Policy," Department of
the Army, July 26, 2010, https://www.army.mil/article/42866
/army_total_force_policy.

55 "nor was the brigade mobilized to play any part in the fight against
ISIS": The 155th Brigade did send soldiers into Syria but only in
individual capacities and small groups, and ostensibly only in a
training capacity. The brigade did train Syrian surrogates fighting
Bashar al-Assad's regime and ISIS, but that training was conducted
in Kuwait and Jordan, not in Syria.

56 "'We've proudly represented Mississippi in past deployments and
will continue to do so now'": "National Guard's 155th Mobilize in
the Spring," *Mississippi Clarion-Ledger*, October 23, 2017, https://
www.clarionledger.com/story/news/local/2017/10/23/national
-guards-155th-mobilize-spring/791646001/.

56 "'combined forces contingency operation designed to deter and
react to possible threats within the Middle East region'": William
Moore, "'Dixie Thunder' Deployment: National Guard Preparing for Spring Deployment to Middle East," *Tupelo (MS) Daily*

Journal, March 9, 2018, https://www.djournal.com/news/national
-guard-preparing-for-spring-deployment-to-middle-east/article
_cfb0c76b-0b9c-57b1-a24b-b069d45a7af8.html.

57 "describes the mission as": "Task Force Spartan," U.S. Army Central, as of April 16, 2019, https://www.usarcent.army.mil/About
/Units/Task-Force-Spartan/.

57 "the budget says": *FY 2016 President's Budget: Justification for Component Contingency Operations Overseas Contingency Operation Transfer Fund (OCOTF),* Department of Defense (DOD), Contingency Operations (Base Budget), March 2015, 13.

58 "the Army's new label": In presenting the Army's "prevent, shape, win" construct that started the long road to a post perpetual war and counter-insurgency model, then chief of staff of the Army, General Raymond T. Odierno, wrote in 2011 that "we must be ready to win decisively and dominantly. If we do not, we pay the price in American lives. When MacArthur said, 'In war there is no substitute for victory,' he was making a plain statement of fact. Nothing else can approach what is achieved by winning, and the consequences of losing at war are usually catastrophic. With so much at stake, the American people will expect what they have always expected of us: to never lightly enter into such a terrible endeavor, but once there to win and win decisively." See General Raymond T. Odierno, Chief of Staff of the Army, "CSA Editorial: Prevent, Shape, Win," U.S. Army, December 16, 2011, https://
www.army.mil/article/71030/csa_editorial_prevent_shape_win.

58 "first tank-heavy brigade to deploy to the Middle East since the 2003 Second Gulf War": Sergeant Brittany Johnson, "155th Armored Brigade Combat Team Takes Over Operation Spartan Shield Mission," DVIDS, July 15, 2019, https://www.dvidshub
.net/news/284584/155th-armored-brigade-combat-team-takes
-over-operation-spartan-shield-mission; Kyle Rempfer, "This Is What Army Central Is Doing in Some of the 'Most Volatile and Contested' Parts of the World," *Army Times,* October 9, 2018, https://www.armytimes.com/news/your-military/2018/10/09
/this-is-what-army-central-is-doing-in-some-of-the-most-volatile
-and-contested-parts-of-the-world/; and Todd South, "Largest Guard Armored Unit Deployment in a Decade Wraps Up, an Even Bigger One Is on the Way," *Army Times,* April 15, 2019, https://www.armytimes.com/news/your-army/2019/04/15
/largest-guard-armored-unit-deployment-in-a-decade-wraps
-up-an-even-bigger-one-is-on-the-way/.

58 "brigade went to climate-controlled warehouses where their *wartime* stocks": Sergeant Brittany Johnson, "155 Draws Army Prepositioned Stock," DVIDS, July 3, 2018, https://www.dvidshub .net/news/283156/155-draws-army-prepositioned-stock.

60 "the 155th fanned out": For the 155th Brigade, those included the major exercises Desert Observer with Kuwait, Iron Union 8 with the United Arab Emirates (a command post exercise in Kuwait), Bright Star 18 in Egypt, Eastern Action 19 in Qatar, and Inferno Creek 19 in Oman. Soldiers in small groups also trained Iraqi, Jordanian, Kuwaiti, Saudi Arabian, and United Arab Emirates militaries.

60 "from Tajikistan in Central Asia, to Egypt in North Africa, to Oman on the Indian Ocean periphery": South, "Largest Guard Armored Unit Deployment in a Decade Wraps Up."

60 "strategic deterrence initiative": Ibid.

60 "'the most strategically important region in the world today'": Rempfer, "This Is What Army Central Is Doing in Some of the 'Most Volatile and Contested' Parts of the World."

61 "The *New York Times* used it to describe twenty-seven countries and regions in relation to U.S. national security. During that same time period, the *Washington Post* used it to describe twenty-two countries and regions": This is according to a digital keyword search of the newspaper archives, reviewing every article posted to NYTimes.com between January 1 and December 31, 2018. An entry was only counted if "strategic" was used as a direct description of the value of the location itself, e.g., "the strategic city of Ghazni," "China, a strategic rival," "Germany's strategic culture," or "Basra, a strategically important port." We repeated the same search for WashingtonPost.com.

63 "the so-called armored brigade combat teams": Each of these heavy brigades consists of seven battalions: three armor or mechanized infantry (so-called combined arms), one "cavalry" (an armored reconnaissance unit), one long-range artillery, one engineer, and one brigade support battalion. Maintenance and sustainment is the greatest weakness of the Army armored force; consequently each battalion itself contains its own maintenance and sustainment company. See "Armored Brigade Combat Team," December 1, 2016, U.S. Army, https:// www.army.mil/standto/2016-12-01; and Major Brett Lea, "1st Stryker Brigade Combat Team Converts to Armored Brigade,"

Army News Service, June 20, 2019, https://www.army.mil
/article/223475/1st_stryker_brigade_combat_team_converts
_to_armored_brigade.

63 "sixteen heavy brigades to cover the entire world": The Army has
thirty-one brigade combat teams (BCTs)—armored and mechanized, infantry, artillery, engineering, aviation, and other types—in
the active component and twenty-seven in the National Guard.
(There are none in the Army Reserve.) There are a combined
sixteen armored, nine mechanized, and thirty-three infantry
BCTs. See "Army Announces Conversion of Two Brigade Combat Teams," U.S. Army, September 20, 2018, https://www.army
.mil/article/211368/army_announces_conversion_of_two_brigade
_combat_teams. See also "The U.S. Military's Force Structure: A Primer," Department of the Army, 2016, https://www
.cbo.gov/sites/default/files/114th-congress-2015-2016/reports
/51535-fsprimerbreakoutchapter2.pdf; Colonel Dawson A. Plum-
mer, Major K. Derrick Rice, and Captain Horace H. Peek V,
"Force Modernization of the Armored Brigade Combat Team,"
U.S. Army: Fort Benning, Winter 2019, https://www.benning
.army.mil/Armor/eARMOR/content/issues/2019/Winter
/1Peek-Rice-Plummer19.pdf.

63 "only about a third of the people are even assigned to combat
units—that is, the fighting brigades": Roughly half are in support
units; the rest belong to units that perform various headquarters
and overhead functions.

64 "for every shooter in the field, there are twelve others who are
either in support positions or out of the fight": According to U.S.
Special Operations Command, as of February 2018, a total of
7,457 special operators were deployed around the world. At that
time the total of special operations forces was 71,900 men and
women in uniform, including the reserves, plus 6,700 government
civilians and an estimated 14,000 contractors for a grand total of
92,600 people. This 12-to-1 ratio does not even count that every
special operations "team"—that is, the smallest element—includes
20 percent communications and medical specialists. (In actuality,
an Army twelve-man Special Force A Team can include up to two
communicators and two medics, or 40 percent.)

64 "Mark Esper told *Defense News*": Jen Judson, "Army Mulls
Pulling Back on Missions to Reduce Demand on Force," *Defense News*, February 15, 2018, https://www.defensenews.com

/land/2018/02/15/army-mulls-pulling-back-on-missions-to
-reduce-demand-on-force/.

66 "two years before Donald Trump was even president": Moore,
"'Dixie Thunder' Deployment."

chapter six BEYOND THE WAR MACHINE

69 "lower standards have cost more due to less capability and greater
attrition": "Army leadership lowered standards from FY 2005–
2008, while swelling pay and benefit packages. As a result, first
term attrition appreciated by 3.4 percent, costing the Army at
least 13.7 billion dollars over six years." Quote in Major Colby
K. Krug, "Sustaining the Quality of the All-Volunteer Force: A
Cost-Effective Approach," SAMS Monograph, Army Command
and General Staff College, May 2016, https://apps.dtic.mil/dtic
/tr/fulltext/u2/1022059.pdf.

69 "the Army doles out": The U.S. Army's FY 2020 Defense Budget submitted to Congress requested $191.397 billion, of which
$63.385 billion would be allocated to personnel.

69 "military's own polling shows": William M. Arkin, "Fewer Americans Want to Serve in the Military. Cue Pentagon Panic," *Guardian*, April 10, 2019, https://www.theguardian.com/commentis
free/2019/apr/10/fewer-americans-serve-military-pentagon
-panic.

69 "20 percent of the total of $750 billion goes for personnel": The
FY 2020 overall Defense budget requested $155.779 billion for
personnel out of the total $718.349 billion budget. That's 21.69
percent.

69 "costs about $8 billion annually": This is the total for all "family
support initiatives," including child care and youth programs ($1.4
billion), schools ($2.4 billion), commissary ($1.3 billion), "morale,
welfare and recreation" ($1.6 billion), and family services ($1.7
billion), which adds up to $8.4 billion.

69 "a draft would both enhance national security while even solving
many of the nation's nonmilitary problems": Bob Hennelly, "What
Does Memorial Day Mean to a Country Where One Percent Serve?,"
Salon, May 26, 2019, https://www.salon.com/2019/05/26/what
-does-memorial-day-mean-to-a-country-where-one-percent
-serve/; Jennifer Mittelstadt, "Ending the Draft Will Be Considered Unthinkable 50 Years from Now," Vox, April 3, 2019,
https://www.vox.com/2019/3/27/18185871/military-draft

-conscription; Gil Barndollar, "If We're Headed for Regime Change in Iran, Get Ready for a Military Draft. We'll Need One," *USA Today*, May 31, 2018, https://www.usatoday.com /story/opinion/2018/05/31/iran-regime-change-american -troops-military-draft-column/656240002/; Sean Mclain Brown, "Should the United States Reinstate the Draft?," Military.com, May 17, 2018, https://www.military.com/undertheradar/2018/05/17 /should-united-states-reinstate-draft.html; Daniel Barkhuff, "Want to Change Our Gun Culture and Stop Mass Shootings? Think About Bringing Back the Draft," Daily Beast, April 23, 2018, https://www.thedailybeast.com/want-to-change-our-gun -culture-and-stop-mass-shootings-think-about-bringing-back -the-draft; Major General Dennish Laich, "Should the U.S. Bring Back the Draft?," *New York Times* Upfront, January 8, 2018, https:// upfront.scholastic.com/issues/2017-18/010818/should-the-u-s -bring-back-the-draft.html#1150L; Sol Gittleman, "The Path to Peace: Bring Back the Draft," *Boston Globe*, November 4, 2017, https:// www.bostonglobe.com/opinion/letters/2017/11/04/the-path -peace-bring-back-draft/wa0YpXPuOLSb9WhDOzn0rI/story .html; Clyde Haberman, "John Kelly Suggests More Americans Should Have the Honor of Serving. He's Right," *New York Times*, October 24, 2017, https://www.nytimes.com/2017/10/24 /opinion/john-kelly-suggests-more-americans-should-have -the-honor-of-serving-hes-right.html?module=inline; Todd South, "Bringing Back the Draft," *Military Times*, July 25, 2017, https:// www.militarytimes.com/news/2017/07/25/bringing-back-the -draft/; Liel Leibovitz, "To Make America Great Again, Let's Bring Back the Draft," Tablet, April 21, 2017, https://www.tabletmag .com/jewish-news-and-politics/230393/bring-back-the-draft; and "Why Don't We Have Mandatory Military Service in the United States?," Quora, 2017, https://www.quora.com/Why-dont-we-have -mandatory-military-service-in-the-United-States (accessed May 28, 2019).

70 "seven out of ten young people": Miriam Jordan, "Recruits' Ineli-gibility Tests the Military," *Wall Street Journal*, June 27, 2014, https:// www.wsj.com/articles/recruits-ineligibility-tests-the-military -1403909945.

70 "wouldn't even be able to meet the requirements to be a soldier": Michelle Obama even bought into this notion, announcing in 2010 that she was throwing her support behind a national effort to improve physical fitness, citing numbers that indicated that too

many young people could not qualify for military service. "This epidemic . . . impacts the nation's security, as obesity is now one of the most common disqualifiers for military service. The physical and emotional health of an entire generation and the economic health and security of our nation is at stake," said Mrs. Obama. See "First Lady Michelle Obama Launches Let's Move: America's Move to Raise a Healthier Generation of Kids," The White House, February 9, 2010, https://obamawhitehouse.archives.gov /the-press-office/first-lady-michelle-obama-launches-lets-move -americas-move-raise-a-healthier-genera.

73   "ten times the area covered by its World War I counterparts": In World War II, just 36 soldiers covered a full square kilometer. In World War I, they needed 404 men to defend the same amount of space.

74   "determine replenishment needs": Historically, how close troops stood to each other had the greatest impact on how many of them got killed. A total of 342,785 U.S. ground force troops (including the Army Air Forces) died in World War II; another 634,068 were wounded. It's an enormous number, though greatly reduced from World War I ratios due to less geographic density, even with the greater lethality of forces.

In World War I, 117,000 American soldiers died, but overall 9 million soldiers died, the vast majority of them German and Russian. Trench warfare and chemical weapons, as well as French introduction of mechanized armor, had the biggest impact in the death of soldiers per square kilometer. All of these numbers are derived from Trevor N. Dupuy, *The Evolution of Weapons and Warfare* (New York: Bobbs-Merrill, 1980) and other papers of Dupuy's Historical Evaluation Research Organization (HERO).

79   "With the cloud and with soldier-level computing devices, it's not so far away": Michelle Tan, "Army Unveils New Plan to 'Win in a Complex World,'" *Army Times*, November 13, 2014, http:// archive.armytimes.com/article/20141013/NEWS/310130024/.

79   "some 2.77 million service members served overseas": Jennie W. Wenger, Caolionn O'Connell, and Linda Cottrell, "Examination of Recent Deployment Experience Across the Services and Components," RAND Corporation, March 2018, https://www.rand .org/pubs/research_reports/RR1928.html.

79   "At no time were there more than 165,000 troops inside Iraq": The exact number was 165,607 U.S. armed forces personnel. But that does not include another 154,825 private contractors,

including 26,869 U.S. nationals contractors. See "Department of Defense Contractor and Troop Levels in Afghanistan and Iraq: 2007–2018," Congressional Research Service, May 10, 2019. See also Chairman of the Joint Chiefs of Staff Navy Admiral Mike Mullen, "Department of Defense News Briefing with Admiral Michael Mullen at the Pentagon, Arlington, Va.," U.S. Dept. of Defense, November 17, 2008, https://archive.defense.gov/Transcripts /Transcript.aspx?TranscriptID=4318.

80 "At no time were there more than 102,000 soldiers in Afghanistan": Note that peak Afghanistan deployment was a different year than peak Iraq deployment. As of September 2011, U.S. Defense had 102,077 personnel in Afghanistan. See "Counts of Active Duty and Reserve Service Members and APF Civilians: By Location Country, Personnel Category, Service and Component," Defense Manpower Data Center, September 30, 2011. See also Amy Belasco, "Troop Levels in the Afghan and Iraq Wars, FY 2001–FY 2012: Cost and Other Potential Issues," Congressional Research Service, July 2, 2009.

According to the Congressional Research Service, "In late 2017, the DOD stopped reporting the number of U.S. military personnel deployed in support of operations in Afghanistan, Iraq, and Syria as part of its quarterly manpower reports and in other official releases." See "Department of Defense Contractor and Troop Levels in Afghanistan and Iraq: 2007–2018," Congressional Research Service, May 10, 2019.

chapter seven WAR PLAYS OUT IN KOREA

82 "at the very moment Japanese prime minister Shinzo Abe was meeting with the new president in Florida": Ju-min Park, "New Nuclear-Capable Missile Test a Success, North Korea Says," Reuters, February 12, 2017, https://www.reuters.com/article/us-north korea-missiles-nk-idUSKBN15R10O.

82 "Trump said in a statement": Kanga Kong and Isabel Reynolds, "North Korean Nuclear Ambitions to Be Defining Issue for Trump," Bloomberg News, February 11, 2019.

82 "two underground nuclear tests and fired two dozen missiles of various types": "Military and Security Developments Involving the Democratic People's Republic of Korea: Report to Congress," Office of the Secretary of Defense, December 15, 2017.

82 "in a 2017 New Year's address": Kim Jong Un, "Kim Jong Un's

2017 New Year's Address," The National Committee on North Korea, January 2, 2017, https://www.ncnk.org/sites/default/files /KJU_2017_New_Years_Address.pdf.

83 "he said, evoking the darkest possible picture": Andrew Rafferty, "Panetta: Trump Is Risking Nuclear War with North Korea," NBC News, April 14, 2017, https://www.nbcnews.com/politics /politics-news/panetta-warns-trump-be-careful-north-korea -n746666.

83 "said then chairman of the Joint Chiefs of Staff General Joseph Dunford": Jim Garamone, "U.S. Doesn't Have Luxury of Choosing Challenges, Dunford Tells Aspen Crowd," DOD News, July 23, 2017, http://www.jcs.mil/Media/News/News-Display /Article/1255656/us-doesnt-have-luxury-of-choosing-challenges -dunford-tells-aspen-crowd/.

84 "how two U.S. Army officers recently described North Korea": Captain Joseph Schmid and Captain Adam Wilson Jr., U.S. Army, "Calling for Improvements on US Army's Cannon Artillery," *Fires: A Joint Publication for U.S. Artillery Professionals*, November– December 2017, https://sill-www.army.mil/fires-bulletin-archive /archives/2017/nov-dec/nov-dec.pdf.

84 "wrote *Forbes* magazine": Niall McCarthy, "Why the North Korean Artillery Factor Makes Military Action Extremely Risky," *Forbes*, October 2, 2017, https://www.forbes.com/sites /niallmccarthy/2017/10/02/why-the-north-korean-artillery -factor-makes-military-action-extremely-risky-infographic/#3b 5f3938317e.

84 "the *New York Times* reported": Motoko Rich, "In North Korea, 'Surgical Strike' Could Spin into 'Worst Kind of Fighting,'" *New York Times*, July 5, 2017, https://www.nytimes.com/2017/07/05 /world/asia/north-korea-south-us-nuclear-war.html.

84 "Another news report": Rei, "North Korean Artillery and the Concept of 'Flattening Seoul'—a Breakdown," Daily Kos, April 25, 2017, https://www.dailykos.com/stories/2017/4/25 /1656090/-North-Korean-artillery-and-the-concept-of -flattening-Seoul-a-breakdown.

This 500,000 number seems to derive from a Department of Defense report, *2000 Report to Congress Military Situation on the Korean Peninsula.* That report states: "North Korea fields an artillery force of over 12,000 self-propelled and towed weapon systems. Without moving any artillery pieces, the North could sustain up to 500,000 rounds an hour against Combined Forces Command defenses for several hours. The artillery force includes 500 long-range systems deployed over the past decade. The proximity of these long-range systems to the demilitarized zone (DMZ) threatens all of Seoul with devastating attacks." *2000 Report to Congress Military Situation on the Korean Peninsula,* Department of Defense, September 12, 2000, https://archive.defense.gov/news/Sep2000/korea09122000.html.

84 "Congressional Research Service gave credence": "The North Korean Nuclear Challenge: Military Options and Issues for Congress," Congressional Research Service, November 6, 2017.

84 "'the fourth-largest conventional military in the world'": "Statement of Admiral Harry B. Harris Jr., U.S. Navy, Commander, U.S. Pacific Command, Before the House Armed Services Committee on U.S. Pacific Command Posture, 14 February 2018," https://docs.house.gov/meetings/AS/AS00/20180214/106847/HHRG-115-AS00-Wstate-HarrisJrH-20180214.pdf.

85 "Saddam was said to have": Jack Anderson and Dale Van Atta, "Saddam Pulls Back Elite Forces," *Washington Post,* November 5, 1990, https://www.washingtonpost.com/archive/lifestyle/1990/11/05/saddam-pulls-back-elite-forces/c45adf43-b9f7-4c29-9d3f-6cbf033faa27/?utm_term=.65d53f60fab9. See also Elaine Sciolino, "Arab of Vast Ambition: Saddam Hussein," *New York Times,* August 5, 1990, https://www.nytimes.com/1990/08/05/world/arab-of-vast-ambition-saddam-hussein.html.

86 "just for 'effect'": "It's a great psychological effect," former B-52 crew member Major Dick Cole said. "You scare the hell out of them." See Joseph B. Treaster, "Bombers: Giant B-52 Grows Old Virulently," War in the Gulf: U.S. Aims and Achievements, *New York Times,* January 22, 1991, https://www.nytimes.com/1991/01/22/world/war-in-the-gulf-bombers-giant-b-52-grows-old-virulently.html.

88 "stated most succinctly": "Statement by Secretary of Defense Jim Mattis," U.S. Dept. of Defense, August 9, 2017, https://www.defense.gov/News/News-Releases/News-Release-View/Article/1273247/statement-by-secretary-of-defense-jim-mattis/.

89 "approximately 600—are long-range enough to hit the metropolitan area": These include self-propelled 170mm guns and some 200 large-caliber (240mm and 300mm) multiple-launch rocket systems.

90 "When North Korea assembled about 400 of these guns": "Military and Security Developments Involving the Democratic

People's Republic of Korea: Report to Congress," Office of the Secretary of Defense, December 15, 2017. See also "North Korea Uses Live Fire Exercise to Display Military Might," BBC News, April 28, 2017, https://www.bbc.com/news/av/world -asia-39743574/north-korea-uses-live-fire-exercise-to-display -military-might.

90   "an even greater number of guns failed": Schmid and Wilson, "Calling for Improvements on US Army's Cannon Artillery."

90   "killing two South Korean marines and two civilians": Joseph S. Bermudez Jr., "The Yŏnp'yŏng-Do Incident, November 23, 2010," *38 North*, January 11, 2011, https://www.38north.org /wp-content/uploads/2011/01/38North_SR11-1_Bermudez _Yeonpyeong-do.pdf.

90   "wildly off the mark": The longer range 300mm KN-09, with a range of up to 200 km (125 miles), though being the only significant new ground forces weapon introduced in the 2010's, exists in only small numbers. The South Korean Ministry of National Defense 2016 White Paper says that North Korea possesses only about 10 operational launchers.

90   "were duds and failed to explode": Joseph S. Bermudez Jr., "The Yŏnp'yŏng-Do Incident, November 23, 2010," *38 North*, January 11, 2011, https://www.38north.org/wp-content/uploads /2011/01/38North_SR11-1_Bermudez_Yeonpyeong-do.pdf.

92   "he was 'confident'": Cheryl Pellerin, "U.S., South Korean Military Leaders Reinforce Alliance," U.S. Dept. of Defense, August 24, 2017, https://dod.defense.gov/News/Article/Article/1288096 /us-south-korean-military-leaders-reinforce-alliance/. Notes.docx. By "defended area," Admiral Harris meant South Korea, the United States, U.S. territories, and U.S. bases in Japan and Guam.

92   "have built is a multilayered ballistic missile defense system": *Missile Defense Review 2019*, Office of the Secretary of Defense, n.d., https://www.defense.gov/Portals/1/Interactive/2018/11 -2019-Missile-Defense-Review/The%202019%20MDR_Exe cutive%20Summary.pdf. See also "Republic of Korea—Aegis Combat System," Defense Security Cooperation Agency, June 9, 2015, https://www.dsca.mil/major-arms-sales/republic -korea-aegis-combat-system; "Japan—Aegis Weapon System Upgrade," Defense Security Cooperation Agency, December 10, 2012, https://www.dsca.mil/major-arms-sales/japan-aegis-weapon -system-upgrade; and Jeffrey W. Hornung, "Japan's Aegis Ashore Defense System," RAND Corporation, August 20, 2018, https://

www.rand.org/blog/2018/08/japans-aegis-ashore-defense
-system.html.

92 "South Korea also has two other indigenously made surface-to-air missiles": Finally, ground-based interceptor missiles in Alaska can intercept long-range ballistic missiles at their apogee, traveling roughly 15,000 miles per hour in space and maneuvering to collide with North Korean warheads.

92 "According to the Missile Defense Agency": Cheryl Pellerin, "Missile Defense Agency Budget Addresses Escalating North Korea, Iran Threats," U.S. Dept. of Defense, April 14, 2016, https://www.defense.gov/News/Article/Article/721122/missile -defense-agency-budget-addresses-escalating-north-korea -iran-threats/.

93 "was reportedly successful": Aegis was successfully tested on October 20, 2015; December 10, 2015; February 3, 2017; and October 15, 2017. There were three more successes, on September 11, 2018; October 26, 2018; and December 10, 2018, but it failed in tests on November 1, 2015; June 21, 2017; and January 31, 2018. See "Navy Aegis Ballistic Missile Defense (BMD) Program: Background and Issues for Congress," Congressional Research Service, updated April 25, 2019.

93 "MDA claimed": "Terminal High Altitude Area Defense (THAAD)," Missile Defense Agency, https://www.mda.mil/system/thaad .html (accessed on May 20, 2019).

93 "according to the manufacturer": "Patriot Saves Lives by Downing More Than 100 Ballistic Missiles in Combat," Raytheon, May 2, 2017, raytheon.mediaroom.com/2017-05-02-Patriot-saves-lives -by-downing-more-than-100-ballistic-missiles-in-combat. See also Tom Kington, "Raytheon Touts Patriot Anti-Missile Performance in Yemen War," *Defense News*, July 12, 2016, https://www .defensenews.com/digital-show-dailies/farnborough /2016/07/12/raytheon-touts-patriot-anti-missile-performance -in-yemen-war/.

93 "both of them part of the counter-battery network": Eighth Army, "CONUS based artillery unit conducts live fire mission," U.S. Army, September 22, 2017, https://www.army.mil /article/194245/conus_based_artillery_unit_conducts_live_fire _mission.

94 "Army major Jeremy F. Linney bragged": Sergeant Brandon A. Bednarek, 210th Field Artillery Brigade Public Affairs, "Rotational MLRS Battalion Arrives in Korea," U.S. Army, June 1 2015,

https://www.army.mil/article/149591/rotational_mlrs_battal
ion_arrives_in_korea.

94 "conventional wisdom is that the bunkers": Simon Scarr, Weiyi
Cai, Wen Foo, and Jin Juw, "North Korea's Other Threat," Re-
uters, May 26, 2017, http://fingfx.thomsonreuters.com/gfx/rngs
/NORTHKOREA-MISSILES/010041BR2VH/index.html.

96 "calling attention to Kim Jung Un's hapless conscript force":
Jim Garamone, "Troxell: U.S., South Korean Troops on DMZ
'Ready,'" U.S. Dept. of Defense, October 31, 2017, https://dod
.defense.gov/News/Article/Article/1358874/troxell-us-south-
korean-troops-on-dmz-ready/.

chapter eight THE POWER OF THE NETWORK

98 "the State Department assured": "Sweden—Patriot Configu-
ration-3+ Modernized Fire Units," Defense Security Cooperation Agency, News Release 18-01, February 20, 2018, https://
www.dsca.mil/major-arms-sales/sweden-patriot-configura
tion-3-modernized-fire-units.

98 "one commentator wrote": Dave Majumdar, "Sweden Wants
Lockheed Martin's Patriot PAC-3 Missile Defense System," *National Interest*, February 22, 2018, https://nationalinterest.org
/blog/the-buzz/sweden-wants-lockheed-martins-patriot-pac-3
-missile-defense-24610.

98 "said Swedish Defense minister Peter Hultqvist": Jay Nordliner,
"Sweden, Jolted Awake," *National Review*, January 3, 2018, https://
www.nationalreview.com/2018/01/defense-sweden-light
-threats-putins-russia/.

99 "Russian submarine was supposedly detected": "Sweden Says Has
Proof of Foreign Submarine Intrusion in October," Reuters, November 14, 2014, https://www.reuters.com/article/us-sweden
-submarine-idUSKCN0IY0U720141114.

99 "Some defense commentators argued that": Dave Majumdar,
"Sweden Wants Lockheed Martin's Patriot PAC-3 Missile Defense System," *National Interest*, February 22, 2018, https://national
interest.org/blog/the-buzz/sweden-wants-lockheed-martins
-patriot-pac-3-missile-defense-24610.

99 "directly threatened the country": Kaliningrad (54.7065° N,
20.511° E) to Stockholm (59.3326° N, 18.0649° E) is 333 miles
as the crow flies.

99 "Opponents fretted about": Gerard O'Dwyer, "Patriot System

Gets Caught Up in Swedish Politics," *Defense News*, July 6, 2018, https://www.defensenews.com/global/europe/2018/07/06 /patriot-system-gets-caught-up-in-swedish-politics/.

100 "incorporated into the same army, if only in name": That coalition included Argentina, Australia, Bahrain, Bangladesh, Belgium, Canada, Czechoslovakia, Denmark, Egypt, France, Greece, Hungary, Italy, Kuwait, Morocco, Netherlands, New Zealand, Niger, Norway, Oman, Pakistan, Poland, Qatar, Saudi Arabia, Senegal, South Korea, Spain, Sweden, Syria, United Arab Emirates, the United Kingdom, and the United States.

101 "later it joined the American-led coalition against ISIS": "79 Partners United in Ensuring Daesh's Enduring Defeat," Global Coalition, https://theglobalcoalition.org/en/partners/ (accessed on May 13, 2019). See also "Sweden," Operation Inherent Resolve, March 16, 2016, https://www.inherentresolve.mil/About-CJTF -OIR/Coalition/Coalition-Display/Article/695786/sweden/.

101 "Officially the country": "Current International Missions" (as of October 2017), Swedish Armed Forces.

101 "to fight pirates": "Somalia (EUNAVFOR)," Swedish Armed Forces, n.d. (2019), https://www.forsvarsmakten.se/en/archived -pages/about/our-mission-in-sweden-and-abroad/completed -operations/somalia-eunavfor/ (accessed May 11, 2019).

102 "Sweden participated in the international action in Libya": "Libya— UP," Swedish Armed Forces, n.d. (2019), https://www.forsvars makten.se/en/archived-pages/about/our-mission-in-sweden -and-abroad/completed-operations/libya-up/ (accessed May 11, 2019); and Heavy Airlift Wing, (HAW), "SAC Milestones 2006," Strategic Airlift Capability, n.d. (2019), https://www.sacprogram .org/en/Pages/SAC-Milestones-2006-.aspx (accessed May 11, 2019).

102 "Sweden even quietly dispatched": Tim Ripley, "Sweden Sends Surveillance Aircraft to Eastern Mediterranean," *Jane's Defence Weekly*, May 1, 2019, https://www.janes.com/defence-news/news -detail/sweden-sends-surveillance-aircraft-to-eastern-mediterranean ; and David Cenciotti, "Why Is a Swedish ELINT Aircraft Operating off Lebanon and Syria These Days?," The Aviationist, May 2, 2018, https://theaviationist.com/2018/05/02/why-is-a-swedish -elint-aircraft-operating-off-lebanon-and-syria-these-days.

102 "described itself as 'international by design'": Håkon Lunde Saxi, "The UK Joint Expeditionary Force (JEF)," IFS (Norway) Insights, May 2018, https://forsvaret.no/ifs/Publikasjoner /ifs-insights-kronologisk-(2010-)/saxi-the-uk-joint-expeditionary

-force-(jef). Sweden also hosted U.K. Royal Marines in an exercise, the first-ever major war game undertaken on its territory. Tim Ripley, "UK Royal Marines to Exercise in Sweden," *Jane's Defence Weekly*, February 14, 2019.

102 "earning its special status": Ryan C. Hendrickson, "History: Sweden's Partnership with NATO," NATO, July 1, 2007, https://www.nato.int/docu/review/2007/Military_civilian_divide/NATO_Sweden/EN/index.htm.

102 "'Our cooperation with NATO'": Nicholas Fiorenza, "'Trident Juncture' CPX Ends with NRF Certification," *Jane's Defence Weekly*, November 27, 2018; "Trident Juncture 18," Swedish Armed Forces, n.d. (2019), https://www.forsvarsmakten.se/en/activities/exercises/trident-juncture-18/ (accessed May 10, 2019).

104 "spends more money on weapons than any other country in the world": "Global Arms Trade: USA Increases Dominance; Arms Flows to the Middle East Surge, Says SIPRI," Stockholm International Peace Research Institute (SIPRI), March 11, 2019, https://www.sipri.org/media/press-release/2019/global-arms-trade-usa-increases-dominance-arms-flows-middle-east-surge-says-sipri.

104 "the top ten": "SIPRI Military Expenditure Database: Data for All Countries 1949–2018," Stockholm International Peace Research Institute (SIPRI), https://www.sipri.org/databases/milex (accessed on May 13, 2019).

105 "$151 billion worth of arms from the United States alone": The Congressional Research Service numbers add up to approximately $151.656 billion for the years 2000–2018, citing notifications to Congress and the Defense Security Cooperation Agency's *Historical Facts Book*. The total is calculated from $12.656 billion for 2000–2009 plus $139 billion for 2009–2018. See Christopher M. Blanchard, "Saudi Arabia: Background and U.S. Relations," Congressional Research Service, September 21, 2018 (with revisions). See also Clayton Thomas, "Arms Sales in the Middle East: Trends and Analytical Perspectives for U.S. Policy," Congressional Research Service, updated October 11, 2017.

105 "formed its own alliance of countries": Farea al-Muslimi, "On the Ground in Yemen: Q&A with Farea al-Muslimi," International Peace Institute: Global Observatory, July 23, 2018, https://theglobalobservatory.org/2018/07/on-the-ground-in-yemen-qa-with-farea-al-muslimi/.

105 "a disaster in every way": Daniel L. Byman, "Saudi Arabia and the United Arab Emirates Have a Disastrous Yemen Strategy," Brookings Institution, July 17, 2018, https://www.brookings.edu /blog/order-from-chaos/2018/07/17/saudi-arabia-and-the-united-arab-emirates-have-a-disastrous-yemen-strategy/; Gregory D. Johnsen, "No Clean Hands: Reaction and Counter-Reaction in the Iranian-Saudi Proxy War in Yemen," Just Security, November 21, 2018, https://www.justsecurity.org/61576/setting-record -straight-iran-saudi-arabias-proxy-war-yemen/; "Yemen Crisis: Why Is There a War?," BBC News, March 21, 2019, https://www .bbc.com/news/world-middle-east-29319423; and *Al-Qaida in the Arabian Peninsula (AQAP)*, Office of the Director of National Intelligence (ODNI) counter-terrorism guide.

105 "many paid mercenaries": Jeremy Binnie and Ashley Roque, "Unauthorised Weapons Transfer Report Fuels Debate over Washington-Riyadh Relations," *Janes Intelligence Weekly*, February 7, 2019, https://www.janes.com/article/86229/unauthorised-weapons -transfer-report-fuels-debate-over-washington-riyadh-relations; and Nima Elbagir, Salma Abdelaziz, Mohamed Abo El Gheit, and Laura Smith-Spark, "Sold to an Ally, Lost to an Enemy," CNN, February 2019, https://www.cnn.com/interactive/2019/02/middle east/yemen-lost-us-arms/.

105 "unable to seize or retain territory and unable to operate as a whole": "Saudi Arabia Can't Win Its Own Battles," War Is Boring, May 20, 2017, https://warisboring.com/saudi-arabia-cant-win -its-own-battles/; and Peter Salisbury, "The New Front in Yemen," *Foreign Affairs*, June 27, 2018, https://www.foreignaffairs.com /articles/middle-east/2018-06-27/new-front-yemen.

105 "unable to properly utilize precision weapons": "Saudi Military Helicopter Crashes in Yemen, Killing 12 Officers," Reuters, April 18, 2017, https://www.reuters.com/article/us-yemen -security-saudi-idUSKBN17K1W0. See also "Yemen's Houthi Rebels 'Shoot Down Apache Helicopter in Hodeida,'" The New Arab, March 17, 2017, https://www.alaraby.co.uk/english /news/2017/3/16/yemens-houthi-rebels-shoot-down-apache -helicopter-in-hodeida; and "Yemeni Forces Down Saudi Apache helicopter: Report," PressTV, June 1, 2018, https://www .presstv.com/Detail/2018/06/01/563519/Yemen-Saudi-Arabia -war-Apache-helicopter-drone-Hudaydah.

105 "the war drags on": Tristan Dunning, "Yemen—the 'Worst

Humanitarian Crisis in the World' Continues," Parliament of Australia, December 6, 2018, https://www.aph.gov.au/About _Parliament/Parliamentary_Departments/Parliamentary_Library /pubs/rp/rp1819/Yemen#_Toc531793286; and Dylan Welch, Kyle Taylor, and Dan Oakes, "Australian Army Veterans Advising Foreign Army Accused of War Crimes," Australian Broadcasting Corporation, December 14, 2018, https://www.abc.net.au /news/2018-12-14/australian-army-veterans-advising-foreign -army-accused-war-crime/10611142.

105 "One U.S. general calls it": Major General Margaret Woodward, "I Ran the Air War over Gaddafi. Here's Why the US Should Stop Backing the Yemen War," Defense One, February 27, 2019, https:// www.defenseone.com/ideas/2019/02/i-ran-air-war-over-gaddafi -heres-why-us-should-stop-backing-yemen-war/155198/.

105 "labels Saudi performance 'incompetent and cruel'": Byman, "Saudi Arabia and the United Arab Emirates Have a Disastrous Yemen Strategy."

105 "Former CIA analyst Ken Pollack": Kenneth M. Pollack, "The U.S. Has Wasted Billions of Dollars on Failed Arab Armies," *Foreign Policy*, January 31, 2019, https://foreignpolicy.com/2019/01/31 /the-u-s-has-wasted-billions-of-dollars-on-failed-arab-armies/.

105 "dependent on the U.S. Air Force for aerial refueling": In 2015 alone, the first full year of Saudi Arabia's Operation Restoring Hope, the U.S. Air Force operated sixty American aerial refueling tankers in Qatar, flying 14,700 sorties. That's an average of forty flights a day, the airplanes filling the gas tanks of twelve different nations' aircraft. Most of those missions were over Syria, Iraq, and Afghanistan, but the tankers also refueled Saudi and other Saudi coalition airplanes bombing Yemen. See Technical Sergeant Terrica Y. Jones, 379th Air Expeditionary Wing Public Affairs, "KC-135s Surpass 100,000 Combat Hours," U.S. Air Force, January 8, 2016, https://www.af.mil/News/Article -Display/Article/641977/kc-135s-surpass-100000-combat -hours/.

106 "dependent on U.S. intelligence for targeting information": There have also been reports that Israeli intelligence has assisted Saudi Arabia. See Jack Kennedy and Firas Modad, "Proposed US Legislation Unlikely to Affect Saudi Ability to Pursue Yemen Campaign or Crown Prince's Domestic Position," *Jane's Defence Weekly*, November 30, 2018, https://www.janes.com /article/84931/proposed-us-legislation-unlikely-to-affect-saudi

-ability-to-pursue-yemen-campaign-or-crown-prince-s
-domestic-position.

106 "one observer said": Missy Ryan, "As crisis intensifies, what's at stake in America's military partnership with Saudi Arabia?," *Washington Post*, October 12, 2018, https://www.washingtonpost.com /world/national-security/as-crisis-intensifies-whats-at-stake-in -americas-military-partnership-with-saudi-arabia/2018/10/12/ 3ce0994e-cd75-11e8-a3e6-44daa3d35ede_story.html?.

106 "stated matter-of-factly": Paul Iddon, "Saudi Arabia Can't Win Its Own Battles," War Is Boring, May 20, 2017, https://warisboring .com/saudi-arabia-cant-win-its-own-battles/.

106 "Even those elements that supposedly did perform": Rajiv Chandresekaran, "In the UAE, the United States has a quiet, potent ally nicknamed 'Little Sparta,'" *Washington Post*, November 9, 2014, https://www.washingtonpost.com/world/national -security/in-the-uae-the-united-states-has-a-quiet-potent-ally -nicknamed-little-sparta/2014/11/08/3fc6a50c-643a-11e4-836c -83bc4f26eb67_story.html. See also Taylor Luck, "New Arab Military Force to Reckon with as 'Little Sparta' rises," *Christian Science Monitor*, February 28, 2019, https://www.csmonitor.com/World /Middle-East/2019/0228/New-Arab-military-force-to-reckon -with-as-Little-Sparta-rises.

chapter nine CONVERGENCE

109 "a 'gold standard'": Evan Munsing and Christopher J. Lamb, "Joint Interagency Task Force–South: The Best Known, Least Understood Interagency Success," *Strategic Perspectives* 5 (Institute for National Strategic Studies, National Defense University), June 2011. http://ndupress.ndu.edu/Portals/68/Documents/stratper spective/inss/Strategic-Perspectives-5.pdf.

110 "'converging threat networks'": "About Us," Joint Interagency Task Force South, 2019, https://www.jiatfs.southcom.mil/ About-Us/.

110 "It is a nexus": Admiral Kurt W. Tidd, SOUTHCOM commander, closing reports at the National Defense University "Beyond Convergence" conference, October 18, 2016, https://www.southcom .mil/Media/Speeches-Transcripts/Article/1035575/adm-tidd -prepared-remarks-for-ndu-beyond-convergence-conference/.

111 "George Tenet . . . said in February 2002": *Current and Projected National Security Threats to the United States*, Hearing Before the Select

Committee on Intelligence of the United States Senate, 107th Congress, February 6, 2002, https://www.intelligence.senate.gov /hearings/current-and-projected-national-security-threats-united -states-february-6-2002. See also "DCI Worldwide Threat Briefing 2002: Converging Dangers in a Post 9/11 World," Testimony of Director of Central Intelligence George J. Tenet Before the Senate Armed Services Committee, Central Intelligence Agency, March 19, 2002, https://www.cia.gov/news-information/speeches -testimony/2002/dci_speech_02062002.html.

111 "he said, opened the way for future Al Qaedas": "Military Command Nominations," Senate Armed Services Committee, July 26, 2002, https://www.c-span.org/video/?171500-1/military-command -nominations.

111 "The convergence theory was that": "National Drug Control Strategy," The White House, February 2003, https://www.state .gov/documents/organization/17757.pdf.

111 "famously wrote": John Arquilla and David Ronfeldt, *Networks and Netwars: The Future of Terror, Crime, and Militancy*, RAND Corporation, 2001, 197, https://www.rand.org/pubs/monograph _reports/MR1382.html.

111 "'striking new and powerful alliances'": Joint Chiefs of Staff, *Countering Threat Networks*, Joint Publication 3-25, December 21, 2016, 88, https://www.jcs.mil/Portals/36/Documents/Doctrine/pubs /jp3_25.pdf.

112 "which identified nearly half of the sixty-three top drug-trafficking organizations": "Strategy to Combat Transnational Organized Crime," The White House, July 25, 2011, https://2009-2017.state .gov/p/us/rm/2011/169045.htm.

112 "officers and liaisons from more than twenty partner nations": Known countries include: Argentina, Brazil, Canada, Chile, Colombia, the Dominican Republic, Ecuador, El Salvador, France, Guatemala, Jamaica, Mexico, the Netherlands, Panama, Peru, Spain, and the United Kingdom.

112 "the Joint Chiefs of Staff later wrote": Joint Chiefs of Staff, *Countering Threat Networks*.

112 "The task force commander in 2017 stated": Claudia Sánches-Bustamante, "JIATF South, an Interagency and International Coalition with a Tactical Mission," Diálogo, April 5, 2017, https:// dialogo-americas.com/en/articles/jiatf-south-interagency-and international-coalition-tactical-mission.

113 "what its commander calls": Ibid.

113 "He said that JIATF South": Munsing and Lamb, "Joint Inter-agency Task Force–South," 1.

113 "Admiral Craig S. Faller credited the Task Force": Posture Statement of Admiral Craig S. Faller, Commander, United States Southern Command Before the 116th Congress, Senate Armed Services Committee, February 7, 2019, http://www.defense assistance.org/primarydocs/190207_sasc_southcom.pdf/.

114 "6 percent of the total": Ibid.

114 "a government best of the best": Inspector General, U.S. Dept. of Defense, *Independent Auditor's Report on the FY 2016 DoD Performance Summary Report for the Funds Obligated for National Drug Control Program Activities*, DODIG-2017-047, January 30, 2017, 13, https://media.defense.gov/2017/Jan/30/2001714313/-1/-1 /1/DODIG-2017-047.pdf; and U.S. Dept. of Defense, *FY 2015 DOD Counterdrug Performance Summary Report*, 10.

115 "A third of these 449 eyes-on cases got away": This is calculated as 449 – 318 = 131 misses or 29 percent.

115 "*This* is a 'success rate of 71 percent'": *FY 2017 Budget and Performance Summary, Companion to the National Drug Control Strategy*, Executive Office of the President of the United States, December 2016, 48–49, https://obamawhitehouse.archives.gov/sites/default/files/ondcp /policy-and-research/fy2017_budget_summary-final.pdf.

115 "Admiral Faller told Congress in early 2019": Posture Statement of Admiral Craig S. Faller, February 7, 2019.

116 "9.4 percent of the entire American population": "Drugfacts, Illicit Drug Use," NIH: National Institute on Drug Abuse, June 2015.

116 "$19 billion to $29 billion in annual revenue": *Joint Message from Assistant Secretary John Morton, U.S. Immigration and Customs Enforcement, and Director Grayling G. Williams, DGS Office of Counternarcotics Enforcement*, U.S. Department of Homeland Security, n.d. (2017), https://www.ice.gov/doclib/cornerstone/pdf/cps-study.pdf.

116 "*Country Reports on Terrorism*": "Country Reports on Terrorism 2017," U.S. Department of State, September 19, 2018, https:// www.state.gov/reports/country-reports-on-terrorism-2017/.

117 "State Department's list": "Terrorism Designations FAQs," U.S. Department of State, January 21, 2017, https://web.archive .org/web/20171125201335/https://www.state.gov/j/ct/rls/fs /fs/266912.htm.

117   "offered an estimate in 2018": Bruce Hoffman, "The Resurgence of Al-Qaeda," Lowy Institute, March 13, 2018, https://www .lowyinstitute.org/the-interpreter/resurgence-al-qaeda.

117   "on the path to defeat": Leon Panetta, *Worthy Fights: A Memoir of Leadership in War and Peace* (New York: Penguin Press, 2014), 400.

117   "A UN Security Council document estimated in 2018": "Overview of the Threat—Status of Islamic State in Iraq and the Levant," United Nations Security Council, July 27, 2018, 5, https:// undocs.org/pdf?symbol=en/s/2018/705.

117   "The State Department pegged the number at": Department of State, "Country Reports on Terrorism 2017," U.S. Department of State, September 19, 2018, https://www.state.gov/reports/country -reports-on-terrorism-2017/.

117   "the Pentagon said": Christopher M. Blanchard and Carla E. Humud, "The Islamic State and U.S. Policy," Congressional Research Service, updated September 25, 2018, https://fas.org/sgp/crs /mideast/R43612.pdf.

117   "Brett McGurk estimated": [Ambassador] Brett McGurk, "Combatting ISIS," C-Span, August 4, 2017, https://www.c-span .org/video/?432179-1/brett-mcgurk-briefs-reporters-combat ing-isis-state-department. See also Brett McGurk, Office of the Special Presidential Envoy for the Global Coalition to Counter ISIS, "Update on the D-ISIS Campaign," U.S. Department of State, December 11, 2018, https://www.state.gov/update-on-the -d-isis-campaign-2/.

117   "Defense Department inspector general said": Lead Inspector General /Report to the United States Congress, *Operation Inherent Resolve, Operation Pacific Eagle–Philippines*, U.S. Dept. of Defense, April 1, 2018–June 30, 2018, https://media.defense.gov/2018 /Aug/07/2001951441/-1/-1/1/FY2018_LIG_OCO_OIR3 _JUN2018_508.PDF.

117   "An estimated 5,600 ISIS fighters were estimated": Richard Barrett, "Beyond the Caliphate: Foreign Fighters and the Threat of Returnees," The Soufan Center, October 2017, https://the soufancenter.org/wp-content/uploads/2017/11/Beyond-the -Caliphate-Foreign-Fighters-and-the-Threat-of-Returnees -TSC-Report-October-2017-v3.pdf.

118   "The best estimate seems to be 7,000 to 9,000": "Country Reports on Terrorism 2017," U.S. Department of State, Department of State, September 19, 2018, https://www.state.gov/reports /country-reports-on-terrorism-2017/.

118 "At a conference . . . in March 2017": "Caribbean Regional Seminar on Countering Transregional-Transnational Threats, Summary Proceedings, Bridgetown, Barbados, 21–23 March 2017," William J. Perry Center for Hemispheric Defense Studies, *Proceedings*, 2017 edition, no. 1 (June), https://www.williamjperrycenter.org/sites/default/files/publication_associated_files/Proceedings%201.pdf.

118 "The Joint Chiefs of Staff affirmed this worldview": Joint Chiefs of Staff, *Countering Threat Networks*.

119 "nineteen different 'counter-campaigns'": These include Combating Trafficking in Persons (CTIP), Counter Corruption (CC), Counter Drug (CD), Counter Human Trafficking, Counter-IED (CIED), Counter–Improvised Threat (C-IT), Counter Insider Threat Program (CITP), Counter Insurgency Targeting Program (CITP), Counter Malign Foreign Influence, Counter Narcotics (CN), Counter Narco-Terrorism (CNT), Counter Piracy, Counter Proliferation, Counter Terrorism (CT), Counter Threat Finance (CTF), Counter Threat Network (CTN), Counter Transnational Organized Crime (CTOC), Counter Unmanned Aerial Systems (C-UAS), Counter Violent Extremism (CVE), and Countering WMD (CWMD).

119 "Defense Threat Reduction Agency": From the DTRA budget: "DTRA future transformation to a focus on counter threat networks. The Defense Threat Reduction Agency (DTRA) supports the nation's only Research, Development, Test & Evaluation (RDT&E) program focused specifically on combating and countering the threats posed by weapons of mass destruction (WMD), improvised explosive devices (IEDs), and asymmetric techniques, tactics, and procedures." *Defense Threat Reduction Agency, Fiscal Year (FY) 2019 Budget Estimates*, Research, Development, Test and Evaluation (RDT&E), U.S. Dept. of Defense, *Defense-Wide* 5 (February 2018), v.

119 "Joint Improvised-Threat Defeat Organization (JIDO) for IEDs": According to Pentagon documents, improvised threats include: Home-Made Explosives (HME), Vehicle-Borne IED (VBIED), Unmanned Aerial Systems (UAS), Vehicle-Attached IED (VAIED), Anti-Armor IED (AIED), Buried IED, Radio Controlled IED (RCIED), Person-Borne IED (PBIED), Booby Trapped Structures (BTS), Improvised WMD, Water-Borne IED (WBIED), and Tunnels.

More recently Counter-IED has been subsumed into Counter-Improvised Threat (C-IT), including even border tunnels, allowing the counterers to fight in the United States as well as overseas.

120   "Counter Malign Influence, and even renamed Counter Iran Threat Networks": "DTRA is uniquely positioned to support CCMDs to compete against adversaries short of armed conflict and to counter malign foreign influence where it is detrimental to U.S. interests," according to *Statement of Vayl Oxford, Director, Defense Threat Reduction Agency, Testimony Before the Subcommittee on Intelligence and Emerging Threats and Capabilities, House Armed Services Committee, April 3, 2019*, House Armed Services Committee, embargoed until April 3, 2019, at 2:30 p.m., https://docs.house.gov/meetings/AS/AS26/20190403/109251/HHRG-116-AS26-Bio-OxfordV-20190403.pdf.

120   "the Pentagon warns": "Central American Regional Countering Transregional-Transnational Threats Seminar, Antigua, Guatemala, 20–22 June 2017," William J. Perry Center for Hemispheric Defense Studies, *Proceedings*, 2017 edition, no. 2 (August), file:///C:/Downloads/803941.pdf.

120   "Pentagon marketers noted in their Caribbean presentation": "Caribbean Regional Seminar on Countering Transregional-Transnational Threats, Summary Proceedings, Bridgetown, Barbados, 21–23 March 2017."

121   "Other 'counter' campaigns that bubble up": See in particular, *2017–2017 Theater Strategy*, SOUTHCOM, April 4, 2017, https://www.southcom.mil/Portals/.../USSOUTHCOM_Theater_Strategy_Final.pdf; *Department of Homeland Security Strategic Plan, Fiscal Years 2012–2016*, Department of Homeland Security, February 2012, https://www.dhs.gov/sites/default/files/publications/DHS%20Strategic%20Plan.pdf; and Maria Kingsley, "Transnational Threats," in *Transregional Threats and Maritime Security Cooperation*, Center for Naval Analysis (CNA), DOP-2017-U-015955-Final-2, August 2017, 8, https://apps.dtic.mil/dtic/tr/fulltext/u2/1040063.pdf.

121   "Joint Chiefs of Staff said in a new 2018 manual": *Joint Operations*, Joint Chiefs of Staff, Joint Publication 3-0, January 17, 2017, incorporating change 1, October 2018.

122   "Army general Paul M. Nakasone . . . said": C. Todd Lopez, "Persistent Engagement, Partnerships, Top Cybercom's Priorities," U.S. Dept. of Defense, May 14, 2009, https://dod.defense.gov/News/Article/Article/1847823/persistent-engagement-partnerships-top-cybercoms-priorities/.

122   "saying in its *Summary of the 2018 National Defense Strategy*":

Summary of the 2018 National Defense Strategy of the United States of America: Sharpening the American Military's Competitive Edge, U.S. Dept. of Defense, n.d. (January 2018), The actual strategy is classified. Only the summary has been publicly released.

chapter ten A GLOBAL SECURITY INDEX

124 "Trump called the military leadership 'embarrassing'": Benjy Sarlin and Alex Seitz-Wald, "Donald Trump Praises Putin, Hillary Clinton Defends Email," NBC News, September 8, 2016, https:// www.nbcnews.com/politics/2016-election/trump-praises-putin -clinton-defends-email-n644621.

124 "he would fire Obama's generals": Jeremy Herb, "'Embarrassing to Our Country': Trump Suggests He'll Fire Top Generals," Politico, September 7, 2016, https://www.politico.com/story/2016/09 /trump-suggests-fire-the-generals-227862.

124 "Washington insiders had made the U.S. 'a mess'": Donald J. Trump, Twitter, August 9, 2016, https://twitter.com/realdonaldtrump /status/762981606755856384.

124 "called the nation's capital a 'swamp'": Donald J. Trump, Twitter, October 18, 2016, https://twitter.com/realdonaldtrump/status /788543616926912512.

124 "insulted national security leaders by name": Others included former Secretary of State (and retired Army general) Colin Powell; retired Marine Corps general John R. Allen, who commanded U.S. forces in Afghanistan; and former deputy director of the CIA Michael Morell. See Donald J. Trump, Twitter, July 29, 2016, https://twitter.com/realDonaldTrump/status /759024055123009536; and Donald J. Trump, Twitter, August 7, 2016, https://twitter.com/realDonaldTrump/status/7624253718 74557952. See also Jasmine C. Lee and Kevin Quealy, "The 598 People, Places and Things Donald Trump Has Insulted on Twitter: A Complete List," *New York Times*, May 24, 2019, https://www .nytimes.com/interactive/2016/01/28/upshot/donald -trump-twitter-insults.html.

124 "questioned the competence of U.S. intelligence": Trump, for instance, said that there wasn't enough evidence to hold Russia accountable for shooting down a commercial airliner over Ukraine the previous year. See Tal Kopan and Jim Sciutto, "Donald Trump Says Russia Isn't to Blame for MH17, Despite Evidence," CNN, October 15, 2015.

124 "he would approve of the use of torture": CIA director John Brennan even laid down the gauntlet publicly, telling NBC News that the Agency wouldn't engage in "enhanced interrogation"—torture —even if Trump were elected president. "I will not agree to carry out some of these tactics and techniques I've heard bandied about because this institution needs to endure," he said. Richard Engel and Robert Windrem, "Director Brennan: CIA Won't Waterboard Again—Even if Ordered by Future President," NBC News, April 10, 2016, https://www.nbcnews.com/news/us-news/director -brennan-cia-won-t-waterboard-again-even-if-ordered-n553756.

124 "wrote George W. Bush speechwriter David Frum": David Frum, "The Worst Security Risk in U.S. History," *Atlantic,* July 19, 2018, https://www.theatlantic.com/ideas/archive/2018/07/putin -trump/565604/.

124 "said a former Justice Department counterintelligence chief": "Trump 'a Clear and Present Danger': Former DOJ Counterintel Chief," MSNBC (*The Rachel Maddow Show*), January 14, 2019, https://www.msnbc.com/rachel-maddow/watch/trump -a-clear-and-present-danger-former-doj-counterintel-chief -1425919555601.

124 "Members of Congress introduced legislation": "Rep Lieu and Sen Markey Reintroduce Bill to Limit President's Ability to Launch Nuclear First Strike," Ted Lieu, Congressman for California's 33rd District, January 29, 2019, https://lieu.house.gov /media-center/press-releases/rep-lieu-and-sen-markey-reintroduce -bill-limit-president-s-ability.

125 "the world's most dangerous online persona": "The Most Dangerous People on the Internet in 2017," *Wired*, December 28, 2017, https://www.wired.com/story/most-dangerous-people-internet -2017/.

125 "entered the Arctic Circle for the first time since the fall of the Berlin Wall": Megan Eckstein, "Truman Strike Group Headed Home After 'Dynamic' Deployment," USNI News, December 11, 2018, https://news.usni.org/2018/12/11/truman-strike-group -headed-home-after-6th-fleet-dynamic-deployment; Megan Eckstein, "Truman CSG: Arctic Strike Group Operations Required Focus on Logistics, Safety," USNI News, November 6, 2018, https:// news.usni.org/2018/11/06/truman-strike-group-operating -in-arctic-circle-required-more-consideration-of-logistics-safety; "USS Harry S. Truman Strike Group Joins NATO for Trident Juncture," Navy News Service, October 25, 2018, https://www

.navy.mil/submit/display.asp?story_id=107550; "U.S. Forces Ready for NATO Exercise Trident Juncture 18," Navy News Service, October 22, 2018, https://www.navy.mil/submit/display .asp?story_id=107514; and "Harry S. Truman Strike Group Enters Arctic Circle, Prepares for NATO Exercise," Navy News Service, October 19, 2018, https://www.navy.mil/submit/display .asp?story_id=107489.

125 "the *Truman* and its full strike group": Petty Officer 3rd Class Thomas Gooley, "HST Strike Group Enters Arctic Circle, Prepares for NATO Exercise," DVIDS, October 19, 2018; https:// www.dvidshub.net/news/printable/297015.

126 "Russian defense minister Sergei Shoigu decried NATO military activity": "Russia threatens response to huge NATO exercise, says its new weapons will be unrivaled anywhere," Associated Press, October 25, 2018, https://www.militarytimes.com /news/your-military/2018/10/25/russia-threatens-response-to -huge-nato-exercise-says-its-new-weapons-will-be-unrivaled -anywhere/.

126 "Moscow instead announced that it would conduct its own . . . drill": "Russia Reacts to Trident Juncture 18," Warsaw Institute, November 1, 2018, https://warsawinstitute.org/russia -reacts-trident-juncture-18/.

126 "they sent two Tu-160 long-range bombers": "Russia Responds to NATO Drill in Its Backyard," TRT World, November 2, 2018, https://www.trtworld.com/europe/russia-responds-to-nato -drill-in-its-backyard-21298.

127 "cut off nineteen years from its forty-year year projected life span": Yasmin Tadjdeh, "BREAKING: New Trump Budget Cuts Navy Shipbuilding, Aircraft Procurement," *National Defense*, March 12, 2019, http://www.nationaldefensemagazine.org/articles /2019/3/12/just-in-new-trump-budget-reduces-navy-ship building-aircraft-procurement.

127 "said Elaine Luria": Megan Eckstein, "After Hearings, Lawmakers Call Truman Carrier Retirement Plan 'Ridiculous,'" U.S. Naval Institute News, March 28, 2019, https://news.usni.org/2019 /03/28/after-navy-hearings-lawmakers-still-call-truman-carrier -retirement-plan-ridiculous.

127 "He called the habit . . . 'faith-based'": Captain Robert C. Rubel, U.S. Navy (Retired), "Retiring the Truman Early Is a Necessary Strategic Decision," U.S. Naval Institute, *Proceedings* vol. 145/3/1,393 (March 2019), https://www.usni.org/magazines

/proceedings/2019/march/retiring-truman-early-necessary
-strategic-decision.

128 "wrote another bureaucratic fighter": Seth Cropsey, "Retiring
the USS Harry S. Truman Is a Terrible Idea," *National Review*,
April 8, 2019, https://www.nationalreview.com/2019/04/uss
-harry-s-truman-aircraft-carrier-retirement-terrible-idea/.

128 "sending Vice President Mike Pence to Norfolk": Ben Werner,
"Pence: No Early Retirement for USS Harry S. Truman," USNI
News, May 2, 2019, https://news.usni.org/2019/04/30/pence
-no-early-retirement-for-uss-harry-s-truman.

128 "He never mentioned Russia": The White House, "Remarks by
Vice President Pence to Crew Members of the USS Harry S.
Truman, Norfolk, VA," April 30, 2019, https://www.whitehouse
.gov/briefings-statements/remarks-vice-president-pence-crew
-members-uss-harry-s-truman-norfolk-va/.

130 "Clapper didn't disagree": Senate Armed Services Committee,
Hearing on "Global Threats," February 9, 2016, https://www
.c-span.org/video/?404436-1/james-clapper-testimony-global
-threats.

130 "there were fewer terrorist attacks and fewer people were killed
by terrorism than in 2016": There were 26,400 people killed in
10,900 terrorist attacks worldwide in 2017. That's a 27 percent
and 23 percent drop, respectively, when compared with 2016. See
"Global Terrorism in 2017: Background Report," START, National Consortium for the Study of Terrorism and Responses
to Terrorism, August 2018, https://www.start.umd.edu/pubs
/START_GTD_Overview2017_July2018.pdf. See also "Annex
of Statistical Information: Country Reports on Terrorism 2017,"
U.S. Department of State, September 2018, https://www.state
.gov/documents/organization/283097.pdf.

130 "fewer countries experiencing terrorism": In 2016, there were
terrorist attacks in 106 countries. In 77 of those countries at least
one citizen died from terrorism. In 2017 that number dropped to
attacks in 98 countries, with people dying in 67. See *Global Terrorism Index 2017*, Institute for Economics & Peace, November 2017,
visionofhumanity.org/app/uploads/2017/11/Global-Terrorism
-Index-2017.pdf. See also "2018 Global Terrorism Index Fact
Sheet," Institute for Economics & Peace, December 5, 2018.

130 "fewer hostage takings": In 2016, 15,500 people were taken hostage, compared with 8,900 in 2017. That's a year-over-year de-
crease of 43 percent. See *Annex of Statistical Information: Country*

Reports on Terrorism 2016, U.S. Department of State, July 2017, https://www.state.gov/wp-content/uploads/2019/04/National-consortium-2016.pdf; and *Annex of Statistical Information: Country Reports on Terrorism 2017*, U.S. Department of State, September 2018, https://www.state.gov/wp-content/uploads/2019/04/crt_national_consortium.pdf.

130 "A total of ninety-four countries became safer": By way of comparison with regard to terrorism, in 2016, seventy-six countries got safer and fifty-three countries had their security deteriorate, according to the Global Terrorism Index. See "Global Terrorism Index 2018," Institute for Economics & Peace, December 2018, visionofhumanity.org/app/uploads/2018/12/Global-Terrorism-Index-2018-1.pdf. See also "Global Terrorism Index 2016," Institute for Economics & Peace, February 2017, visionofhumanity.org/app/uploads/2017/02/Global-Terrorism-Index-2016.pdf.

130 "conflicts involving terrorists, rebels, and other 'non-state' actors increased significantly": There were fifty-three state-based wars fought in 2016, the most since the end of the Cold War. That number dropped slightly to forty-nine in 2017. However, non-state conflicts increased from sixty-two in 2016 to eighty-two in 2017. See Kendra Dupuy and Siri Aas Rustad, *Trends in Armed Conflict, 1946–2017*, Peace Research Institute Oslo (PRIO), May 2018, https://reliefweb.int/sites/reliefweb.int/files/resources/Dupuy%2C%20Rustad-%20Trends%20in%20Armed%20Conflict%2C%201946–2017%2C%20Conflict%20Trends%205-2018.pdf.

130 "civilian casualties from warfare and terrorism also declined": Terrorism killed 5,000 fewer people in Iraq and 1,000 fewer people in Syria in 2017 than in 2016. See "Annex of Statistical Information, Country Reports on Terrorism 2017," U.S. Department of State, September 2018, https://www.state.gov/documents/organization/283097.pdf.

ISIS, which is the biggest perpetrator of terrorism, attacked less often in 2017, and when they did attack, they killed fewer people. Between 2016 and 2017, ISIS attacks dropped 23 percent and they killed 53 percent fewer people. See *Annex of Statistical Information: Country Reports on Terrorism 2017*, National Consortium for the Study of Terrorism and Responses to Terrorism, September 2018.

131 "security declined in North America more than any other region in the world": "The Most Peaceful Countries in the World 2018," *Global Finance*, June 12, 2018. and "Is the World Getting Safer

or More Dangerous?," Bellwood Prestbury, September 2, 2017, https://www.bellwoodprestbury.com/your-challenges/insights /article/is-the-world-getting-safer-or-more-dangerous-320/.

131 "violence cost the world less money": The global economic impact from violence dropped 42 percent in one year from $14.3 trillion in 2016 to $52 billion in 2017. See "2018 Global Terrorism Index Fact Sheet," Institute for Economics & Peace, December 5, 2018.

131 "Raw violence . . . has generally been trending down": According to the Global Terrorism Index, 2014 was the most dangerous year on record for terrorism; however, not every metric has been trending down. In the year 2016, nearly a dozen more countries experienced terrorist attacks. See *Global Terrorism Index 2017*, Institute for Economics & Peace, November 2017.

131 "a record 104,000 civilians were killed": Dupuy and Rustad, *Trends in Armed Conflict, 1946–2017*.

131 "a spike in drug trafficking into the U.S.": Director of National Intelligence James R. Clapper, "Worldwide Threat Assessment of the US Intelligence Community," Testimony before the Senate Select Committee on Intelligence, February 9, 2016, https:// www.dni.gov/files/documents/SASC_Unclassified_2016_ATA _SFR_FINAL.pdf.

131 "record number of undocumented minors crossed the U.S.-Mexico border": "Unaccompanied Alien Children Released to Sponsors by State," Office of Refugee Resettlement, U.S. Department of Health and Human Services, September 27, 2019, https:// www.acf.hhs.gov/orr/resource/unaccompanied-alien-children -released-to-sponsors-by-state. See also "Southwest Border Unaccompanied Alien Children Statistics FY 2016," U.S. Customs and Border Protection, January 20, 2017, https://www.cbp.gov /site-page/southwest-border-unaccompanied-alien-children -statistics-fy-2016.

131 "millions were driven out of their homes to seek asylum": The UN measured 60 million displaced people worldwide. See Clapper, "Worldwide Threat Assessment of the US Intelligence Community."

131 "the 'invisible enemy'": "Photographing the 'Invisible Enemy,' Ebola" (video), UN News, February 10, 2015, https://news.un .org/en/audio/2015/02/596972.

131 "killed more than 10,000": In 2016, infectious disease was touted as "the neglected dimension of global security," according to the National Academy of Medicine and the Commission on a Global

Health Risk Framework for the Future. See *The Neglected Dimension of Global Security: A Framework to Counter Infectious Disease Crises* (uncorrected proofs), Commission on a Global Health Risk Framework for the Future, 2016, https://nam.edu/wp-content/uploads/2016/01/Neglected-Dimension-of-Global-Security.pdf.

In 2017, the CDC called health security "an unfinished journey" as it warned of a growing global threat from drug resistance that could trigger an outbreak like the 1918 plague or bioterrorism. See Michael T. Osterholm, "Global Health Security—An Unfinished Journey," *Emerging Infectious Diseases* 23, supplement 1 (December 23, 2017), https://www.ncbi.nlm.nih.gov/pmc/articles/PMC5711312/.

136   "a set of Easter bombings in Sri Lanka": "The Man Who Might Have Stopped Sri Lanka's Easter Bombings," BBC News, May 31, 2019, https://www.bbc.com/news/stories-48435902.

138   "calling for a refocus of the military away from unconventional to conventional war": Helene Cooper, "Military Shifts Focus to Threats by Russia and China, Not Terrorism," *New York Times*, January 19, 2018, https://www.nytimes.com/2018/01/19/us/politics/military-china-russia-terrorism-focus.html.

chapter eleven CIVILIAN CONTROL OF THE MILITARY

140   "who had defeated two World War II veterans in 1992 and 1996": Bill Clinton defeated President George H. W. Bush in 1992 and then Senator Bob Dole in 1996. And that was despite being vilified by Republicans as a Vietnam War draft dodger.

140   "Jones 'was astounded'": Bob Woodward, *Obama's Wars* (New York: Simon & Schuster, 2010), 39.

141   "one of the smartest men ever to wear the uniform": Robert M. Gates, *Duty: Memoirs of a Secretary at War* (New York: Knopf, 2014), 293.

141   "Blair had met Obama only once": Woodward, *Obama's Wars*, 58.

141   "wartime was no time for a learning curve": Gates, *Duty*, 259–60. Serving chairman of the Joint Chiefs of Staff Admiral Mike Mullen agreed, arguing that the wars in Afghanistan and Iraq "simply wouldn't allow for a months-long interregnum" while new people were appointed and new policies formulated.

141   "had barely 'crossed paths'": Gates, *Duty*, 287.

141   "also didn't know the president": Leon Panetta, *Worthy Fights: A*

Memoir of Leadership in War and Peace (New York: Penguin Press, 2014), 193–95, 203.

141 "Obama reasoned": Gates, *Duty*, 260; Ben Rhodes, *The World as It Is: A Memoir of the Obama White House* (New York: Random House, 2018), 35; and Janet Napolitano, *How Safe Are We? Homeland Security Since 9/11* (New York: PublicAffairs, 2019), 56.

141 "Obama told Gates": Gates, *Duty*, 270.

141 "thought that retired general Jones would 'give him'": Woodward, *Obama's Wars*, 38.

142 "Panetta would 'secure the support of . . . agency veterans'": Panetta, *Worthy Fights*, 203.

142 "a 'heat shield against the agency'": Peter Baker and Mark Mazetti, "Brennan Draws on Bond with Obama Backing C.I.A.," *New York Times*, December 14, 2014, https://www.nytimes.com/2014/12/15/us/politics/cia-chief-and-president-walk-fine-line-.html.

142 "they had never managed anything": Gates would later write that they "seemed to lack an awareness of the world they had just entered" and that they micromanaged military matters. See Gates, *Duty*, 288, 291, 338, 352, 475. Panetta also complained about the White House staff, saying that he had to submit speeches for White House approval; Panetta, *Worthy Fights*, 232.

143 "he just didn't know who his ideological allies were": As one former top White House staffer later wrote, "most of the people who filled the top positions of Obama's State Department or Pentagon were people he had never actually met." See Rhodes, *The World as It Is*, 49.

143 "the D.C. metropolitan area boasting the highest median household income in the entire country": According to the most recent government survey, the median household income in Washington, D.C., ranked number one compared to every other state with $82,372 per year. Maryland, adjacent to and a commuter state for D.C., ranked number two with $80,776. By comparison, the national average was only $60,336. Additionally, several D.C.-neighboring areas in Virginia topped the country's list for highest income by county. See "2017 American Community Survey Single-Year Estimates," United States Census Bureau, September 13, 2018, https://www.census.gov/newsroom/press-kits/2018/acs-1year.html. See also "Five-Year Trends Available for Median Household Income, Poverty Rates and Computer and Internet Use," United States Census Bureau, December 6, 2018, https://

www.census.gov/newsroom/press-releases/2018/2013-2017
-acs-5year.html.

chapter twelve AN ALTERNATIVE

149   "when President Trump said he was going to withdraw from
       Syria": President Trump actually first stated his desire to end U.S.
       fighting in March 2018. See "Remarks by President Trump on
       the Infrastructure Initiative," The White House, March 30, 2018,
       https://www.whitehouse.gov/briefings-statements/remarks
       -president-trump-infrastructure-initiative/.

149   "the retired general wrote": Secretary of Defense James Mattis,
       Letter to the President, December 20, 2018.

150   "remarking that 'everybody else got the oil'": Carol D. Leonig
       and Philip Rucker, 'You're a Bunch of Dopes and Babies': In-
       side Trump's Stunning Tirade Against Generals," *Washington Post*,
       January 17, 2020, https://www.washingtonpost.com/politics
       /youre-a-bunch-of-dopes-and-babies-inside-trumps-stunning
       -tirade-against-generals/2020/01/16/d6dbb8a6-387e-11ea
       -bb7b-265f4554af6d_story.html.

151   "the organization was broken and 'on the run'": Jim Garamone,
       "Mattis Says Operations Against ISIS Will Change in 2018," U.S.
       Dept. of Defense, December 29, 2017, https://www.defense.gov
       /Explore/News/Article/Article/1406064/mattis-says-operations
       -against-isis-will-change-in-2018/.

152   "John Bolton went as far as to say": "Bolton: U.S. Forces Will Stay
       in Syria Until Iran and Its Proxies Depart," *Washington Post*, Sep-
       tember 24, 2018.

152   "The professional military . . . says": *Summary of the 2018 National
       Defense Strategy of the United States of America: Sharpening the Amer-
       ican Military's Competitive Edge*, U.S. Dept. of Defense, n.d. (Janu-
       ary 2018), https://www.defense.gov/Portals/1/Documents/pubs
       /2018-National-Defense-Strategy-Summary.pdf.

153   "Mattis himself said as Secretary": Secretary of Defense James N.
       Mattis, "Remarks by Secretary Mattis on the National Defense
       Strategy," U.S. Dept. of Defense, January 19, 2018, https://dod
       .defense.gov/News/Transcripts/Transcript-View/Article/14200
       42/remarks-by-secretary-mattis-on-the-national-defense-strategy/.

155   "make the details of air strikes an official secret as well": Tara Copp,
       "Pentagon Strips Iraq, Afghanistan, Syria Troop Numbers from
       Web," *Military Times*, April 18, 2018, https://www.militarytimes

.com/news/your-military/2018/04/09/dod-strips-iraq-afghanistan
-syria-troop-numbers-from-web/.

158 "his willingness to choose the most audacious option, about his
recklessness, that worried them": I wrote about this in William M.
Arkin, "With a New Weapon in Donald Trump's Hands, the Iran
Crisis Risks Going Nuclear," *Newsweek*, January 13, 2020, https://
www.newsweek.com/trump-iran-new-nuclear-weapon-increases
-risk-crisis-nuclear-1481752.

EPILOGUE

163 "reassured the public in the Pentagon's first Covid-19 press conference": Jim Garamone, "DOD Updates Coronavirus Situation,
Guidance," U.S. Dept. of Defense, March 9, 2020, https://www
.defense.gov/Explore/News/Article/Article/2106218/dod-updates
-coronavirus-situation-guidance/.

164 "'We continue to improve our ability to defend the U.S. homeland'": Jim Garamone, "U.S. Potential Target for Malicious Actors,
DOD Official Tells Congress," U.S. Dept. of Defense, March 11,
2020, https://www.defense.gov/Explore/News/Article/Article
/2109639/us-potential-target-for-malicious-actors-dod
-official-tells-congress/.

164 "'working to keep America safe'": Charles Pope, "Goldfein Em-
phasizes Protecting Force from COVID-19 While Fulfilling All
Missions, Operational Priorities," U.S. Air Force, March 18, 2020,
https://www.af.mil/News/Article-Display/Article/2117268
/goldfein-emphasizes-protecting-force-from-covid-19-while
-fulfilling-all-mission/.

165 "Military forces throughout the country were prepared": William M. Arkin, "Exclusive: As Washington DC Faces Coronavirus Spike, Secret Military Task Force Prepares to Secure the
Capital," *Newsweek*, April 16, 2020, https://www.newsweek.com
/exclusive-washington-dc-faces-coronavirus-spike-secret-military
-task-force-prepares-secure-1498276; and William M. Arkin,
"Exclusive: Inside the Military's Top Secret Plans if Coronavirus Cripples the Government," *Newsweek*, March 18, 2020,
https://www.newsweek.com/exclusive-inside-militarys-top
-secret-plans-if-coronavirus-cripples-government-1492878.

166 "'This is not the first war we've ever been in'": David Vergun,
"Esper Lists DOD's Top Priorities During COVID-19 Pandemic,"
U.S. Dept. of Defense, March 24, 2020, https://www.defense.gov

/Explore/News/Article/Article/2123100/esper-lists-dods-top
-priorities-during-covid-19-pandemic/.

166 "said the force would remain on watch": Terri Moon Cronk,
"Navy Officials Announce 3 COVID-19 Cases Aboard USS Theodore Roosevelt," U.S. Dept. of Defense, March 24, 2020, https://
www.defense.gov/Explore/News/Article/Article/2123759/navy
-officials-announce-3-covid-19-cases-aboard-uss-theodore-roosevelt/.

167 "Admiral Gilday wrote in an open letter to the force": "Chief
of Naval Operations Statement on USS Theodore Roosevelt,"
Commander, U.S. Pacific Fleet, March 26, 2020, https://www
.cpf.navy.mil/news.aspx/130579.

167 "in his now-famous memo": Matthias Gafni and Joe Gorofoli,
"Exclusive: Captain of Aircraft Carrier with Growing Coronavi-
rus Outbreak Pleads for Help from Navy," *San Francisco Chronicle*,
March 31, 2020, https://www.sfchronicle.com/bayarea/article
/Exclusive-Captain-of-aircraft-carrier-with-15167883.php.

168 "the world would never go back to what it had been":"What We're
Learning About National Security from COVID-19" (interview
with Michael Chertoff), The Cipher Brief, April 9, 2020, https://
www.thecipherbrief.com/what-were-learning-about-national
-security-from-covid-19.

168 "'final nail in the coffin of the post-9/11 era'":John D. Negroponte
and Edward M. Wittenstein, "Coronavirus Signals We Must Shift
from Terrorism to New Bipartisan Intelligence Priorities," *USA
Today*, April 29, 2020, https://www.usatoday.com/story/opinion
/2020/03/30/coronavirus-new-intelligence-agenda-needed-column
/2935817001/.

169 "he told *60 Minutes*": "Fighting an Unseen Enemy: How the
Military Is Protecting Itself from the Coronavirus Pandemic,"
60 Minutes (CBS News), April 26, 2020, https://www.cbsnews
.com/news/us-military-army-readiness-coronavirus-60-minutes
-2020-04-26/.

169 "Bernie Sanders said": "Bernie Sanders Addresses the Nation
on the Health and Economic Crisis," Bernie (Friends of Bernie
Sanders), March 12, 2020.

169 "Joe Biden urged": "Joe Biden: The Virus Lays Bare the Short-
comings of the Trump Administration," CNN, March 15, 2020,
https://www.cnn.com/2020/03/15/opinions/joe-biden-opinion
-virus-lays-bare-shortcomings-of-trump-administration/index.html.

170 "More Guardsmen and women were mobilized": William M.
Arkin, "The Military Hasn't Saved Us From Pandemic—Nor

Should It," *Newsweek*, May 25, 2020, https://www.newsweek
.com/military-hasnt-saved-us-pandemicnor-should-it-1506272.

171 "treated a total of 161 patients": Information provided by the
U.S. Navy. See also Associated Press, "Navy Hospital Ships, Once
Through Critical, See Few Patients," *New York Times*, April 30,
2020, https://www.nytimes.com/aponline/2020/04/30/us/ap
-us-virus-outbreak-hospital-ship-few-patients.html.

173 "And Tier 4 was everybody else": Jim Garamone, "DOD Starts
Tiered COVID-19 Testing Process to Ensure Safety," U.S. Dept.
of Defense, April 22, 2020, https://www.defense.gov/Explore
/News/Article/Article/2160008/dod-starts-tiered-covid-19
-testing-process-to-ensure-safety/; and Barbara Starr, "How the
Coronavirus Pandemic Has Shaken the US Military," CNN, April
26, 2020, https://www.cnn.com/2020/04/25/politics/corona
virus-impact-us-military/index.html.

173 "'We have more than two carriers in the inventory'": "5 Things
to Know About the Military's Coronavirus Response from Defense Secretary Mark Esper," *CBS Evening News*, April 1, 2020,
https://www.cbsnews.com/news/coronavirus-military-response
-defense-secretary-mark-esper-5-things-to-know/.

174 "the Army announced": Corporal Hannah Clifton, 38th Infantry Division, "38th Infantry Division Soldiers Come Home,"
Indiana National Guard, April 9, 2020, https://www.in.ng
.mil/News-Article-View/Article/2144058/38th-infantry-division
-soldiers-come-home/.

175 "those directives having no impact on his ability to wage war":
Corey Dickstein, "Pentagon: US Troops in South Korea Are
Combat Ready Despite Lack of Major Training Events," *Stars and
Stripes*, January 28, 2020, https://www.stripes.com/news/pacific
/pentagon-us-troops-in-south-korea-are-combat-ready-despite
-lack-of-major-training-events-1.616598.

175 "*doubling* the counter-narcotics missions in Latin America": "Remarks by President Trump, Vice President Pence, and Members of
the Coronavirus Task Force in Press Briefing," The White House,
April 7, 2020.

176 "General John Hyten said": "Fighting an Unseen Enemy: How
the Military Is Protecting Itself from the Coronavirus Pandemic,"
60 Minutes (CBS News), April 26, 2020, https://www.cbsnews
.com/news/us-military-army-readiness-coronavirus-60
-minutes-2020-04-26/.

INDEX

ABOUT THE AUTHOR

William M. Arkin has been working in the field of national security for more than forty-five years as an Army intelligence analyst, author, activist, and journalist. He has authored or coauthored more than a dozen books; two of them (*Top Secret America* and *Nuclear Battlefields*) have been national bestsellers. He is well known for his many revelations of many secret government programs, and his award-winning reporting has appeared on the front pages of *The Washington Post*, *The New York Times*, and the *Los Angeles Times* and on the cover of *Newsweek* magazine. He has also been a columnist for *The Washington Post*, the *Los Angeles Times*, *The Guardian*, and the *Bulletin of the Atomic Scientists*. Arkin worked for NBC News as an on-air analyst and investigative reporter for three decades. His career has been unique, consulting and working for groups as diverse as Greenpeace, the Natural Resources Defense Council, and Human Rights Watch; as well as for the U.S. Air Force. He has made multiple trips to war zones in Iraq, Afghanistan, Lebanon, Israel, and Africa. He lives in North County, San Diego.

Research assistant E. D. Cauchi holds a Bachelor of Arts in world history from the University of Toronto and a Master of Science from the Columbia University Graduate School of Journalism. She lives in New York with her husband, Frank.